CASE STUDIES IN
CULTURAL ANTHROPOLOGY

GENERAL EDITORS

George and Louise Spindler

STANFORD UNIVERSITY

THE SAMBIA

THE SAMBIA
Ritual and Gender in New Guinea

GILBERT HERDT

The University of Chicago

The Adaptable Courseware Program consists of products and additions to existing Wadsworth Group products that are produced from camera-ready copy. Peer review, class testing, and accuracy are primarily the responsibility of the author(s).

Foreword

ABOUT THE SERIES

These case studies in cultural anthropology are designed to bring to students, in beginning and intermediate courses in the social sciences, insights into the richness and complexity of human life as it is lived in different places. They are written by men and women who have lived in the societies they write about and who are professionally trained as observers and interpreters of human behavior. The authors are also teachers, and in writing their books they have kept the students who will read them foremost in their minds. We believe that when an understanding of ways of life very different from one's own is gained, abstractions and generalizations about social structure, cultural values, subsistence techniques, and the other universal categories of human social behavior become meaningful.

ABOUT THE AUTHOR

Gilbert H. Herdt was born the eldest of four children in Oakley, Kansas, in 1949. He grew up in a small farm town his grandparents—first-generation immigrants from Germany and White Russia—helped homestead. His early schooling was near Wichita, where his father was a research engineer for the Boeing Company. He finished high school in California, and began undergraduate work there. Geology, history, and geography were his initial interests, but after his first course, he knew he wanted to be an anthropologist. Clinical psychology was his second love. His first field work as an undergraduate was with Japanese-Americans in the San Francisco Bay Area. His master's thesis (1972) was based on a year of field work in a large psychiatric ward, studying rituals of psychotherapy. The same year he began two years' graduate study in cultural anthropology and New Guinea studies at the University of Washington, where he received a Ph.C. (1973). He was awarded the 1974 Fulbright predoctoral fellowship to Australia and became a graduate student in the Department of Anthropology of the Research School of Pacific Studies, in The Australian National University. He spent two years studying the Sambia tribe of the Eastern Highlands in Papua New Guinea, after which he received his Ph.D. from the ANU in 1978. Following this he was awarded an Individual Postdoctoral fellowship of the National Institute of Mental

Health, which he used in cross-training into psychiatry and gender research at the University of California, Los Angeles (1978–1979). From 1979 to 1985 he taught at Stanford University. Since then he has been Associate Professor on the Committee on Human Development at The University of Chicago. To date, Herdt has made seven field trips to the Sambia and has published several books and various articles on them, focused on psychological and clinical studies of gender, symbolism, and sexual identity development. Besides his research in the Pacific area, he teaches seminars on clinical interviewing and is beginning comparative work on the psychocultural bases of gender and sexuality in Western culture.

ABOUT THE BOOK

This study of ritual homosexuality as preparation and training for warrior status and warfare among the Sambia of Highland New Guinea is remarkable for several reasons. It is a detailed ethnographic report, based on participant observation, of long-term institutionalized homosexuality, but it goes well beyond ethnography and engages in depth with the larger problem of gender identity and its formation. Professor Herdt shows how important culture is in the formation of gender identity and in the display of sexuality in social contexts. He raises key questions about both our cultural assumptions concerning sexual behavior and gender identity and our scientific theories about sexual processes.

This study shows that it is entirely possible—in fact among the Sambia it is required—to move from exclusive homosexual behavior to exclusive heterosexuality. Among the Sambia, adult males are husbands, fathers, and warriors who must always be prepared for war. They do not as adults engage in homosexual practices and in fact look down upon the occasional adult male who does so, at least one who does so habitually. All of these very masculine, heterosexual males, however, have spent years engaging in homosexual acts required of them as preadult initiates, during which time they avoided women and learned to be antagonistic toward them.

In this case study Professor Herdt combines theoretical concerns with ethnographic reporting. He draws from models and theories in cultural anthropology, psychoanalysis, clinical psychology, and from new perspectives on symbolism and meaning. Symbolic and semiotic anthropology would seem to be natural companions of psychoanalytic and clinical thought. They are often, and surprisingly, kept separate or exclusive in the interpretation of cultural phenomena. Professor Herdt combines these approaches in his analysis of Sambian culture and individual behavior.

As with all good anthropological studies of other cultures, we learn about ourselves as well as about the people studied. This case study serves as an especially exotic mirror to reflect upon our own sexual beliefs and practices. All cultures polarize phenomena in nature and in humans as normative or

deviant. The Sambia polarize male and female, masculine and feminine behaviors. But they do not polarize or oppose homosexuality and heterosexuality
as permanent and irretrievable assignments as we often do. In Western culture, one who engages in homosexual behavior or who has experienced feelings that we culturally define as homosexual can become identified with a
lifelong, specific role—the homosexual or gay—both in social definition and
personal identity. For the Sambia this is unthinkable, because all adult males
should pass from exclusive homosexual behavior in their preteen and adolescent years to exclusive heterosexual activity as adults during the period
when the gender identity of the individual is consolidated. Moreover, the
Sambia completely lack our category and role of the lifelong homosexual (sex
with the same sex) or gay (a social identity and lifestyle based on same-sex
attraction).

The Sambia and other non-Western peoples do not split off sexuality from
the rest of social life. For them, sex and marriage go hand in hand with rituals
and politics and time-honored traditions. They cannot be gay or lifelong
homosexuals because their culture does not categorize people or gender in
this way. Their sexuality is contextualized and a part of broader patterns
directly bearing upon individual development. But neither are they slaves to
custom. They learn and experience and adapt, having the opportunity to
recreate their own way of fitting into ongoing cultural traditions.

Polarization and categorization seem to be characteristic of not only our
thinking about sex, but also about religion, politics, marriage, and relations
with the Soviet Union. We tend to assign people, events, and actions to
permanent classes or categories in which we like to believe they will remain
permanently. We are labelers and we often substitute labels for understanding. This can and does do violence to the more complex realities of personal,
social, and political life.

The Sambia have a long history totally unrelated to ours. They are one of
many tribes in the hinterland and along the southwestern coast of New Guinea
who practice ritual homosexuality—or did practice it until recently. These
tribes speak non-Austronesian languages, are sparsely populated, warlike,
and involved in elaborate male ritual cults. It seems probable that the ancestors of these groups may have come to New Guinea as recently as 10,000
years ago (or less), and that they were pushed to the margins of their geographic area by later invasions and migrations of larger Highlands tribes
belonging to a different cultural tradition. Professor Herdt has expanded upon
this thesis in *Ritualized Homosexuality in Melanesia* (1984).

However remote the Sambia may seem to us as we sit reading about them
in libraries, at home, or on the campus grass, and however distant from our
own history they may be, the implications of their way of life for us and our
culture are profound. We cannot copy the cultures of others. Cultures do not
work properly out of context. But we can ask new questions about our own
culture. We can question our assumptions and our prejudices. We can question our very way of thinking.

This case study is worthy of your thoughtful attention. It will be harder to absorb than a relatively simple report on a way of life, for it is much more than that. But the effort will be worthwhile.

GEORGE AND LOUISE SPINDLER
Series Editors
Calistoga, California

Acknowledgments

Field research among the Sambia from 1974 to 1976 was mainly supported by the Australian-American Education Foundation and the Department of Anthropology, Research School of Pacific Studies, the Australian National University, and I wish to kindly thank these institutions. Subsequent research trips in 1979, 1981, 1983, and 1985 have been funded by the National Institute of Mental Health, the Department of Psychiatry at UCLA, the Wenner-Gren Foundation for Anthropological Research, the Spencer Foundation, and Stanford University, and I gratefully acknowledge their assistance. For financial and administrative support in recent field research and in the preparation of this monograph, I am indebted to the Department of Anthropology, Stanford University. Sincere thanks go to members of the New Tribes Mission of Papua New Guinea, whose help and kindness have been invaluable. I wish also to extend thanks again to the Department of Anthropology and Sociology, the University of Papua New Guinea, and to the Institute of Papua New Guinea Studies and its Director, Professor Andrew Strathern, for their support of my research. Several scholars have read or discussed with me pieces of this study in previous forms, and I wish especially to thank Derek Freeman, James L. Gibbs, Jr., Theodore and Ruth Lidz, Kenneth E. Read, Robert J. Stoller, Donald F. Tuzin, and the late George Devereux. I am most grateful to George and Louise Spindler for their incisive editorial advice and for their long friendship. For detailed and helpful criticisms of this manuscript I wish to thank Gregory Guldin, Fitz John Poole, and George Westermark. Finally, as always, I thank the Sambia most of all—for their generosity, friendship, and belief in me remain central to my life and to my work.

Contents

List of Illustrations

Introduction

The Sambia are a warrior tribe who inhabit isolated areas of the Southeastern Highlands of Papua New Guinea. They number somewhat over 2000 people spread thinly over a vast jungle rain forest. Their hamlets are tiny, and from the air they appear dotted in little clusters over adjacent mountain ridges of narrow river valleys. On all sides the Sambia are surrounded by similar tribes belonging to the Anga language family. These groups number from several hundred to several thousand and they extend from the Highlands to far south on the Papuan Gulf of New Guinea. All of these tribes were enemies. Warfare among them was chronic and is believed to reach back into the ancient past.

In this book we will journey to their world. You will find the Sambia fascinating and exotic. But their significance for us lies not in their exoticness as much as in how they construct gender and sexual identity. The Sambia case study can teach us all something basic about the power of society to structure masculinity and femininity, sex differences and sexual development. You will discover how warfare made their behavioral environment dangerous for them. So challenging was it that males were brought up to be fierce and aggressive warriors who, if necessary, must be able to kill at any time. This fierce masculinity goes hand in hand with sexual antagonism between men and women. Men are initiated into a secret society that practices male homosexuality as the normal way to become masculine. You will also see the problems this creates for boys' development—because they grow up in one world, that of the women, but are then forced into a new world, that of the men, wherein they acquire a secret identity and warrior status.

In 1974 I first began living with the Sambia. I spent nearly two years with them. I was 25 and green to New Guinea. Eventually I became proficient in their language, which belongs to a main language family called Anga. Nothing was known of their language or culture at the time. Negative stereotypes and folklore pictured them as murderous guerrilla warriors, thieves, and worse. I found their aggressive reputation to be warranted. Yet I discovered a private side of them never hinted at in the racist stereotypes: their warmth and friendliness. This is not surprising. Their enemies were terrified of them. In public the Sambia men put on a showy and aggressive front, but in private and with friends they reveal their talkative hospitality, humor, and common sense. You will learn in later chapters that these two sides of their personality are directly related to the two different worlds they share in, the men's and the women's.

Warfare was officially stamped out six years before my arrival. The warriors live in peace now. How has it affected them? Their war raids are gone. They can no longer use violence to redress wrongs or seek revenge on distant enemies. Gone too are the constant bow-and-arrow fights between neighboring hamlets within the Sambia Valley. These fights had been the key contest of masculine "strength" to see which warriors and villages were the strongest. The suffering of war and the ever-present fears of attack are over. And yet, in 1974, everywhere I visited among the Sambia and neighboring tribes, men still carried their bows. The initiates who lived in the men's houses were still being trained in the martial arts. They were expected to learn the ways and ritual lore of warriorhood. The boys still practice warrior games and are still trained to be aggressive fighters. This is because the Sambia still fear their enemies. They feel there is a chance that the government authorities might someday vanish, leaving a gap that warfare will again fill.

The Australians managed the old colonial government of New Guinea. After World War I and the defeat of Germany, Northern New Guinea, Germany's former colony, became a mandated territory of Australia. England's former colony, Papua—Southern New Guinea—also because a part of the single territory, Australian New Guinea. Until the 1920s the Highlands were believed to be uninhabited. Gold prospectors exploring the hills, however, discovered myriad tribes, some in the tens of thousands, in great valleys there. The Australian patrol officers went to each interior part of the country to stop warfare and establish administrative posts. The Sambia were one of these—the last Eastern Highlands population to be contacted and controlled in the late 1950s and early 1960s. No outsiders were allowed in the area until about 1968, when it was officially "derestricted."

When I began my search for the Sambia, I wanted to study traditional initiation rites. I'd considered several areas of the world, such as the Amazon and Africa, before settling on Papua New Guinea. Letters from anthropologists and missionaries led me to the Anga groups, which were still said to do secret cult initiations. The search required taking successively shorter flights, first to Port Moresby, the capital of Papua New Guinea, then to Goroka, the capital of the Eastern Highlands Province, and lastly to the Mountain Patrol post, a small administrative center with a tiny grass airstrip high in the mountains. From there I walked over several mountain ranges. The Australian officer found some men to go with me and loaned me the native interpreter, a Sambian man, because I did not speak the language. Thus began my first patrol of the whole area, which took weeks of walking, to visit each tribal group. The Sambia were the last group I visited before selecting a village in which to live for two years.

After these weeks of patrolling and that one last long hike, three days from the patrol post, we descended into the first Sambia village. It was Nilangu, which later was to become my home. People were dressed entirely in traditional garb. No one spoke English and only a handful of men spoke Pidgin, the local trade language. They knew I was coming because such news spreads like wildfire through the area. Crowds were all around. The war leaders looked fierce with their bodies painted and bows in hand. But so many people smiled and seemed open and friendly. The village occupies an extraordinary location, at an elevation of 6000 feet, literally perched on a mountain ridge like an eagle's nest. It was beautiful, an anthropologist's dream. And the people seemed genuinely pleased that I was there.

I wanted, right then and there, to unpack my bags and settle into Nilangu. People greeted me and we shook hands. The village seemed like it could be a home. The men's clubhouse caught my eye; I walked over and peered into the doorway. And then, to my amazement, out blasted the Beatles' song, "I Wanna Hold Your Hand." Oh hell, I thought. Had I come all this way to find the same old junk of civilization, here, back in these isolated mountains, thousands of miles from home? I stepped back, disbelieving and exasperated.

But I was wrong. The radio was a fluke, its owner the only man to return from coastal work with a music box. (It broke in a few weeks.) Everything else seemed traditional: the men who went hunting, the women in the gardens, the initiates hiding behind their bark capes from the women. Kanteilo, the old man and aging war leader who was to become my village sponsor and "father," stepped forward. He showed me around, pointing out things with meaningless words. He gave me bananas and corn to eat; the old fox was buttering me up so I would stay. I was impressed and intrigued with what was to me an odd mixture of rugged individualism and personal warmth.

This warmth was reflected in how the men loved to talk and sing together. On patrol, as we climbed up and down jungle mountains and through swamps, the men never tired of chattering. They would prop up each other's dwindling energy at the day's end by singing in unison as we slogged up one last mountainside. In the clubhouse the talking was more intimate and cordial, but no less constant. They asked me a thousand questions, and I was exasperated at being unable to communicate.

While on this patrol I heard a rumor that the Sambia would initiate their boys soon. Because of this I set up camp there. Would I get to see their marvelous initiations? I asked the Nilangu villagers if I could live with them. They were thrilled; it meant status, money, medical supplies, and who knows what other riches to them, for, with my tennis shoes and kerosene lamps, I was obviously rich. Smoking my pipe and sharing food dispelled the other rumors that I was a missionary or government patrol officer (see Photo 1). Everyone helped construct a house in the center of the hamlet, using local trees, bamboo, and grass thatching. Until then, though, I had to live in the men's clubhouse.

The clubhouse was a spartan place where I hung my hat for a month till my house was built. I slept there, ate what others ate, and began to learn the language. The place was damn uncomfortable: fleas, constant smoky fires,

*Photo 1. The anthropologist takes morning coffee beside a mumu (feast) pit
(1979) (Photo courtesy of Dr. Robert J. Stoller)*

drafty, and noisy. It was difficult to get a good night's sleep, especially when
a large, ugly flying fox bat kept flapping up to the house late at night to feed
on a nearby banana tree.

What had I come to see? My interest in anthropology stemmed from a
fascination with the power of ritual events and symbols to shape people's
behavior, even their deepest experience. I wanted to know how identity—
which is such an elusive concept—was changed by initiation. I read the anthropological literature in vain for this information. An occasional writer
described the local meanings of ritual transitions, yet I wanted to go further
and combine social descriptions of the collective rituals with studies of how
individuals experience them. I had done something similar three years before
in my first fieldwork project on a large psychiatric ward in California, which
stimulated my interest in identity rituals. Could I use the same interview
techniques in New Guinea? Experts were skeptical, and I must admit that I,
too, was unsure. Yet I had just read two books that made me hopeful: Robert
Levy's (1973) *The Tahitians*, a marvelous study of how Tahitians subjectively
experience their social practices and themselves, and Robert LeVine's (1973)
Culture, Behavior and Personality, which brilliantly outlined the use of psy-

choanalytic methods across societies to understand how personality and culture mutually interact and influence, for example, the meaning of customs (such as initiation rites) at conscious and unconscious levels of awareness. Thus I resolved to make a try at studying both Sambia individuals and their collective rituals.

The new initiates into the men's house interested me most. How did the rituals affect them? What did it change inside of them: their masculine identity or self-esteem, their identification with rituals and associations with their age-mate peers? Could rituals alter their feelings about themselves, even at unconscious levels such as in their dreams? I knew that it would take a long time to grasp these problems because they require a deep knowledge of the language and culture. As I learned NeoMelanesian Pidgin, I began simple talk with others. Then I began to learn the Sambian language. In about three months I was having detailed conversations; in six months I could understand some ritual talk; and in 10 months I was fluent enough to interview in depth without a translator. But even so, when boys told me of their experiences, how could I know how much their stories matched the real ritual events? Or, if they had had idiosyncratic experiences, how was I to understand how typical were their experiences? I will return to these problems later.

The difficulties I faced changed somewhat after my first initiation experience in December 1974. A marriage ceremony was to be held in our village. The fourth-stage initiates (there were six of them) between the ages of 18 and 25 were to be released for the first time in years from ritual taboos. In the hours before we went into the forest for secret purificatory rites, the men decided to wait in my house while the rituals were being prepared. The youths to be initiated were nervous. So was I, but for a different reason: I didn't know if I would be accepted. Should I go with them? Would they let me—a stranger—accompany them to their sacred ceremony? What would I do if they said no? But they put me at ease. Weiyu—who has since become a close Sambia friend—asked me if I would join in the ceremony. Several older men disagreed with this but my sponsor, Kanteilo, who was the main elder and big man, said it was all right. Soon these youths started talking among themselves, expressing how they felt about what was to happen. It seemed so natural—their talking, their anxiety and shame, and their great anticipation—but I had not been trained in anthropology to expect such shared feelings. Here was a backstage sharing of experience and thoughts that surely reflected the men's subjective identities. They were, they said, scared to see the women after avoiding females all these years. But an hour later there they were in the ritual, being instructed in heterosexual coitus, the taboo on adultery, and the secret ritual practice of drinking white tree sap to replace their semen. When they spoke of women, the older men were angry, even repulsed; when they said the word "vagina," they spat compulsively. I was stunned by their strong negative emotions and amazed to learn that they secretly drank tree sap. My friends' initiation thus constituted my own initiation as a field anthropologist: What on earth did all this mean?

That is, in short, the key question of this case study: What do these initiation rites mean for Sambia? In particular, what do they mean for their gender and sexuality? At the time of my initial fieldwork, no one knew much of initiation rites among the Anga tribes. Certainly nothing was known scientifically about their sexuality. My discovery of widespread cults of institutionalized homosexual activity has altered our understanding (Herdt 1984). At the time I lacked scientific training on sexual behavior and identity. But as I learned more of the meaning of the ritual practices, it became clear that I had to study these cultural and psychological spheres of gender behavior and identity, because to understand Sambia ritual requires knowing their underlying ideas about gender.

Sambia are preoccupied with the differences between maleness and femaleness. Men perceive these differences to be the product of biological forces active both in natural species and in humans. On the one hand, Sambia believe femaleness to be an innate, natural essence, which in humans inevitably results in adult femininity and parturition. Maleness, on the other hand, is a weak and tenuous essence that does not naturally produce adult masculinity. Unless men intervene with ritual procedures that protect boys from female contamination, boys stay small and weak and ultimately die. Only through oral homosexual inseminations that artificially create maleness are boys believed able to attain adult manhood. The process begins in the initiation rituals described below. Yet while homosexuality is begun through initiation, it is far more than a ceremony. Born from the trauma of separation from mother and secret threats, homoeroticism is seductive, powerful, and sometimes cruel. For some 10 to 15 years, Sambia boys engage in homosexual activities on a daily basis, first as the fellator (insertee) and then as the older fellated (insertor). At marriage (usually between the ages of 18 and 25 years), youths become true bisexuals for a time. With fatherhood, however, homosexuality should cease; men should become exclusively heterosexual in their sexual behavior. The cycle begins again when a new crop of boys is initiated into the ritual cult. And so it is today.

It is with the meaning of this ritualized pattern that we shall be concerned, with the various ways this old-fashioned initiation influences the growth of masculine roles. And, behind that, we will be concerned with its growing impact upon the boys' subjective sense of themselves: what their maleness means for them and the ways this sense of masculine self is special in its capacity to make a man sexually excited first by boys and then by women.

Sambia pose a challenge to our Western notions of what makes men and how their sexuality is formed. Sambia homoeroticism belongs to a social tradition, as we shall see; yet it is more than the sum of custom or myth. It is a human reality, a whole way of life secretly suffered and enjoyed. And like elsewhere in Melanesia, its puzzling outcome *is* exclusive heterosexuality—but of a special and rather restrictive sort. In the conclusion I will argue that this developmental pattern belongs to a lifelong pattern of psychological and cultural forces.

To fully grasp the Sambia initiations means also knowing something about their reporter and interpreter—me. Perhaps the background noted above on the circumstances of my original fieldwork helps clarify who I was when first starting the research. Yet my perspective on anthropology is that we need to know even more about the subjective identity of the field worker. Anthropologists have in general mentioned themselves in their accounts of other cultures. This is necessitated by our field method, participant-observation, which is essentially a subjective method. We live with the natives in their villages. We eat and talk with them. We make friends and sometimes enemies too. In a word, we become involved—subjectively involved—with the people we study. We have feelings about them. Our studies are not scientific experiments, but rather holistic accounts, creative interpretations. This interpretative image is presently the subject of much debate in anthropology. How personal and subjective should the field worker be in describing events and communications? Usually, when ethnographers mention themselves and their situations, what they have to say is chatty and peripheral. My perspective is somewhat different.

It seems essential to describe some of our field experiences as anthropologists in order for readers to fully understand our views on the culture we studied. Sometimes in this book I will be self-revealing. This personal material is not extraneous or peripheral to the initiation data. For I was not a cold machine—an unfeeling robot—who witnessed the ritual nose-bleedings I will describe. It was my self, my feelings of shock and concern and understanding, which emerged as I recorded the events, that made this study possible. My feelings resonated to those of the Sambia themselves—their shock, fear, anger, and sorrow in the rituals. Did they not sense this? Is this not part of the reason they trusted and permitted me to be the first outsider to see their secret rites? So, I sometimes will describe my reactions to the events to serve as a bridge for you so you can understand how the rituals created feelings in all the participants. These emotions are at the very core of the phenomenon we want to understand. By inserting my subjectivity into this case study, however, you should not think that what you will read is fiction or poetry. The extreme view of reflexivity suggests that objectivity isn't possible. I am not going to that extreme. My view is that with training and discipline we can study the feelings of others and ourselves as a part of the culture we work in. This view represents a shift in our awareness of how to study culture. By studying this side of initiation—its power to create a new identity in people— we see better the mutual interaction between the ethnographer's experience and how it emerges from long-term and sensitive relationships with informants. This process is what interests me most.

I went to the Sambia to understand what it would be like to grow up in a small village and be initiated into manhood. Though I knew that Sambia practiced ritual initiation, I did not know about their secret cult. Indeed, they hid the homosexual activities from me for some months, as I explain in Chapter 5. I did not expect them to be secret sharers in that ancient tradition— now virtually vanished elsewhere in New Guinea—of ritualized homosexuality. These practices surprised me, even as a trained student of anthropology. They sometimes disturbed and even shocked me, for as a stranger and as a young single male I felt alone and vulnerable. I was eventually entrusted by my friends and admitted into the cult initiations. In these ways I became a participant-observer of Sambia initiations. My empathy and curiosity and friendship admitted me to the rituals. Those attitudes also influenced my rapport with individuals, making this report far richer. But even so I did not become a real "member" of the ritual cult—for I was never initiated into it—and I believe that I remained self-conscious and objective in my desire to study, not use, the Sambia for understanding what it was like for them to experience ritual.

I was permitted into the initiations on one condition: that I not allow the women and children, or the outside authorities, to learn the true identities of the persons and events. Over the years many conversations with Sambia have helped me understand their concerns about this. Hence, all of the names below are pseudonyms, and certain background details are altered to protect people.

By the time these fieldwork observations were made, the Sambia, like ourselves, were in the throes of change. America was suffering the effects of the Vietnam War. The United States and the USSR made a space connection; the events of Watergate forced Nixon out and Ford in; the greatest economic recession since World War II occurred after an Arab oil embargo. Papua New Guinea, coasting along on a wave of Australian political change and the death rattle of colonialism, gained independence in 1975. In that year the Sambia performed their twenty-third initiatory cycle of the twentieth century. The anachronism of a late-twentieth-century tribal initiation seemed fitting to the still rugged and isolated Eastern Highlands. Here, we are no different from Sambia: the world is moving too fast for us.

This case study has been written primarily with the beginning student in mind.* My scholarly writings are readily available for those wishing to pursue selected topics further (Herdt 1977, 1980, 1981, 1982a, 1982b, 1982c, 1984). From time to time I will refer to these other publications and, where the comparative viewpoint is interesting, I shall also refer to selected works in New Guinea studies at large. These comparative glances will, I hope, amplify general theories related to the Sambia case study, such as those concerning sexual antagonism, pollution beliefs, and ritual homosexuality.

Ritualized homosexuality is unusual but not rare in Melanesia; the best indication is that 10 to 20 percent of all these traditional cultures historically practice this form of gender and sexual development (Herdt 1984). Today, however, culture change has destroyed most of these customs. Yet Melanesia is a vast area of enormous cultural diversity: over 1000 different languages and hundreds of distinct cultures. In cross-cultural perspective, Sambia ritual practices belong to this culture-specific pattern of initiation rites, secret male cults, and small-scale patrilineal† villages involved in rampant warfare among

---

* Photographs published in this study were taken in 1975. They are published here for the first time with permission of Sambia leaders because the key actors are now adults and unrecognizable or are deceased.

† See the Glossary in the back for definitions of this and other technical terms.

men and sexual antagonism between men and women. These groups live primarily in southwestern and coastal New Guinea and among the adjacent Anga area where isolation and recent contact preserved the ritualized homosexual practices. Vast parts of island New Guinea lack some or all of these traits, and ritual homosexuality is absent from the mainstream Central Highlands area.

Still other tribes, such as in the Western Highlands, lack initiation rites altogether; whereas in the mainstream Eastern Highlands, initiation cults like those of Sambia are performed but without homosexual activity. The Western Highlands groups differ in other ways too, for they are highly populated (for example, the Melpa people there number 100,000), warfare is different there than elsewhere, and men engage in widespread ceremonial exchange competitions called *Moka* or *Tee*, through which they achieve prestige status and attain gender identities consonant with their achieved social positions. In short, whereas homosexual initiation for Sambia is crucial in the psychosocial development of masculine identity, in the Western Highlands ceremonial exchanges facilitate similar identity outcomes. On the collective level, both types of societies can be seen as having successfully achieved specific adaptation to the behavioral and cultural environments in which they live. Keep in mind, then, that the Sambia identity mechanism—rituals of gender transformation—is but one of several alternative ways in which masculine gender roles are accommodated to social structure and notions of what is male and female. This leads me to my last point: the relationship between this case study and our present Western views on sex and gender.

Western culture still views sex and gender as "natural"—a part of nature, reproduction, biological drive—and less a product of society. The extreme form of this perspective suggested that females are weak, temperamental, dumb, uncreative, and best confined to mothering and the home. Males were seen as biologically superior, stronger, more active and intellectual, and natural warriors and breadwinners. These sexist stereotypes were ingrained in American society and in Western culture more broadly until the 1920s and 1930s; however, they are still around. These cultural beliefs deprive women of educational and work opportunities on the basis of received cultural wisdom. Anthropology was a strong instigator of change in relation both to sexual and racial discrimination. Our great thinkers—such as Franz Boas, Ruth Benedict, Margaret Mead, Edward Sapir, and others—directly argued against this biologism. Margaret Mead in particular paved the way with new insights into the cultural structuring of gender through her studies of adolescence and sex roles in Samoa and New Guinea. Of course, there are weaknesses in these studies; they were done more than 50 years ago. Yet her basic relativist theory—that culture shapes sexual identity and gender roles—remains central even though still controversial in the social sciences.

Such questions raise the general problem of cultural relativism when studying human behavior. Relativism is a basic working principle in anthropology. This view sees human customs as meaningful and coherent in their native social context. Thus, we cannot wrench such practices as warfare, sexuality, or child-rearing out of the cultures in which they occur without doing violence to their meaning and contribution to the society as a whole. And so it is with such a controversial topic as homosexuality: it must be understood in its own time and place, by the actors themselves. It is but one among many life-designs humans have created in adapting to conditions the world over. We must see how our own views on homosexuality compare to those of other cultures before judging them. We shall return to this comparison in Chapter 7.

It is fitting to refer back to that early gender research here, in another study of New Guinea, because basic and far-reaching changes in society's ideas of sex roles are occurring all around us. The cultural institution of the family is changing as never before. More women are working and more men are taking a greater role in child-rearing. There is more divorce than ever, so there are more single parents. Abortion and contraceptives are emotionally charged topics. People no longer feel compelled to marry or to have children. The Gay Movement and the Women's Movement are vocal and active parts of society. Gays demand equal treatment and the recognition of their alternative life-style which goes beyond sexual activity to embrace a new social identity. Lesbian mothers have become an important topic for debate too.

Such issues are changing male and female roles in the United States, signaling a change in our consciousness about sex and gender. The Sambia case study provides a different perspective for us to reflect on this change. Sometimes, indeed, the most objective way to reexamine such social issues is to stand outside of them for a moment, to consider how another culture has dealt with the basic question of how to be human in a very different way.

Recent anthropological research in New Guinea indicates the limitations of our Western model of gender. The extraordinary degree to which New Guinea cultures polarize and exaggerate differences between the sexes is essential to understand. We see in their sex stereotypes the hard impact of warfare, a problem to which we shall return later. Contrary to our own view, such cultures as the Sambia see homosexuality not as a negation of masculinity but as the only means through which it is attained. The customs and myths perpetuated by these men's societies emphasize masculinity and its characteristics, such as the penis, so we may refer to these as phallic cults. They are not completely alien to our tradition. In Western culture, the Ancient Greeks practiced a similar form of ritual homosexuality. We will study the Greeks and other cultural examples in Chapter 7. In this book, however, we will concentrate on the Sambia system in order to see how gender is created in the members of a phallic cult that still lives today.

1/The behavioral environment

You are asked to grant as a fact, for the moment, that some generations ago but no more than 200 years, bands of fierce warriors and their families—perhaps refugees of a great war in Papua or perhaps fed up with too much war—ventured from the coastal hinterland over three mountain ranges to a virgin rain forest valley, there to chase out a handful of hunting and gathering people and settle. They were an unnumerous, unorthodox, unpowerful group, ancestors of present-day Sambia. You will meet their descendants and study the legacy of their culture in this book.

The pioneers founded tiny hamlets atop steep mountain ridges for defense. Using stone axes they hacked out the jungle, cleared land, and planted the first gardens. Until the harvest, hunting and foraging provided the only food. Death—from sickness, accidents, famine—eliminated many. Sambia say only the strongest survived. Their famous ancestor and culture-hero, Numboolyu, lived during this time. Legends say he founded the great cultural institutions such as initiation rites, performed miraculous feats, and fathered many children. He survived his peers; indeed, the name Numboolyu means "he who outlived others in a great plague." Two villages were eventually founded, and soon they were at war. Thus, Sambia say, began their society, an extremely isolated group of some 2400 hunters and agriculturalists inhabiting the southwestern corner of Papua New Guinea's great Eastern Highlands.

In this chapter we are concerned with more than the mountain setting of the Sambia; we will see the role that warfare played in structuring the behavioral environment and consciousness of the people. For, above all other factors, warfare violence shaped society and the individual. We will need to keep this dual vision of the individual and the group in mind, for the one affected the other and, together with culture and the environment, these elements formed the totality we will study. The *behavioral environment* will refer to ecology, technology, and those group perceptions and responses to the landscape that provide the context for individual development. *Culture*, on the other hand, refers primarily to those symbolic values and beliefs learned and transmitted across generations through interactions with other members of society. Later we will study warfare as an historical current in the behavioral and cultural constitution of Sambia: at the time of its founding, at initial contact with outsiders in the early 1960s, and today.

THE LANDSCAPE

Sambia are a rugged mountain people whose remote homeland is one of the world's great rain forest landscapes. The entire tribal population is spread over a territory of hundreds of square miles in a corner of the Eastern Highlands Province. (See Map 1.) The landscape is rugged: high mountain ranges soaring to 11,000 feet (the same altitudinal range as the Swiss Alps) pitched between swift natural river systems, the land an uneven green canopy as far as the eye can see. Surrounded on all sides by jagged peaks of the impressive Kratke Mountains, Sambia territory is impenetrable except by mountain trails. There are no roads. Hamlets are built in the elevation range of 3000 to 6000 feet. Gardens are cultivated up to about 7000 feet. Pandanus nut groves are tended and harvested to an elevation of about 8000 feet. Men hunt in clan territories extending to peaks of 9000 feet and more, an eerie no-man's-land of dense vegetation, fog, and silence. Rainfall is heavy at 150 inches a year. The rainy season creates ever-increasing wetness over nine months of the year, whereas the brief dry season (often confined to a few afternoons in June) is broken by morning fog and sudden cloudbursts in the late afternoon.

A turbulent land it is, whose terrific rain and dreadful fog were once referred to as "Frankenstein country" by a patrolling Australian officer, a man who could abide the biting fog only by taking cognac in his morning tea. Though lush and forbiddingly beautiful, the area seems anomalous because of its high elevation, cool climate, and heavy rain forest set almost dead center on the equator, creating unusual climatic conditions. These include extraordinary temperature changes each day: cold, hot, rainy, sunny; occasional earth tremors, landslides, and creeks that flood constantly in the monsoon; spectacular rain and electrical storms creating veritable light shows at night, with thunderbolts reflecting off mountains miles away, beneath a dark cloak of glittering diamonds. Against such a backdrop one feels acutely the smallness of the human element compared to the vastness of nature. No wonder Sambia refer to themselves as squatters in the nest of the proud harpy eagle (a clan totem), as cousins of the tree-dwelling possum.

To understand the local economy and settlement patterns, we must grasp an image of the landscape. We can do no better than the mental map of Sambia themselves, a folk image of their geography. Through this map we will see how three basic pursuits—food getting, residence, and defense—are organized.

Suppose we take a bird's-eye view of the Sambia River Valley, what do we see? Very little differentiation in flora or fauna at first. We notice the high mountains with their green carpets soaring above the ever-constant river, which dominates the landscape of the valley floor. In between the peaks and river are garden patches intermixed with bands of grassy meadows. And, of course, there are the hamlets, easily recognizable from great distances by stately groves of feathery mint-green bamboo growing in and around them.

The valley can thus be viewed as a series of five concentric circles of ecological zones climbing from the river to the mountain peaks, thousands

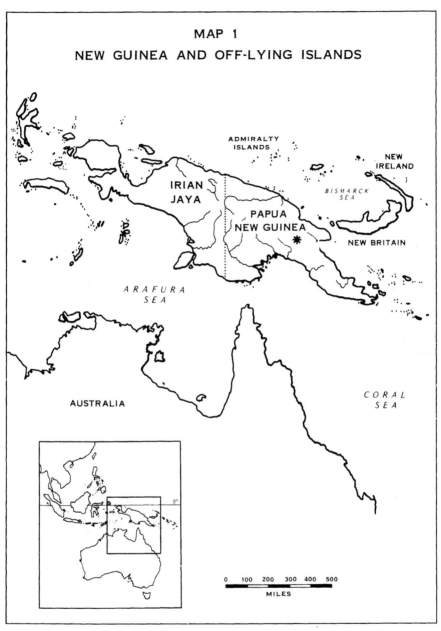

MAP 1
NEW GUINEA AND OFF-LYING ISLANDS

ADMIRALTY
ISLANDS

NEW
IRELAND

IRIAN
JAYA

BISMARCK
SEA

PAPUA
NEW GUINEA

NEW BRITAIN

ARAFURA
SEA

CORAL
SEA

AUSTRALIA

0°

0   100   200   300   400   500
MILES

Map 1

of feet above. Each of these provides valued resources which can be outlined here:

Wunyu-wulu (riverine land).   This zone refers to banks and marshes of watercourses, primarily adjacent to the river on the valley floor, so it is at the lowest altitude. During the monsoon the river sometimes rages and overflows its banks. These narrow muddy flood plains provide rich soil for pandanus fruit and banana trees, taro, and the cane reeds women use in making grass skirts. From the riverbanks, freshwater eels are trapped; when smoked they provide delicious treats. In the dry season some areas of the river are dammed to catch the local scavenger fish, which is also smoked and eaten. Children love to play in small creeks hereabouts by day, and women hunt frogs in them by torchlight at night.

Wungul-kwaku (habitation area).   Here we have the hamlet living space and its adjacent gardens. When Sambia use the term *wungul-kwaku*, they have in mind "cleared areas," swept clean and without vegetation, such as the small central plaza space in the center of the hamlet wherein children play and oldsters chat or do busywork. Village habitations are built hundreds of feet above the river bottom, on mountain ridges, to prevent surprise attacks. One can thus look down and across vast distances from the hamlet. Huts are built in a line formation and are fortified against attack by tall concentric barricades of bamboo groves, cordylines (waxy-leafed trees of many colors, sometimes called palm-lilies), wild sugar cane, and various trees. Bamboo groves are also the resting places of hamlet spirits *(aatmwogwambu)* who protect the village and are associated with the ritual cult. Gardens of sweet potatoes, sugar cane, and European-introduced vegetables such as corn and green beans surround the village. Nearby mountain streams provide sweet drinking water; lower in the valley these creeks demarcate clan territories, gardens, and the riverfront property.

Angoolendoowi (edgeland forest).   The middle area of mountainsides beyond and above hamlets forms a sort of random patchwork of secondary forest and occasional grassland. Here the virgin rain forest has been cleared for garden land. Initiates like to hunt small game here. Some pandanus, areca or betel nut (which is chewed and is mildly narcotic), and other special trees are planted around gardens for their foodstuffs. Today, this zone is the prime area for coffee growing, which was introduced in the 1970s as a cash crop. Small plots of taro are planted here and there. But the larger individual and hamlet-communal gardens are the key food supply. These yam and taro plantations are also used for ritual feasts. Pigs forage nearby, though Sambia have few pigs. Ramshackle pig-herding huts are built nearby for older women who take on this chore. More common are the garden huts that provide alternate residences for families during planting and harvest times. Finally, the higher grounds of edgeland forest provide flat spaces for sacred ritual dancegrounds during male initiation, and every hamlet boasts one of these.

Koonai-wumdu (pandanus-nut forest).   Above the edgeland forest we move into deep rain forest. Only men and older initiates usually venture here to hunt; at harvest times, however, men take their families temporarily to live in pandanus-nut houses, which are sturdy cabins constructed of pandanus materials. Nearby forests have mixed varieties of oak, pine, beech, and other broad-leafed trees sheltering thick vines with beautiful forest orchids. All pandanus trees are individually owned and tended by men. Their nuts are highly valued and taste like coconut. Sambia regard them as protein sources equivalent to certain meats, to mother's milk, and to semen, as we shall see. "Harmless" cold swamp bogs are used for planting taro gardens. Some bogs, however, are believed inhabited by "evil" nature spirits that can engulf men and are very much feared. Possum-hunting parties operate out of the pandanus-nut houses too. Pandanus groves are strange places, silent and fogbound with enormous trees—eerie and jagged monstrosities growing in deep forested swamplands that extend a mile or so up into colder cloud forest country. In this zone, men say, the elusive cassowary (an ostrichlike bird) can be trapped, and here she mingles with fierce male forest spirits *(ikeiaru)*. Both these creatures are respected and even feared and occupy important roles in Sambia mythology.

Kai-wumdu (high forest hunting territory).   Great expanses of wild mountain terrain slope upward to the peaks above the pandanus. The area is perpetually foggy, so it is damp with mossy surfaces and thick undergrowth. Gnarled and crooked cedar and other trees are festooned with liverworts and lichens. Limestone outcrops create rock shelters and shadowy caves that Sambia dread—the hiding places of ghosts and forest spirits. Village clans as a group own large tracts of this forest, for which they will wage war to protect their exclusive hunting rights for possum, cassowary, and birds. To travel here one must crisscross high and treacherous tree bridges, often wet or mossy. Hunting lodges of poor construction provide temporary shelter during times of ceremonial hunts. Though miserable abodes, perpetually cold and damp and without barriers against the terrible leeches that thrive in this zone, men may spend weeks in them. The possum they catch and smoke here are crucial for ritual feasts. This high roof of the world is indeed a kind of masculine testing ground unknown to women and children.

POPULATION GROUPINGS

The patterns of population and settlement of the Sambia and their neighbors are similar throughout the region. Here I will concentrate on only the Sambia, while in the next section we will examine wider regional patterns.

Today, the Sambia live in six different population areas organized around river valley systems. These six population clusters can be called *subtribes*. Each is made up in turn of one or more social units referred to as *phratries*, which are themselves composed of different hamlets.

Phratries are social units that group people according to their common geographic territory, an image of common origin and fictitious ancestors, shared ritual customs and identity. In some cases there are minor dialect differences between phratries. Nevertheless, Sambia of all six subtribes speak one language and recognize other speakers as similar to themselves and distinct from neighboring tribal groups. Each phratry is composed of two or more hamlets, which, in general, vary in size from about 40 to 150 persons. The end of warfare has created several large *composite hamlets* (based on the merging of two previously separate hamlets) like Nilangu, my fieldwork site, which numbers about 160 people. In all there are 10 phratries and some 40 different Sambia hamlets scattered throughout the six valleys. These phratries range in size from the Yulamwi, with about 80 people, to the Wunyu-Sambia, with 421 people in the Upper Sambia Valley. These river populations are the focus of a person's social affiliations and interactions throughout life. Each valley's hamlets are usually within sight and earshot of each other; by contrast, valleys are separated, depending on the particular area, by the mountains and by walking distances of from three hours to two days. Within the social universe of each valley, marriage and initiation co-occur, so men are linked to each other by ties of kinship, marriage, and/or co-initiation. Within this cluster, hamlets often fought against one another in ceremonialized bow-and-arrow fighting; while at other times, when necessary, they united in defense against attack by outside groups. However, in the Sambia Valley and one other valley, the social situation is more complex due to the presence of three different phratries in the same broad valley. Traditionally, then, a river valley population had a string of neighboring hamlets with their own common forest and riverine territories, who also shared ritual dancegrounds and fightgrounds.

Sambia River Valley   The focus of this ethnography is the Sambia River Valley and its hamlets (see Map 2). This area is my principal research population and it was the center of my first fieldwork from 1974 to 1976, on which most of this report is based. To understand the Sambia ritual initiatory cult, we will want to study how the valley is internally divided.

The Sambia River Valley is a long, thin, partially deforested habitational zone, falling between two mountain chains, the Green Mountains and the Blue Mountains. The Sambia River headwaters flow from the northerly Papuan Vailala Divide, a 10,000-foot mountain pass that separates Sambia from their neighbors, the Wantukiu tribes. Politically and ecologically, the valley can be divided into an upper and lower area. The Upper Sambia Valley contains two different phratries: on the western bank the Wunyu-Sambia, with six hamlets (total population 421); and on the eastern bank the Seboolu, with four hamlets (total population 411). In the early 1970s a new settlement sprung up on the valley floor near the local Christian mission. This mission is about a 45-minute walk from my village. The Middle Valley has a small phratry, the Yulami (population 98), the original inhabiting group mentioned above—remnants of the hunters and gatherers chased out long ago. These three phratries together number 930 persons in all, and they constitute my major research population.

The population density of Sambia is low. Estimates place it at between four and five people per square mile. However, the density dramatically increases if we study only the total land mass that is ecologically utilized. The Middle and Upper Sambia Valley, for example, is an area whose total exploited land base is about 24 miles (6 km wide by 10 km long, or 60 km^2). This utilized area mass yields a population density of just over 38 persons per square mile, which represents a truer population density picture. Even assuming this higher density, however, Sambia still have vast unused forest preserves available to them for future use.

Farther south, an hour south of the Yulami over a steep mountain range, is the Sambia River Delta, which is, more properly speaking, the drainage

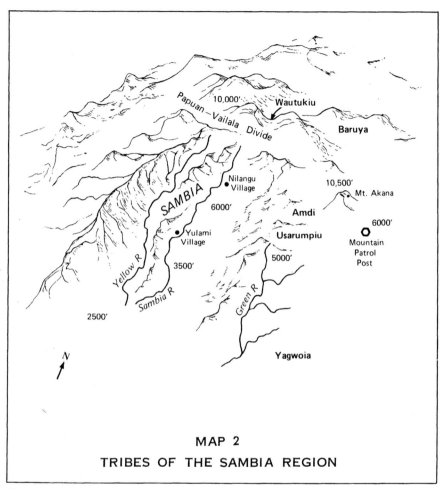

MAP 2

TRIBES OF THE SAMBIA REGION

Map 2

basin of the river. This area is inhabited by the Moonagu phratry, with six small hamlets (total population about 300). The Moonagu are distinct from the Upper Valley and traditionally had few social contacts with them. But they fraternize with the Yulami people, and in 1975 due to social changes they joined the initiations we will study below.

ECONOMY

Like other New Guinea peoples, Sambia are subsistence horticulturalists. Food is plain but usually plentiful. Sweet potatoes and taro are the main staples, and yams are a seasonal feast crop. Many other green vegetables are cultivated too, and mushrooms and palm hearts are gathered from the forest on an irregular basis.

Sambia practice slash-and-burn gardening. After a garden is exhausted it will be left dormant for a few years. Gardening is done in shifting swidden cycles, with garden plots cut out of virgin rain forest and secondary forest. Gardens are cultivated up to two hours' walking distance from the village. All slash-and-burn was formerly done with stone tools. Until recently (around 1960), Sambia probably had to gather wild foods much more than now. Sambia themselves say that the introduction of steel axes has made food more plentiful and easier to obtain.

Sambia traditionally had a simple technology. Their greatest number of implements were the weaponry used in war. Arsenals included stone and wooden clubs, pineapple-shaped clubs, and stone axes, all crafted for killing in intertribal wars. Men still carry bows and arrows wherever they go. There are over 20 types of arrows, according to whether the shaft is straight or barbed, long or short, of hard or soft wood. Bows are made of wood from an extremely hard palm tree. Barbed or hooked arrows are for killing men and pigs. Blunt-nosed arrows are used for killing birds, while multipronged arrows are used to kill wild pigs.

In gardening, however, there are really only two key instruments, and these reflect the strict sex-role dichotomy: stone (and today steel) axes for men and digging sticks for women. Men say it used to take as long as two weeks to fell a large tree with their old-fashioned axes. Nowadays, they can chop down the same-sized tree with a steel axe in only a few hours. Bamboo knives, cassowary bone awls, and other simple tools were also employed in butchering and cooking animals. Grass skirts woven by women and bark capes made by men (from bark of the local mulberry tree) provide the main clothing.

Men and women have sharply defined places in the behavioral environment. Their society dictates that men be warriors and hunters (skill with bow and arrow being the critical sign of competence both in war and the hunt), while women be mothers and gardeners. While these roles are rationalized by economic and social needs, Sambia themselves view gender roles as conditioned by nature.

All economic activities are strictly regulated on cultural-based gender principles governing the division of labor. Men fell trees and clear brush; women burn off the debris, till the soil, plant, weed, and harvest. Men hunt, women do not. From childhood onward boys are prepared to use weapons in hunting and war, whereas girls do domestic chores such as babysitting and learn more about gardening. Hunting remains even today an important economic pursuit, for it provides most meat protein as well as the possum meat used for ceremonial gifts.

Both hunting and gardening are intermixed as economic routines all year round. But there are also marked climatic seasons—dry and rainy periods—that strongly influence subsistence activities and family life. During the light monsoon the weather is normally wet, so people stay closer to home in the hamlet. During the short-lived dry season, hunting parties are launched and men live for weeks in the forest. When new gardens are cultivated by the whole community, people also live away from hamlets for long periods of

TABLE 1   SEX-TYPING IN GARDENING ROUTINES

Routine	Plant	Putative "Sex" of Plant	Cultural Actor			
			MEN	WOMEN	INITIATE	CHILD
1. Scaling trees			x			
2. Clearing grass				x		
3. Loping off small trees/branches			x			
4. Burning vegetation				x		
5. Digging soil	Sweet potato	Female		x		x
6. Weeding						
	Taro	Male	x			
	Leafy greens, reeds, flowers	Female		x	x	
				x		x
	Sugar cane	Male	x	x	x	
	Banana trees	Male/ female	x	x	x	x
	Pandanus trees	Female	x	x		
7. Harvesting	Sweet potato			x		
	Taro		x			
	Sugar		x			
	Greens		x			

time in garden houses. Finally, ritual initiations and trading parties to other villages lead men away from the village. A good deal of time is thus spent removed from the hamlet over the course of a year.

Gardening routines are rigidly sex-typed. Being the main staple, sweet potatoes are the most common type of garden. They are planted in large tracts by a nuclear family, or a man and his wives, on his own clan land. If the bush is virgin forest, it is much harder work to clear. If it is secondary forest—the site of an old garden—the land will have lain fallow for five to ten years and, though still heavily forested, it is easier to till than virgin land. Men do all the chopping of trees; they climb up and cut off branches. Women cannot do this. Then the tree is slashed around its base, partially burned, and is left standing for firewood. All other activities related to sweet potatoes are mainly done by women, as shown in Table 1. Other crops, such as sugar cane, allow more gender flexibility as to who does the work.

Part of the reason for the rigid sexual division of labor is that all natural species are identified as being either "male" or "female." Sweet potatoes, for instance, are said to be soft and lie in the ground horizontally; so they are categorized as female. Taro is hard and grows vertically; so it is seen as being male. Therefore, women must tend sweet potatoes while men cultivate taro. We will see other examples of this sex-biased imagery, which I call *genderizing*, in Chapter 4. There we will also see how sex taboos and men's fears of women's pollution restrict both gardening activity and sexual behavior on a daily basis. And in Chapter 5 we will study ceremonial hunting and ordinary gardening in preparation for collective initiations.

Hunting is critical for two reasons: it provides most of the meat and it is a source of masculine prestige. Since Sambia have very few pigs, pork plays but a small role in gift-giving and feasts to mark ceremonies. For instance, in 1975, Nilangu—the largest hamlet in the valley—had a total pig population of about 15. Compare this puny figure with the Western Highlands Enga tribe, who have hundreds of pigs in each small settlement (Meggitt 1974). This is probably because Sambia is heavily forested, and has little grassland, in which pigs thrive best. Possum and similar marsupials are the game men hunt. This marks off the fringe-area Sambia from other more powerful and populous Central Highlands groups. Sambias emphasize possum hunting over pig husbandry, which reinforces the rigid sex-role dichotomy: men must hunt to provide meat for initiations and marriage exchanges since they cannot rely on vast pig herds, raised primarily by women but distributed by men, as elsewhere in New Guinea (see Brown 1978; A. J. Strathern 1972). Hunting is thus a central context for proving manhood.

There are three main types of hunting: the hunt with bow and arrow, trapping, and the scaling of trees to roust possum and bag them. There are no natural predators in Highlands New Guinea except man, who hunts and kills many species. Only the cassowary and wild boar are of any real danger to men. Bow-hunting is mainly used for birds. Trapping is done by snares or spring-traps, which are the only means of catching the elusive cassowary—so powerful and quick a bird that it eludes the bow. Trapping for possum, eel, and birds is respectable enough. In the case of possum hunting, what is most daring and masculine is to catch the prey with one's naked hands. This brings the greatest prestige. Men watch their forests daily so they know the ins and outs of game, including their lairs and trails. Possum are nocturnal mammals that forage high in trees. Men scale trees—some over 100 feet tall—aided only by vines. Then they grab the possum or roust them to the ground, where another hunter clubs them. Traditionally, a marriage gift of possum meat required long ropes of dried possum (cured over weeks for preservation in the high forest), some ropes being 20 feet long, which hold between 30 and 60 possum. No wonder these hunts required months of daily possum hunting for the bachelor, his clansmen, and age-mates (men initiated together, who call each other *ginyoko*). We shall see later how ritual initiation encourages boys to be strong hunters and virile men.

THE GENDER PROBLEM

The sexual polarity of Sambia economic roles is a powerful fact in the behavioral environment. Men spend most time with other men, and women and children are more often together. The sexes economically complement rather than cooperate in this division of labor. Perhaps because of the long-standing identification of one sex with certain routines, the opposite sex comes to envy them their power in that domain. The striking thing is a tendency for many activities to be restricted to one sex or the other.

Is it possible that children do not notice this? I think not. They grow up in this environment and come to associate most social and economic activities with gender roles. They tend also to evaluate these routines as being either more or less feminine or masculine. But whose value standard do they use in this evaluating, their mother's or their father's? It matters because their parents' views differ, as we shall see. In a certain sense the answer is: mother's. Yet this cultural identification creates a conflict for the boys, who must become like their fathers and unlike their mothers in every way. The way Sambia resolve this problem through ritual initiation forms the main theme of our case study.

THE REGIONAL PICTURE

Anthropologists have sometimes played down the historical relationship between neighboring tribes in the same geographic region. This is under-standable, since we ethnographers work in only one society for two years or less and often lack detailed observations of intertribal contacts. We emphasize the integrity and autonomy of the group with whom we lived. These view-points can result in a distorted image of a people: we do not see why one group was led historically or politically to behave in special ways that respond to neighboring groups, nor do we see how they emphasize for themselves their distinctive ethnicity by perpetuating certain social practices. So far, Sambia have been presented as an island unto themselves, unconnected to others in time and space. Let us now introduce their historical relation to other groups in the area.

First of all, to recapitulate, Sambia and their Anga neighbors are dwarfed by contrast to the immense tribal populations of the Central Highlands of New Guinea. True, Sambia were notorious warriors whose aggressive rep-utation extended far beyond any world they knew. But still, in comparison to mainstream Highlands societies, Sambia are a fringe-area people. Their language belongs to a completely different language phylum than that of the Highlands; their population is tiny compared to the tens of thousands in other Highlands groups like the Dani or Enga; they hunt far more than these others; they scarcely raise pigs and lack pig feast ceremonies; and they look south, toward Papuan groups, for their ancestrage and trading ties. At the same time, though, they have been culturally influenced by Highlands neighbors to the north, such as the Fore and Awa, from whom they have imported ritual patterns such as nose-bleeding ceremonies.

In these ways Sambia are but one of a set of seven societies formed with their immediate Anga neighbors in the Mountain District, the most southerly political division of the Eastern Highlands Province. It covers an area of about

8000 square miles and has a total population of 12,000 people, so a low population density (Brookfield and Hart 1971: 96–124). Of these Anga tribes only the Baruya people (Godelier 1969, 1982) outnumber the Sambia. In regional politics Sambia and the Baruya were the local kingpins in war (see Map 2). Although separated by middlemen tribes, each bordered four of the five remaining Mountain District tribes, so they were always involved in shifting alliances with smaller groups in between themselves. Thus, the Amdi tribe would attack the Usurumpia people. Sambia would aid the latter, with whom they intermarried, whereas Baruya would support the Amdi tribe. And so it went. On unconditional terms it was considered dangerous, or in most cases (as for the Amdi and Sambia) suicidal, to travel through these neighboring tribal areas. One's "security circle" (Lawrence 1966)—wherein people were relatively free of fear from being attacked—extended at most to only the territory of a man's phratry. Even within the Mountain District, then, men were extremely vulnerable to ambush or sorcery, so trade expeditions for feathers, bark capes, vegetal salt, and the like were undertaken only in friendly border areas (Godelier 1971). Other social contacts, especially marriage and initiation, rarely extended into friendly communities of the adjacent border tribes.

Despite a tradition of warring intertribal relationships, these seven Mountain District tribes shared important cultural and linguistic patterns, and they all were probably prehistoric migrants from around Menyamya, in South-Central Papua, some 200 years ago. Sambia themselves look to an archaic ritual center there called Kokona as their actual ancestral, as well as spiritual, "origin hole."

In 1976 I did a long patrol leading to this area, visiting the areas around Kokona. Ten Sambia went with me. We saw the basalt pillar outcrops Sambia associate with their sacred myths. Neither my friends nor their fathers had ever visited here, and they were in awe of what they had previously known only from legend. Yet they were frightened as well, afraid they would be attacked by the local people—ancient enemies—the group associated with the original cause for migration generations ago. Old wounds heal slowly. Besides, the Menya were cannibals (Sambia never were), and Sambia distrust headhunters, even those who now wear T-shirts.

The results of this common heritage of regional traditions can be seen in social organization throughout the Mountain District tribes: identical house forms, residential patterns, dress, nearly identical material culture; strikingly similar socialization and sleeping patterns, behavioral gestures, and body language; ritual, marriage, leadership, illness, and mortuary customs that are much alike in form and content. Most impressive of all for this case study is the universal presence of the men's secret societies throughout all these Anga tribes, extending throughout the Mountain District all the way to Menyamya and farther south. My reconnaissance patrols over the years have convinced me that a basic, archaic ritual complex is common to all these tribal groups (see Herdt 1984). It involves both male initiation and ritual homosexual practices of the form to be described below.

There is an old myth Tali and Kanteilo once told me that relates how Sambia followed the east-to-west movement of the sun from their ancestral territory at Kokona to the present-day valley. The sun bore them pandanus fruit and arrows but no stone war clubs. A strange oversight, for Sambia refer to the sun as "our father," the provider of all things—except for the first war club. They acquired such weapons from neighboring tribes. Sambia needed them because their legends say they left their ancestral home following a great war, only to enter the valley and war against its true owners, the Yulami. Soon they were at war with their neighbors too. Perhaps this myth mirrors the fact that Sambia always had two different types of warfare going on: the one, bow and arrow, the other (more deadly) with stone clubs used against other tribes. And perhaps it was not until they came to the Sambia Valley that their environment forced them into just as deadly intratribal war, using stone clubs as weapons against neighbors. This was a harsh reality, yet this is how Sambia associate their origins with ancient warfare, and their need to be strong to survive. Therefore, in that timeless realm of ritual, the old fear of a necessity for war still reigns, a theme we shall see reflected constantly in the next chapter.

2/Warfare and social organization

Warfare and social organization are interwoven in Sambia society and culture. Warfare was the ultimate reality—transcending and influencing everything else in the sense that no one could control its effects—in the behavioral environment. The fear of war breaking out at any time conditioned an aggressive masculine ethos, the special way in which men related to women, and the cultural institutions at large. We will here concentrate on the context of war, social structure, and sexual politics. In the following chapter we will study the effects of warfare on the socialization of children and adolescents into gender roles.

A WAR IS GOING ON

Sambia made prowess in battle a supreme measure of a man's place in this world and his social relationships in it. Their culture is still strongly tied to this mythology of the great warrior. Men were preoccupied with warfare, as the arrangement of their institutions and personal lives reveals. For war had been, as far as Sambia had ever known, chronic, widespread, and destructive. Warfare appropriated so much time. Men spent much of their time keeping watch against surprise attack and preparing for it (for example, by making weapons)—not to mention the long periods in battles and on war parties. Masculine prestige came from one's reputation as a warrior. In so many ways, great and small, men competed with one another for the social praise they constantly sought. Hence, from the time of their youth, men tried to establish their reputations as able marksmen, hunters, and as war leaders *(aamooluku)*.

A war is going on: this is the thought, the psychological perception that underlies much of what occurred in historic Sambia society. War could break out at any time. Political assassinations (either actual or attributed to sorcery) were commonplace. War leaders dominated the scene. When they happened to be shamans *(kwooluku)*, their magic and spirit familiars made them doubly powerful. Women needed armed guards to escort them to their gardens for the same reason. Even children could not play outside the hamlet since parents feared they would be easy targets for payback killings due to the strong value on blood revenge. Men watched their interactions with their wives closely for fear of sorcery practiced by the women in sympathy with their enemies should war break out. When such violence can erupt at any time, one remains constantly on guard.

In this sense there is a deep anxiety about having to defend a stone-age society prone to violence. From childhood onward the hamlets' warriorhood, constant battles, and war tales molded masculine education. The problems surrounding these preparations plague everyone, but they are felt most deeply by men. Masculinity is purchased through war exploits, including the defense of one's hamlet, guarding the innocent. Even today men are the more suspicious of Sambia citizens. In both group situations and individual relationships a wrong or an insult (imagined or real) can provoke quick violence. Without written laws, policemen, or courts, men must rely on their own might and their supporters in defending themselves. The grudges of the past smolder and die slowly. Men are sensitive to abusive language, which makes people cautious even of their words for fear they may unleash violence, or that other secret treachery, sorcery.

Hamlets lived always in military readiness for they felt that only cold-blooded action bought survival in the heat of attack. Beyond the hamlet, all groups were potentially hostile. In such a world the Sambia, like all Melanesians, as Theodore Schwartz (1973: 161) argues, must determine "Who can be trusted? The question is crucial for any culture." This thought underlies many Sambia stories about the past. In the behavioral environment of historic Sambia society, fear of attack always surrounded travel and everyday life.[1]

The need to rely on one's wits, brawn, and stone weapons creates a most watchful anxiety among Sambia men that is alien to most Westerners. Is it not difficult for the middle-class-comforted reader to appreciate the effects of this gut-level anxiety which, after years, becomes a constant murmur in one's insides? (I am sadly reminded that those among us born into the inner-city ghetto are not so unfamiliar with this picture.) But think of close brushes with death, as from accidents, and how these make us watchful about the feared situation of the accident for days afterward. From childhood on, this unpredictable environment promotes a reality-oriented, defensive anxiety reinforced by perceptions and responses of one's own parents: of one's mother, who clutches one during assaults on the hamlet, and of one's father, who leaves the household to fight, returning with wounds or glory, or not returning at all. The suspiciousness infects one's father who is also wary of one's mother, since she is "naturally" polluting and comes from a hostile hamlet. Beyond the hamlet, who is not regarded as potentially dangerous? Children growing

---

[1] Schwartz (1973: 157) states further: "The paranoid ethos in Melanesia derived from the uncertainty of life, from the high mortality rate and short life span, from the many births and relatively few surviving children. It depended on the uncertainty of the yield of productive activities. Perhaps more fundamentally for Melanesia the paranoid ethos related to the extreme atomism of social and political life, to the constancy and omnidirectionality of war and raiding, to the uncertainty of village and clan cohesion. In the Melanesian behavioral environment actuality and fantasy are mutually supportive. The effect is the same: the individual both projects his hostility upon his environment and realistically perceives it there. Projections that find confirmation in actual interpersonal hostility remain projections."

up in such conditions come to have suspiciousness pervade their thoughts and even their dreams.

The unpredictability and constant need for preparedness make men aggressive in their world view. Perhaps this is an inevitable response to both "projected and perceived enemies." People develop a social paranoia that becomes a "variable made constant, *a principle that cannot be relaxed*" (Schwartz 1973: 163, my emphasis). This idea helps us to calculate what the experience of chronic war might have been like. When something is stressed so much, it invades every part of life, gradually creating—from routine conversation and activities—the warrior values that permeate one's outlook on society and the universe.

SOCIAL STRUCTURE

The hamlet is the key unit of social structure. In most matters—such as war, hunting and gardening, marriage arrangements, and property disputes—men look to their hamlets and find mutual interest and support there. Hamlets have their own troubles, of course. Squabbles over gardens, adultery and marital arguments, not to mention petty gossip: all these created problems for peaceful coexistence. At its worst, the disputes led to fighting and a rupture in the hamlet, with the disgruntled faction (usually a clan or clan segment) forming a new hamlet elsewhere. But that was rare. Most Sambia still view their hamlet as home and a haven protecting them from precarious multitudes of enemy groups and evil spirits.

Hamlets have women's (or nuclear family) houses *(aambelangu)* and one or two men's clubhouses *(kwolangu)* associated with rigid taboos of all kinds. Women are felt to be polluting, especially their menstrual blood. Since they can transfer the pollution, they cannot ever enter the clubhouse or go near its male initiates. Women must travel only on specified female paths inside the hamlet, whereas initiates must travel only on physically elevated male paths. Families live in women's houses. Adult men sleep and eat in the male space of the women's house. Their wives, unmarried daughters, and infant uninitiated sons sit in the female space. Women should not interfere with men's activities either, and they are forbidden from touching men's heads, weapons, and ritual ornaments. Somewhat older boys sleep in their fathers' male space.

All initiated unmarried males reside in the men's clubhouse and must avoid women (and to a lesser extent children) at all times. The clubhouse is the real nerve center of masculine activity and secrecy because ritual, warfare, and hunting groups operate from there. During such times men leave their wives and sleep in the clubhouse. This creates a barrier between fathers and sons until the boys are initiated. Boys and women are kept in the dark about some men's activities, especially ritual events. Ordinary activities like gardening and feasts women and children knew of; but all of my male informants

Photo 2. Initiates huddle for taro feast (Sambia Valley initiations, 1975)

disclaim any knowledge of ritual secrets before their initiations. It is as if there are two worlds in their childhoods: that of the men and that of the women.

This sort of men's clubhouse is a distinctive culture-area institution in New Guinea societies. One sees similarities, even striking resemblances, between the male organization and ceremonial behavior surrounding men's clubhouses everywhere on the island. Yes, it is true that some cultures differ in ritual beliefs regarding male cult life; that some groups emphasize warfare much more than others, as, for example, the aggressive Mundugumor versus the peaceful Mountain Arapesh (Mead 1935) in the great Sepik River basin, far north and west of Sambia. And some societies place a larger emphasis on sacred art in the clubhouse or upon mythology told by men; or the women may play a more prominent role in the symbolism of certain male cult rituals (see Herdt 1982a). Yet these differences must not blind us to the cultural patterns that men share through the institution of the clubhouse. These include military training, supervision and education of boys in the masculine realm, the transmission of cultural knowledge surrounding hunting magic and warrior folklore, the organization of hunting, some separation or recognition of the difference between men and women, the socially sanctioned use of ritual paraphernalia and musical instruments such as flutes and bullroarers, and so forth. These distinctive customs anchored the men's world in the clubhouse throughout Melanesia.

The division between men and women in the Sambia hamlet was based also on kinship. A hamlet is organized by the core of its male patrilineal kinsmen (reckoned by genealogical descent from father to son) who were born there and are expected to always reside therein. Hamlets are internally segmented into smaller descent groups. The largest unit of hamlet grouping is the great-clan, which consists of all persons who trace genealogical descent to a known, fictitiously named ancestor. The great-clan is usually named after the founding clan of the hamlet. Its members can also be dispersed in other hamlets. Great-clan leadership is vested in eldest males of its founding clan. The hamlet is made up of one or more great-clans. These great-clans are subdivided into two or more component clans (*iku*, for tree). Clans link persons who can actually demonstrate descent from a known real ancestor (one to three generations back).

Clansmen usually reside in the hamlet of their father or, less commonly, that of their father's brothers, biological or more distantly related, who may reside in a neighboring hamlet of the same phratry. Hence, patrilocal residence—living in father's village—is very high among Sambia, with more than 80 percent of Sambia males residing partrilocally. Clansmen share collective property, especially gardenland and pandanus and forest preserves, as noted above. But the individual clansman also has his own personal property (such as garden plots, pandanus groves), inherited from his father. Sambia have a kinship system that stresses generational relationships. Clansmen refer to one another as "brothers" or "fathers" or "grandfathers," and their related children of the same generation refer to each other as "brother" or "sister." Hamlet play groups of children are thus reared as if they belong to a large extended family. The numerical size of clans and great-clans depends on the hamlet's size and whether the clans are localized in one hamlet or dispersed. Female clansmen do not inherit land property, though they have "use" rights in certain lands. Women are seldom utilized for reckoning descent because they often move out of the hamlet upon marriage. In sum, a hamlet's clan groups are united by an image of common descent as brothers who support one another in economic production, warfare and ritual, as well as in marriage.

The clansmen of a hamlet are also allied in matters of warfare and ritual with those of other (usually neighboring) hamlets who belong to the same phratry. Phratry members are descended from a single, fictitious ancestor, making them "brothers" or "age-mates." Numboolyu is such a mythical ancestor. He came from Kokona, so all his descendants share a common origin. Furthermore, the separate clans of a phratry participate in a structure of rituals, some of which they own as intangible property. Next, and related to ritual identity, is the wearing of a common style of male grass sporran, or grass apron (a kind of grass skirt like a kilt, which in males covers only the genital area; in females, the grass forms a true skirt). This is a sign of their phratry membership and an emblem of ethnic identity in intertribal relationships. In times of war, hamlets of a phratry can call on each other for assistance. These facts reveal how phratry organization is linked to ritual initiation in many ways.

Neighboring hamlets in a valley tend to jointly sponsor collective ritual initiations. These occur every three or four years and are first focused on the construction of a large culthouse (called the *moo-angu*). The culthouse is a production of the locally involved men of the clans of these hamlets, usually at the behest of their elders and war leaders. It is always built adjacent to a danceground (*korumundiku*: dancing, *korumu*; bonfire *diku*). Although each hamlet has a separate danceground, collective initiation is invariably held on a neutral danceground—associated with all the hamlets of a phratry—and situated at a distance from any one of them. This collectivity of neighboring hamlets within a valley, who usually join to cosponsor *bachelor initiations*, I call a danceground confederacy (or simply confederacy).

The confederacy is thus a political and ritual grouping of local hamlets who suspend their intermittent fighting long enough to initiate together. Sometimes these hamlets even feud with others of their own phratry. Hamlets of different phratries, however, fight more frequently and with more bloodshed and vengeance. Still, their joint initiations make their sons age-mates, members of a regional age-set. As adults, some of these men marry their age-mates' sisters and daughters, so they become in-laws. This means that such marriages are contracted with sometime-enemies. So male age-mates not only share in ritual secrets, but they exchange their sisters and clanswomen as pawns to opposing hamlets to obtain wives. No wonder men feared women: their wives often came from enemy groups. Kinship and intermarriage, joint initiation and warfare, all are factors in the functioning of the confederacy.

Within the Sambia tribe there are two types of confederacy organization. The first consists of only one phratry, in one valley. These hamlets, to re-iterate, believe they share common descent, geographic origin, and ritual customs. We best call this unit an *intra*phratry confederacy. The phratry itself is identified with one of its own dancegrounds, and it internally organizes collective initiations only by and for its member hamlets. This form of initi-ation usually occurs in settlements such as the Moonagu phratry in the Sambia River Delta (see Map 2), geographically isolated from other phratries. The second type of confederacy is more complex and powerful. We will study its magico-political form in the Sambia River Valley. This is an *inter*phratry confederacy incorporating hamlets of two or three different phratries. When peace permits, these groups jointly initiate their sons on a single danceground, which thus crosscuts phratry boundaries (see Photo 5, p. 46). Over the past 60 years, Sambia say, their valley held many interphratry initiations. From the 1940s until pacification, however, warfare increasingly blocked these per-formances. This changed in the 1960s, as we shall see. It seems, then, that interphratry confederacies are more unstable than the smaller intraphratry organizations. Yet, in both types of confederacies the initiation program coincided with unpredictable war and peace.

Let us now turn to warfare, to the concept of strength, and to associated male values that Sambia identify with the complex of war.

JERUNGDU AND THE MALE ETHOS

If we would gauge the inner workings of Sambia society through the strivings of its men toward an ideal of masculinity—a state of being both chosen and necessary—we would discover that Sambia belong to that group of warrior cultures that stress ideas about strength. We then must focus our sights on understanding their single most powerful concept: *jerungdu.*

Jerungdu is physical (biologic) strength,* the supreme essence of maleness in body, personality, and spirit. The concept subsumes hardness and resolve, bravery and warlike exploits, among its connotations. *Jerungdu* means the strength to do battle: not just to defend oneself, one's family and property, but to prove or reaffirm the fact of one's masculine powers. Like a silent power behind the throne, ideals of *jerungdu* embody the essence of a masculine state of being, a guide for rhetorically type-casting all others, and the socially necessary way to behave. *Jerungdu* speaks to the hard reality of male existence.

Even though *jerungdu* is believed crucial for the creation and maintenance of masculinity, it is an outstanding problem of male development that this state of being is not natural or innate; it must be achieved. We must understand this belief in its social context.

Jerungdu is a bodily essence, a substance akin to life-force. At bedrock, it is semen *(kweikoonbooku)* that bestows this power. *Jerungdu* is thus a substance uniquely male, produced and transmitted only by men. Here is a simple example. My informant, Tali, when talking about *jerungdu*, said this: "A woman—she has no *jerungdu*. A boy has none. That [*jerungdu*] of a man— semen—they have none of that." Semen creates what Sambia call the "hard" parts of human anatomy: bones and muscle and skin tissue, as well as the brain, spinal column, hair, and fingernails. *Jerungdu* is observable, too, in the virile qualities of large physique, taut skin, shiny face and nose, and sharp eyes. The secondary sex traits of puberty likewise stem from semen. (Not from sperm: Sambia do not recognize conception as we know it.) Semen stimulates the growth of these masculine qualities which, together with the capacity to ejaculate and the willingness to do battle, constitute the culturally shared gender signs of *jerungdu.*

Above all else, the ideals and sentiments of *jerungdu* lead to dominance[2] behavior: males must constantly strive to seem manly. In its simplest form, this is because society—one's parents, siblings, and peers—demands that a male demonstrate his strength to reap the benefits of being a fully masculine adult. It is also because a man believes his life-force and existence hinge on possessing abundant *jerungdu*. This is why the individual is motivated to dominate in warfare and in sexual intercourse. Sambia men (like men elsewhere) rely upon their culture—values, symbols, and myths other men accept—to justify their action for the sake of their own *jerungdu*. And there is conflict, sour grapes, and cruelty in Sambia life as a result. Yet there is also care and pageantry in Sambia relationships; and besides, men feel that their

---

* Throughout the text *jerungdu* and "strength" are used interchangeably in this sense; other connotations will be annotated as appropriate.

[2] I use *dominance behavior* as a descriptive concept in relation to *behavioral outcomes*: the subjective principle that, as a result of his interactions with others, a man should be perceived as more masculine and stronger (possessing more *jerungdu*) than them.

dominance is necessary to defend the community and get done what needs doing. For these reasons, *jerungdu* is not only the key principle of all masculine behavior; it represents a principle of the male cult that can never be relaxed.

Now let us see how this value system influenced society and the individual in the main social institutions: marriage and sexual relationships; religion; leadership and social stereotyping among men; and warfare.

MARRIAGE AND SEXUAL ANTAGONISM

How, where, and when to obtain a wife are among the major problems of masculine life. All men must be married and father children to be esteemed as whole persons, as sons who have become manly adults. Females are in short supply since polygyny allows powerful and senior men to take several wives at the expense of weaker men. Adding to this problem, wives must be obtained from outside one's clan and preferably beyond one's hamlet. So this means women must be traded—sometimes against their will—with other, often hostile groups, in unstable political circumstances. Virtually all marriage is between people in the valley, for intertribal marriage is rare. One relies on the elders of the hamlet to negotiate, persuade, or coerce other men to exchange their daughters or sisters in any of three ways for marriage. Two forms of marriage contract predominate: infant betrothal and brother-sister exchange; the other type, bride service, is a weak third.

Infant betrothal *(ichinyu)* is the most honored, complicated, and traditional marriage practice. It is an old-fashioned custom based on the giving of meat gifts to a woman at the birth of a daughter. Infant betrothal accounts for upward of 40 percent of all marriages in Upper Sambia Valley hamlets. In larger hamlets it occurs between the component clans of a hamlet. It creates political alignments of in-laws between neighboring hamlets. The rule is that a woman obtained as a wife through infant betrothal must be replaced—her daughter or another woman returned by the man recipient or the donor clan group—in the next generation. Besides this expected reciprocity, infant betrothal warms up relations between affines as in-laws are expected to provide food gifts, render assistance, and avoid direct battle with each other in warfare. More broadly, it tends to solidify intrahamlet unity and moderate interhamlet relationships. However, the question always remains: Will such-and-such group give us back a woman in the next generation?

Brother-sister exchange contracts *(yandi-andi)* are less valued socially than infant betrothal, though sister exchange is the more pragmatic and numerous of all presently existing marriages. The principle is simple and less troublesome politically: two individual men (usually acting in concert with their clan brothers) arrange to exchange their sisters (biological or classificatory) as wives to each other. But if for some reason one of the men objects to marrying the woman offered, then he may proceed differently. He can negotiate with a third party to obtain a different woman, trading the woman of the donor group to the third party to conclude the exchange and have a wife. Sometimes, then, as many as six clans are involved in sister-exchange marriage. If there is a discrepancy in the ages of the women's brothers, an exchange is concluded with the older man's promise of his sister later to come to the immature male. For example, a marriageable-aged man may arrange to marry the older, marriageable-aged sister of a boy; the older man then promises to give his younger sister (or another substitute clan sister) to that boy after his puberty for marriage. This introduces the uncertainty of future conditions, as in infant betrothal. The ideal is for men of equal age to have an immediate transaction (though discussed for months or even years in advance) with no further obligation on their part. The advantages are obvious despite the lack of pomp and ceremony accompanying infant-betrothal marriage.

The third form of marriage contract is bride service. If a man is desperate, has no claims on infant girls or available sisters (or willing clansmen to help him with such) for obtaining a wife, he may ingratiate himself to an older man with daughters or sisters in the hope (not promise) that eventually one shall be given (*yashyotwi*) to him. This is an uncommon practice. For one thing, Sambia men are too proud to ingratiate themselves easily. When it occurs, however, the expectation is the same as for infant betrothal: eventually, the recipient must return a daughter or other marriageable woman to his father-in-law's group.

An even rarer form of marriage should be mentioned here: wife-stealing. If one is man enough and brave enough, he may try to steal the woman of another group. Wife-stealing inside the valley is rare but not unknown; indeed, it is so unusual that I would omit it except for its glorified mythology: men feel that, among the best of warriors, it should be counted a daring ideal for them to someday, somewhere, steal the woman of an enemy after doing him in. Wife-stealing was thus a male fantasy of ultimate conquest. (In Upper Sambia hamlets I knew of only a handful of such wives taken over the last two generations; see below.) There is a big payoff for the risks, of course: what is stolen need never be returned.

Since the mid-1970s another form of marriage has been introduced: bride wealth. A man and his clanmates will "pay" for a bride, usually in money. In a few short years this practice has dramatically increased in frequency, but this takes us beyond the period of this study. I shall return to it, however, in the "Afterword."

Not only the character of Sambia social organization but the ideals of masculinity are deeply wedded to this structure of types of marriage. The structural currents are twofold: obtain a wife by infant betrothal and take on a *delayed-exchange* obligation in the next generation; contract a brother-sister marriage and this *direct exchange* requires no further obligation. In either case there is an implied willingness to create social bonds with an individual and/or his group. The most significant form of such relationships is a shaky alliance between the in-laws. Sambia refer to this long-standing relationship between neighboring hamlets as *ninbuninyaalum* ("sister's husband, my in-laws"). Later we will see how ritual homosexuality reflects such alliances.

In many ways marriage relationships provide a "push" to Sambia society and its individuals along a path toward intergroup stability. Yet, the violence of war and the concept of *jerungdu* are factors of dominating that tend to "pull" apart and destabilize the society. For instance, what will become of the boy whose older brother-in-law promised him a wife in a sister-exchange contract but fails to deliver? Will the boy as a man seek revenge, which leads to warfare? The awareness of this "push" and "pull" in Sambia masculine behavior is a definite concern in growing up and in being initiated.

Masculine apprehension is also embedded deeply in male-female relationships, which are highly associated with the economic division of labor. Men feel that maleness is a higher, cleaner, better essence of nature than femaleness; women are only there. Women feel the men are too aggressive and somewhat lazy, yet men must be reckoned with. Masculinity is both a social framework of perceptions and a cultural way of acting, and these emerge in two contrary settings: the women's houses and the men's clubhouse.

Femininity is associated only with the women's houses and the menstrual hut. Women have their own world, which is secret in some respects and off-limits to men. Ritual and military activities derive from the clubhouse, which forms a barrier between men and women. Women are responsible for supplying most garden food, especially during time of war. They were in the past no doubt cynical of these arrangements, since nowadays some women scoff at the men's preoccupation with old war tales. Even men recall that they tired of the constant fighting that disrupted gardening and hunting, making food scarce. But it is the nature of female essence that motivates men's antagonism toward women.

Men cling to a view that masculinity can be depleted: a belief that the male body runs down and wears out, due to the notion of a short supply of semen, *jerungdu*. Women extract this, sapping a man's substance. Through intercourse a wife is believed to draw selfishly on her husband's substance, redoubling her own strength. No wonder women are healthy and outlive us, men say. And recall that wives are of other groups, often from potential enemy hamlets, so they cannot be trusted. Yet only a wife and children bring full manhood. Here we have a basic tension that is central to the male ethos.

Women's sexuality has mysterious origins diametrically opposed to that of men's. Men have body strength sapped to produce children, which depletes them, inducing weakness and old age and death. On the other hand, men feel women bear children and yet remain strong and vital, outliving one and then another husband, to remarry without remorse for insatiable sexual desire and longevity. Note that this view pertains to *marriageable* women; mothers and sisters are not feared in this way. However, the men generalize so: they not only regard women as hostile, even evil, but ironically they see females as inferior, even though their natural powers enable women to procreate and outlive men. We will study these contradictions more fully in the following chapter.

A wife thus brings a man maturity, food, a home, and heirs, all necessary for full manhood. A wife is a man's sexual property, as other men recognize. She draws him into social relationships with others, including in-laws. Relationships to in-laws are demanding and also rewarding. Children bring full adult status to both husband and wife, but that is not all. Sambia do not live only for the enjoyment of their offspring, yet one finds it difficult to imagine them without the bright faces of their children, who so innocently break through the heavy formality of men and women. Sambia look down upon a barren woman and later in life pity her for "her" condition. Men deny sterility in themselves. Jealous male suitors who commit sorcery on the female to spite the marriage are usually blamed. Yet men also recognize barren women as full-time sexual partners, something a nursing mother cannot be. No woman goes unmarried for long. But some men do. And without the advantages of marriage, men are nothing.

Let us summarize. The qualities of Sambia male-female relations may be seen as consequences of warfare, the male concept of *jerungdu*, and the aggressive behavior deriving from its socialization. Male values motivate a struggle for strength. Yet in male-female interactions one sees terrible signs of opposition and fear, such as in men's beliefs about women's bodies. This overall tendency has been called *sexual antagonism* in New Guinea societies. Men and women are not only different, but opposed, and even hostile in some respects. The sexes are at war. Why should this be? Importing women from potential enemy hamlets is a major cause. Marrying spouses—strangers—as pawns in a political tug-of-war between groups is another reason. And the long separation of the sexes during development is a third. This latter idea we will study in the next chapter. But, in general, a man's dominance of others is seen as a confirmation of manhood in his eyes and those of his mates, so the effect of masculine values reaches far into other areas of social action.

MASCULINE VALUES AND GENDER STEREOTYPES

In a company of warriors, there are but a handful of ruling stereotypes. This restrictiveness is understandable: a warriorhood requires hard standards of conduct that keep the ranks in line. Moreover, military rules create *esprit de corps*; they also maintain allegiance to the military club by downplaying men's personal needs (Langness 1967). Such stereotypes affect the wider society, though their restrictions fall hardest on men since women here do not fight in war. Military orders and such standards are common in most of New Guinea Highland societies (see Langness 1972; Koch 1974; Mead 1935; Meggitt 1977; Read 1954; Reay 1959; Sillitoe 1978; A. J. Strathern 1972: 187–91). Such stereotypes manage Sambia social behavior and have many consequences. Gender stereotypes also dictate attitudes about one's position in sexual intercourse. Masculine stereotypes, whether in serious rhetoric or personal jokes, control the degrees of sexual freedom in Sambia society.

The gender stereotypes are thoroughly structured in men's thinking, speech, and institutions. They can be described in two ways: as a set of characteristic gender identity states, *ways of being* male or female; and as a set of distinctive gender statuses, *ways of acting* masculine or feminine. Three verbal categories of being stand out most: *jerungdu*, being strong; *havaltnu*, being equivalent (symmetrical, competitive); and *wogaanyu*, being unmanly (weak, passive). When applied as judgments to others' behavior, the gender stereotypes have strong effects. They occur in both male and female thought, but are most marked in males. Such labelling is usually specific to particular acts in a situation, so it characterizes the situational behavior of individuals rather than their permanent state of being. When a boy shows fear at a masculine act like climbing trees to hunt possum, for example, he will be called *wogaanyu*. Besides this, there are two prominent male-gender role models: the *aamoo-luku* (war leader) and the *wusaatu* (rubbish man). Ideal types they are, but no less powerful because of that. There is a third type, too, the *aambei-wutnyi* (female kind), meaning a gentle man, which is akin to our label of *sissy*; but it is seldom used, being a "quiet category." These labels and sex-role types crosscut all other social, kinship, or ritual status terms among males, from small boys to elders. So the identity categories apply to all males regardless of their age, rank, ritual status, and reproductive status, and are powerful mechanisms for self-control and social regulation.

We need to examine these gender stereotypes and see how they are inter-related, for their sharp edges condition all social interaction, especially in ritual. The logic of ritual takes these categories for granted: it sometimes blows up their significance inside ritual dramas, exploits their mythology in teaching boys about manliness, or deflects attention elsewhere—away from humans to nature or spirits—where the same stereotypes are seen. But what-ever, the logic of ritual never forgets these gender stereotypes.

The essence of *jerungdu*—the state of being physically strong—is observable in one's deeds. In its highest form, *jerungdu* is like our notion of prowess in battle. Yet *jerungdu* also aims men toward masculine competence (as defined by Sambia culture) in hunting, ritual, and sex. It drives men to be strongest, bravest, and best. Stated simply, *jerungdu* means pure masculinity.

Havaltnu, meaning *to be the same (havaltnuntu)*, provides a more complex counterpoint to the concept *jerungdu*. *Havaltnu* can be translated as *like-kind* or *equivalent*, according to the speaker and the context. Age-mates are be-lieved to be *like-kind*. Indeed, we would not go far wrong in seeing age-mates as *sine qua non* persons who must be equivalent. The same idea applies to female age-mates too, though not as rigorously. Equivalence stems from age-mates being of the same sex and having been born in the same time period, therefore being roughly of the same physical size and capacities. These char-acteristics give rise to an expectation—that age-mates should be biologically and socially alike.

Initiation formalizes this standard. Age-mate A is expected to match age-mate B in all accomplishments; so this norm creates competition between them. By contrast, if A's achievements (including physical growth) are not matched by B in scaling trees or marksmanship, then B is socially diminished by comparison to A in the eyes of others. Hence, there is always a tension between age-mates because they are constantly being compared.

That men can be ridiculed in everyday life for their masculine failings testifies to the relentless stress placed on conformity to male ideals. Brief mention of the third verbal category, *wogaanyu*, will highlight this point. *Wogaanyu* has a wide range of negative connotations specifying that various acts are unmanly and therefore *shameful (wungulu).*[3] Physical weakness, fear, laziness, and neglect of ritual or age-mate obligations are all acts that can be labelled *wogaanyu*. Cowardice is most shameful of all. To call someone *wogaanyu* is an insult in face-to-face encounters. It can provoke anger or shame or both in the accused, depending on the status and social bonds between the two men. A father or brother can admonish another man in a way an age-mate dares not. The war leader and rubbish man provide the opposing models for this evaluating. Boys and men are evaluated using these stereotypes; if found lacking, the stigma of the *wogaanyu* accusation falls on them. Even a young war leader's failures could be labelled this way, dared another brave the accusation, tantamount to an insult that could lead to a duel. Yet the accusation need not be made directly. For men, like women, gossip, and their private judgments find currency among them and put pressure on public opinion. Envy and jealousy are no doubt at work in this informal social control process, for when someone grows too strong or too weak, people's words help keep them in line. Being a war leader or simply being male, therefore, demands scrupulous attention to face-to-face interactions at all times, lest a man's behavior betray any sign of unmanly weakness.

As a male acts in one way or another, he communicates being strong, competitive, or unmanly. This is a process in which internal motivations produce behaviors that the society labels according to far-reaching gender standards. Sambia recognize that men have different physical constitutions and personal histories and, if pressed, they will admit that such differences influence male behavior. But they dislike recognizing environmental differences and instead stress the *biological* basis of being strong or weak. They punish boys who act *wogaanyu*, and favor—indeed demand—that their sons show *jerungdu*. Now what matters is how situational gender evaluations are converted into permanent social titles.

Somewhere in a male's development, the signs pointing to a boy's being a war leader or a rubbish man change from being temporary labels into more binding stereotypes. The symptom is no longer odd-man-out: it is what usually happens and becomes expected. Constant acts labelled *jerungdu* by others transform a man into a *strong man*. Being consistently brave in battle leads to being called a *war leader*. Continued acts of weakness lead others to call someone a *rubbish man*, which is defined mainly by being afraid of fights. Therefore, weakness and strength are ultimately judged by perceptions of a man's prowess in battle. Boys are expected to model themselves after the war leader and to despise the rubbish man.

I am speaking of idealizations, not actual behavior. In reality, Sambia recognize that men are weak or strong, rubbish men or war leaders, without

---

[3] Please note that the feeling of shame among Sambia is a powerful experience, more powerful, I think, than our Western label for that emotion. At its extreme, shame can result in suicide or murder. Chapter 4 details how the male cult rituals use shame as a social control.

usually saying so. Here, personal and kinship sentiments intervene, for one may note that a paternal uncle is a rubbish man and still value him affectionately as a hamlet elder. (I cannot know how this changed since pacification, but I am certain men are allowed more freedom in deviating from masculine standards than before.) In the culture of my childhood—Midwestern America, c. 1955—a similar contrast was made between musclemen and sissies, between weakness and strength.

The *war leader* is a label assigned to fight leaders, skilled hunters, and virile men, and this is romanticized among the Sambia. All true warriors are believed to be potent. There is a double sense of this potency: the obvious one is that warriors are surefooted and efficient in manly endeavors. The other sense is of a kind of liquidity or abundance of body fluids—sweat, mucus, blood, urine, and especially semen—which are noticeable and symptomatic signs of *jerungdu*. Sambia believe the war leader has a generous seminal emission every time. Yet—please note—this male essence is contained within a hard, tough, pointed, lean body, taller and bigger than most. Sambia say that the war leader even has an erection going into battle! The war leader should be physically big: broad shouldered, barrel chested, with taut skin, sharp eyes, abundant body hair, a small waist, abdomen, and arse. (A male infant born with body hair is felt to hold promise of being a war leader.) The war leader as a boy is distinguished by his sharpshooting, his love of hunting (birds), his pugnacious, easily angered, quarrelsome nature (he enjoys fighting with other children), and, appropriately enough, his tough quietness. This quietness—the Sambia word is *mangu-tetnyi*—has qualities of arrogance, tight-lipped pragmatism, proud carriage. And humorlessness. Initiates are punished for laughing in public and men rarely crack jokes except in private with their cronies. War leaders do not chatter or make idle conversation (like some men do)—that is too feminine. There is a distinctly antisocial flavor in the extreme form of these traits. Swashbuckling and fearless, war leaders enjoy aggressive confrontations and battles. In their religious belief, Sambia hold that deceased war leaders become the fearsome forest spirits, the *ikeiaru*. Rubbish men never become that. War leaders are proud. They cannot bear being shamed and they become arrogant and withdrawn when ignored. They may be silent in the presence of elder authorities, but they are cagey and distrusted by equals. Here is an apparent paradox I have noticed in several war leaders. Though usually quiet, they are demonstrative when greeting me, grabbing hold of me, big smiles (empty smiles) and sticky praise, touching my body, searching me (frisking me). Sambia, too, note this: the war leader "butters you up"; but later, in a battle, "It's you he'll aim toward killing," they say.

But there is a less extreme form of this ideal. Sambia refer respectfully to their older war leaders as the "mother of our hamlet." This image conveys the sense that, whatever else holds true, the war leader "guards the doorway" (the entrance within the barricades) to the hamlet and is its true protector. All of a war leader's aggressiveness and spite—his *jerungdu*—is to be aimed beyond his group toward enemies. In this sense, too, older war leaders who have proven themselves can relax more as others come up the ranks.

Photo 3. Mon, the dead war leader

Lastly, war leaders are womanizers, but of a special kind. They don't love women—they lust for women. Bearing the very face of manliness, they prefer men and the company of men. They are thought to have been rapacious fellators as boys (hence they possess abundant semen and *jerungdu*). As bachelors, they don't leave boys alone, and enjoy using younger initiates as an erotic outlet whenever the need presents itself. They are also felt to attract women easily, copulating with wives as soon as it is possible to do so. And they then prefer women over boys (since they are said to grow sexually bored with initiates sooner than other men). War leaders enjoy the erotic conquest. They are no friend of women or of femininity. Rather in the manner of collecting possum pelts, or of boasting of their victories—their enemies slain in battle—war leaders take women and acquire them as wives.

An example will help illustrate. Mon, the greatest war leader in the valley, was a remarkable man. You can see his toughness in Photo 3. He died in 1982. But even in his late sixties he was rough and tough, acknowledged as *the* leading elder of Pundei hamlet. He killed at least eight men and was involved in countless battles. He married six times (outliving three of his wives) and fathered over 20 children. Until his death he was one of the three oldest living people in the valley—survivor of wars, epidemics, famines, virtually the last of all his brothers, age-mates, friends, and enemies. Mon acted the part of the ruthless, cold-blooded warrior who for decades led by bluster, guile, intelligence, threats, and his warlike skills. For instance, he proved himself a master of treachery, not above killing a clan brother, Weiyu's father, as described in the next chapter. He held shamanic powers for a time and practiced sorcery to uphold his control. But Mon was never much of a shaman and he preferred the direct force of deeds to magic. How ironic that his son—Sakulambei—is a pseudo-hermaphrodite and powerful shaman (see Chapter 3). Thus, Mon firmly controlled his world for close to half a century.

By contrast, the rubbish man is small and diminutive, afraid of battle, and generally assailed as inferior. A rubbish man, men make clear, *does not kill men*. He is a weakling, the passive follower; he can be pushed around. More than this, the rubbish man stereotype implies cowering and ineptness, making a mockery of manhood: creatures to be ignored, ridiculed, even hated, but not pitied. The very name "rubbish man" connotes femininity by its association with sweet potatoes (*wusaatu*, *wusu*, sweet potato, or food provided by women; *aatu*, hand): females, dirty soil, and soft (feminine, as opposed to hard, masculine, such as taro) tubers. The rubbish man label is a humiliating stigma.

By definition the rubbish man is also *wogaanyu*, unmanly. What does this suggest? He is, mainly, lacking in *jerungdu*. This means more than that he is simply unaggressive, a poor hunter or fighter. He tries to compensate by acting tough with women or children. Yet his gender identity is associated with shortness, small physique, late puberty, laziness, and compensatory loud speech. (To paraphrase Shakespeare, Sambia would say: "Methinks he doth protest his masculinity too much!") The rubbish man is short on semen, manliness. Why? Men say the rubbish man is one who did not ingest enough semen from enough men as an initiate. Like women—who, as inferiors, men identify with the very name of *wogaanyu*—a rubbish man is not tough enough, cannot scale trees, lift heavy items, or tighten a bow. Consequently, men feel he will not acquire a wife quickly. Sambia say the major reason is that women despise the rubbish man, who is too female-like to be exciting to women. In some respects women share the same view. Men can be labelled rubbish men for many reasons, but nowadays two things stand out most: cowardice and being too frequently in women's company. So the rubbish man is not as erotically exciting as a war leader, he finds it harder to get a wife, he fathers fewer children, and—note the ironic stress—he is too comfortable being with women. In such ways the rubbish man is a failure at being ideally masculine.

Sambia manhood values phallicness and checks the weak traits in males. The image of the war leader is strength and courage itself, a symbol of masculinity—of belonging to the fight, the forest, and the company of men. The image of the rubbish man gets no praise and earns the hand-me-down hostility of men and women alike. His weakness and inability to fight invite an early death or another man to steal his wife or his wife to leave him for a stronger hunter and defender. These are bad omens for the rubbish man's personal safety and success in marriage. The message seems clear in its conscious condemnation of the useless rubbish man: of this part of himself a

Sambia must reassure himself that "that stereotype is not me," and, moreover, he must believe it.

Among Sambia, therefore, the state of maleness is not in the gift of nature. Masculinity, in all its aspects, is a personal achievement; it is the highest expression of being toward which a man must strive. Because it is tenuous, men always feel pressure upon themselves as individuals and upon their collective status as a group. The ethic of *jerungdu*, instilled throughout the long initiations into manhood, compels men to be dominant in all manner of interpersonal relationships and activities, thus ensuring that *jerungdu* is a governing cultural principle of Sambia life.

RELIGION

We need to review one final area of Sambia social organization before turning directly to warfare. Religion, like the other social institutions discussed above, was strongly affected by the warrior ethos of men. Along with many New Guinea peoples, Sambia do not distinguish absolutely between the "natural" and the "supernatural." To them, their spirit beings and the forces of nature are real and alive. So we may say that their religion is animistic. Nor is religion cut off from other kinds of social activity. Ritual we can see as a means of attempting to communicate with spirits and with nature, and thereby as a way to control or at least to placate these forces. Since Sambia feel that humans are caught in a world not of their making and over which they have little control, we may also say that they have a fatalistic world view. Their shamans and initiation rites, however, offer hope in the struggle to control the great powers of life and death. Here we shall briefly examine Sambia ideas about spirits, death, and shamanism; in Chapter 5 the initiations are explored in depth.

To understand spirit beliefs, we need to recognize how Sambia connect the soul (*koogu*) to the mind and body. For Sambia, like other New Guinea peoples, the soul is an independent agent, an entity beyond control of the person, and one that, during sleep, wanders about free of the body. Hence, dreams are viewed as real events that occur to the counterpart of one's body, the soul. Likewise, the individual's personality and waking consciousness are different from the soul. Both males and females have souls that are associated with their social personhood, before and after death.

One's soul emerges in the womb, the result of maternal (blood) and paternal (semen) sources. Souls are vaguely sex-linked, such that men believe their own souls are more strongly identified with their fathers, indicating animation—consciousness—attributed to the soul. Thought or personality (*koontu*)*

---

* *Koontu* and *koogu* are different words constructed from the same, common, root prefix morpheme, *koo*, which generally marks male gender. Yet their linguistic closeness probably attests to their psychological closeness.

is distinct also from one's soul. Thought indicates intention and will. Infants, for example, have souls from fetal life onward, though they have little consciousness until around age two, when they can respond to their names and carry out orders such as "fetch that pipe." But not until initiation do boys have much thought *that counts*: that is, they are irresponsible because they are not consciously accountable to ritual and moral norms. We shall see in Chapter 4 the dilemma this age gap poses for their fathers. Finally, spirit familiars (*numelyu*) are acquired later through various initiation ceremonies. These familiars (animals, plants, spirit beings) are counterparts of one's soul. They aid and protect the soul in various ways, can be seen in dreams, and generally support good health and longevity. Shamans in particular rely upon special shamanic familiars for spiritual control of their souls during healing trances and in dreams. The soul, personality, and familiars are basic constituents of the individual person for Sambia. After death, the soul remains as one or another kind of spirit or ghost; the person's spirit familiars are released, eventually to go to another kin's person; and the person's consciousness merely "dies," Sambia say. What remains of known persons are their accomplishments in the physical world and people's memories of the deceased.

Sambia are close to death, and their omnivorous spirits are never far behind. Forest and hamlet spirits are different from ghosts. Their brooding ghosts, nameless spirits of the dead who mercilessly strike the living to devour their innards, are truly dreaded and frightening shades. Sambia hate them, and they sadly mock themselves with the proverb: "We are their meat, their possum and pig, the helpless prey of our ghosts." Ghosts are felt literally to eat the corpses of the deceased. In dreams all images of people eating are interpreted as being ghosts eating human parts; the meat, though disguised as pig or possum, is really the corpse of a targeted person. For the dreamer to partake of this flesh invites feelings of cannibalism, sorcery, and soul-death upon awakening. And people never quite forget this hideous image. Sambia are no friends of their ghosts, nor are they at peace with them (any more than with each other). Ghosts also hover close to hamlets they lived in as humans, sometimes frightening children. By contrast, hamlet spirits are deceased prominent females and forest spirits are bygone big men thought to be generally protective of the village.

Neither in life nor in dreams can ordinary men control spirits. Only shamans can do so. Incantations can be said by sorcerers over the skull and bones of one's ancestors (or deceased kin) to conjure up their ghosts to level sickness and death against one's enemies. Yet because these shades are unruly and unpredictable, Sambia are reluctant to practice the sorcery for fear it will turn back on themselves. Even shamans can only exorcise or outwit the ghosts. Spirits have a greed and envy surpassing men's. At times of death—which exact mourning and wailing for the loss of loved ones—the new ghost is feared for its anger. Sambia believe all deaths are supernaturally caused by sorcery or spirits. So the ghost tries revenge, extending the human norm for blood revenge after death. Indeed, at such times I have seen people travel alone or to their nightly toilet in genuine fear.

Ancestral forest spirits are not as vicious as ghosts to their own kinsmen, but they still are to strangers. These souls of deceased big men guard clan territory. They are said to be envious of any hunter's catch, and many a folktale tells how a lone trapper met an untimely death through the deceptive cries of spirits. Children enjoy such ghost stories with wide-eyed interest. Through these stories they unwittingly learn that their male cross-cousins (from neighboring hamlets) are ambivalent and tricky figures with divided loyalties—sometimes changing from spirits into men—who are never to be fully trusted, as their fathers well know from past battles.

Only the female hamlet spirit, the *aatmogwambu*, whose cries are supposed to animate the sacred flutes (see Chapter 5), is a protector who alerts her hamlet to enemy attack. These spirits are thought to be the souls of prominent deceased women of the hamlet. Notice the differences in the sexes of these spirits. Ghosts are believed to be of both sexes; ancestral forest spirits are almost universally conceived to be only male; and hamlet spirits—as one would expect because of the close association of men with forests, women with hamlets—are normally female. Sometimes people say forest spirits are married to hamlet spirits. Hamlet spirits are named and "owned" by individual clans, in association with the spirit's dwelling place on clan property, which it guards.

Though ghosts seem evil and other spirits are punishing and angry, at least they make men thankful to be alive, and they help explain the otherwise unknowable. Like death.

In greeting death, Sambia reveal a characteristic vitality that is cloaked in masculine bravado. Men and women alike break into soul-wrenching sobs at the news of death. At no time does this occur, and it is otherwise unacceptable for a man to openly cry. Brothers gradually succumb to piteous wailing and outbursts of anger, eventually ending in the frenzied destruction of the gardens of the deceased and a feasting on his food crops. Meanwhile, the widow and female relatives and some male kin too roll in mud to express their sorrow. In a day or two they have exhausted themselves. A hunt is then organized by the sons and brothers to provide gifts of meat for the funeral guests and grieving kin. Finally, with warrior aplomb, all of these sad sentiments are hastily laid to rest at the funeral, a month later. A simple sacrificial act of placation of the ghost, with food offerings, is transformed into an aggressive and noisy chase by men flaunting phallic bamboo poles mounted with bull-roarers, in hopes of banishing forever the now evil ghost from its own home-land. The attempt is always futile; the ghost is here to stay. Yet this ceremonial bluster typifies the dramatic way in which Sambia confront feelings of loss and death in their lives: beginning with wailing, their exhausting lamentations eventually turn into anger, only to recover themselves in the most masculine act of self-assured pride. Are they not trying too hard and protesting too much that in spite of their grief they are in fact masculine?

This attitude toward the dead has its parallel in men's views about death in battle. Most Sambia men are terrified of death, as you can see in their eyes when they discuss the subject. The smallest cuts or colds are cause for concern; and yet, Sambia have a remarkable capacity to endure great pain. Squeamish but obstinate they are. Sickness, pain, and death are for them no strangers; in warfare they are expected. To endure the possibility, men have created mental tricks for drumming up a paradoxical stance in doing battle: turning resolve into recklessness. For instance, a great secret of the men of one hamlet is their consumption of bitter, bright-red juice (consciously compared to menstrual blood) immediately prior to battle, so as to inject into themselves aggressive abandon in the battle-charge, which did frighten enemies. Thus they defend themselves against fear and create fierceness for battle.

What is difficult to grasp is the personal glory—which is a valued end in itself—of being successful in war. This glory entails something else: a capacity to regard one's opponents as inhuman, according to the degree of hostility in the fight. At their worst, Sambia have an extraordinary ability to think of true enemies as targets divorced from any sense of humane empathy at all (Read 1955). But we must remember that many other New Guinea peoples are alike in this regard—nor are we Westerners so different, as recent wars have shown. This suggests my main point here: warfare creates cruelty and preoccupation with the present. Sambia are oriented to the present. They confront the past, the spiritual world, or the future only as a pragmatic matter, rarely as reflections on the existential potentials of life itself. This psychological pragmatism is necessitated by the pervasiveness of warfare in their behavioral environment.

No account of Sambia religion is complete without studying its shamanism, a complex subject mentioned in later chapters. Shamans mediate between this world and that of the spirits. They have the power to heal; to move into trance states; to summon unto themselves their spirit familiars in many forms and shapes; to be possessed by them; and through these beings—while in a trance—to ascend to the realm of the ghosts where they say they can see and hear and feel through the senses of their tiny human counterparts, to engage the spirits and outwit ghosts, and thus retrieve the "stolen" souls of their sick patients over whom they sweat and suffer. These miraculous feats, in states of "magical flight," distinguish true shamans from other healers or sorcerers, who are also present in Sambia society. For here, too, *jerungdu* creates unequal powers in shamans. Thus the shaman is a hero, a person whose great strength is used unselfishly for the good of the group.

I have always felt that their shamans, who sometimes are eccentric and ratty and even crazy, provide great relief to Sambia, the hope of escaping the dark forces of their evil spirits and horrible sicknesses that lead to death. Shamanic cultures are a heroic complex in human society, an archaic and simple way—though one riddled with complex states of mind like trance that we still little understand—of easing suffering and providing encouragement to those who must will themselves to live. Hope is provided for those who survive the problems of constant war, and for those who cannot bear to have survived when their loved ones were so capriciously carried off in death's cruel arms. Sakulambei is such a hero. Like other male shamans, he can perform healing ceremonies both in women's houses and in the clubhouse.

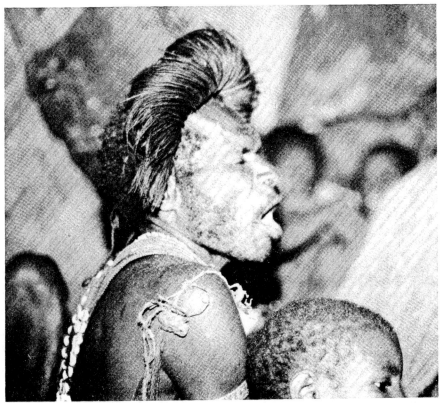

Photo 4. A shaman in trance during healing ceremonies (Photo courtesy of Dr. Robert J. Stoller)

Women shamans, such as Kaiyunango, can only perform in women's houses. Yet she too is no less a heroine in the eyes of women and some men.

Male shamans were also critical in warfare. Much of the reason for this was once succinctly put to me by a renowned war leader. In doing routine genealogy collecting at a distant hamlet, a borderland village near hated enemies, I discovered an inordinate number of shamans (deceased and living) compared to Sambia society at large. When asked about this a war leader (then about 50 years old) said of his community:

> We live near the Amdi—our enemies. They raid us. Who can foresee their attacks? Who could help us? Shamans' dreams foretell raids. . . . If they see [dream] particular enemy warriors, we know those men will die before us.

The shaman was an oracle, then, whose allegedly infallible advice no doubt foretold and even stimulated military activities. From their own divinations and dreams (and those of war leaders and elders), shamans tried to predict the success of a battle or an impending attack. This was their duty as they learned it in initiation rites. Men shamans offer supernatural purification for

Photo 5. Warrior displays on dance-ground (Sambia Valley initiation, 1975)

warriors too by performing healing ceremonies in the clubhouse. Each warrior received protection, and this surely comforted men who faced an early-morning battle. Their persons and weapons also needed cleaning of residues of female pollution. Such traces made warriors weak and vulnerable, for men feel that the "smell of women" attracts arrows to them like a magnet.

After the battle, male shamans did even more. They performed ceremonies to cleanse the blood of slain enemies from the weapons and bodies of living warriors. This purge lessened the possibility of reprisal attacks by the ghosts of their victims. To sum up: a shaman could heal, oraculate, and provide for the magical strengthening and cleansing of warriors. Shamans are colorful figures who require more description, especially women shamans, whom we will study below.

WARFARE: THE BEHAVIORAL CONTEXT

Male values invited the havoc of war. Confrontations between individuals and groups were heavily cloaked in terms of male concepts of weakness and strength. Men confronted one another in a context of power relationships. Male prowess based on the image of the war leader demands that a man not only surpass others, but that he also gets what he wants. In a dispute, a man's opponent must submit to his wishes: this is the ethic of *jerungdu* and of the war leader stereotype. Failure in it signifies weakness, that one is unmanly, a rubbish man. The simplicity of the Sambia model of masculinity makes it applicable to a wide range of encounters, from squabbling over a sweet potato to a full-scale war. Given these values and prestige-seeking, pride and reck-lessness no doubt contributed to warfare. A hamlet daringly flaunted its military might by lining up its warriors to intimidate opponents, daring others to back away from the challenge. Likewise, the dancing and singing contests of contemporary initiations recall more blustering group displays of strength on the dancegrounds of bygone battles (see Photo 5).

Two other factors are important here. First, adding to the severity of all confrontations is the Sambia value of blood revenge: any killing demands a payback killing. Second, even simple disagreements were potentially dangerous and could escalate due to a total lack of third-party redressive mechanisms beyond the hamlet. Once a conflict broke out there was no formal way to de-escalate it. Peaceful mediation of differences between hamlets was rare. Only after a conflict dragged on for months might it be settled by the truce ceremony. And even the truce left lingering animosities more often than not. (See Koch 1974: 159–75, who shows these factors to be common throughout much of Highlands New Guinea.) Finally, although men fought for various reasons—including disputes over women and marriage negotiations, the destructiveness of pigs, slander, and the like—their conflicts were enhanced by cultural ideals that men should dominate others and achieve prestige through the battle. Masculine values thus imply that violence—especially the boisterous intratribal bow fight—was a *normal* means of achieving social recognition.

It is with the meaning of warfare as a background to male initiation and masculine gender that we are primarily concerned. So we must investigate this context—the living meaning of war—even though the battles are gone. There are methodological problems here. I will not fully document Sambia warfare for that would require so many remembered battles, so much tactics and military lore, leading us aside from ritual and gender. Because I arrived after war was suppressed, my description is historical and retrospective for, without direct observations, we can only report others' statements. (See Meggitt's important book, *Blood is Their Argument*, on this point.)

Men were plainly obsessed with war, as their constant and unsolicited recollections showed me during fieldwork. They made references to old battles and nearly fatal brushes with death. Old war leaders delighted in showing their battle scars and, after they trusted me,[4] in listing the names and circumstances of warriors they had slain. Frequent allusions were made to little ambushes and far-off raids, stories they loved. Their tales of warfare sometimes left me doubting—so much so that my skepticism kept me from using these data until later field trips, when I verified the reports. More than with other stories, such as those on rituals, dreams, and myths, men unconsciously

[4] My language, my culture, especially my whiteness—these traits Sambia identified with their Government Patrol Officers, whom they associated with their colonial containment—made initial rapport difficult. I had to overcome that distance enough to allow access to what information they guarded: slain warriors, infanticide, homosexual activities, and sorcery practices, to name but a few things they still hide from outsiders. I did this by assuring them that they could trust me; by opening my house to them; and by assuring their confidentiality.

repress the gory parts of war tales, transforming the once traumatic into drama, a pseudo–art form. The grisly details can be remembered if one prods, particularly when working in a group (where someone may recall them). Then the humor, courage, and glories tend to fade: blood and guts and dismembered bodies are a sobering reminder of those war "games." This unconscious editing was necessary: without the ability to convert great trauma into retrospective triumph, life would be unbearable for men who were so constantly battling. After the facts are studied, it is clear that men imagine war battles to be a kind of gamesmanship: showy, exciting, potentially lethal—the greatest display of power—but still a game.

Sambia distinguish between different modes of warfare, each having its own motives and outcome. These included: the restricted ritualized bow fighting of "little fights"; escalated bow fighting that turned into "big fights"; and intertribal guerrilla raids. I use the adjective *ritualized* with some reservation, for the term implies (as it does also when affixed to *ritualized homosexual practices*) the qualities of gamelike or mechanical behavior. (We need to be cautious in our terminology for this reason: despite his emphasis on the ideal of *equivalence* in Gahuku-Gama ritual fighting, I think Read [1959: 429] went too far in directly comparing it to the "football matches" that came after it was gone.) Nonetheless, some simple term is needed to contrast this limited type of battle with intertribal warfare, in which deadly weapons and homicide were *expected*. In ritual bow fighting with neighboring hamlets, men wanted to bluster and impress more than kill. But if a killing occurred, revenge was demanded. Violence remained a possibility in any martial engagement, no matter how stylized or seemingly harmless. Because the hamlet was a defensive unit, all of its warriors rallied as a defensive force when it was attacked. In interhamlet warfare not involving their own village, the men of a hamlet did not necessarily act as a group. They could split up and even take different sides. This depended on two factors: the intensity of the fighting and individual loyalties to in-laws in the warring villages. Beyond this, groups could limit the fighting by controlling the weapons used against opponents, the level of combat in engagements, and by stressing their kinship to opponents. Sambia were, in short, like other New Guinea peoples who distinguished between restricted and unrestricted warfare.[5]

Interhamlet exchanges of arrows from opposite mountainsides of the valley constituted ritualized bow fighting. Usually such feuds occurred between nearby hamlets of a danceground confederacy. Sometimes the aim was to retaliate for insults or alleged sorcery or adultery. The warriors stood in cleared areas on opposite hillsides and lofted arrows at each other. Some of these clearings were agreed-upon ritual fightgrounds. Exchanges of arrows caused running

[5] Langness (1972: 930) writes: "By restricted warfare is meant that which 1. occurs only for a specific reason; 2. occurs only at specific seasons or times such as headhunting season, initiation period, etc.; 3. is restricted in the sense of having limited goals such as one life for one life, to gain reputation, to obtain wives, etc.; or 4. a combination of these. Restricted warfare, as is implied here, takes place within a public in which there are known rules accepted by all participants. Unrestricted warfare occurs for a great variety of reasons, is not restricted to any special season or motive, and does not take place within a system of rules."

charges to and from the vicinity of the fightground. (Karl Heider [1979] has documented such conflict in his case study on the Dani people, and you can see actual examples in the film *Dead Birds*.) A blinded eye or a festering wound brought on slow and torturous death. These were among the dangers created by this test of strength. In spite of the ideal norm, killings did occur—sometimes following lethal wounds or, at other times, from direct hits in the battle.

It was a masculine prerogative for age-mates and contemporaries of neighboring hamlets to challenge one another with bow. As in the Middle Ages of Western Europe, for instance, Sambia men view the ritualized bow fight as a manly joust. Stone and wooden war clubs—the deadly weapons—were not used since bow fights were not supposed to be lethal. Men stress that "We eat with those people, they aren't enemies; we wouldn't want to kill them." Yet their view about the "accidental" killings in bow fighting is contradictory: yes, they wanted to stand out by being sharpshooters, but no, they did not really want to kill neighbors. So warriors rationalize their killings by saying things like "He stood in front of my arrow" or "He found my arrow." Such fatalistic and pat rationalizations defended the reckless side of bow fights. In the end, local fatalities were ascribed to weakness (in judgment or *jerungdu*) in the wounded man. Proof for this are the living war leaders themselves: they were strong enough to survive.

This ideal of fighting prowess is captured poignantly in men's prized idiom—that ritualized bow fighting is simply their *play activity* (*chemonyi*) or game. Here again we encounter the attitude that bow fighting is only pseudo-war—dangerous but still governed by acknowledged rules. Their viewpoint finds support in observations of masculine development. First as boys, and then as initiates, males engage in rough-and-tumble games like mock bow fights (using play bows and arrows made of bamboo), dirt rock fights, and king-on-the-mountain contests—warriorhood games encouraged by adults (especially men) and accepted as useful pastimes (much as Americans regard such boyish activities). They are games of equivalence. Obviously this training reinforced aggressiveness: It toughens boys, and also stimulates rivalries and dominance between them. Imitating their seniors, boys label one another as weak or strong, as rubbish men or war leaders. Thus, initiates are being prepared for battle.

It was a dangerous step toward adulthood that led initiates directly into bow fighting. Eventually they fought against peers, sometimes those from nearby hamlets with whom they had engaged in the earlier games. Usually this began when they were second-stage initiates. Instructed and supervised by father or brothers or war leaders, the initiates were praised for "standing strong" to protect the hamlet. When the heat was on and the battle thickened, however, they were removed behind the front line of the older, experienced warriors: all except for the best of them, the initiates who would distinguish themselves. With experience and age, they became better bowmen and took risks, until finally the bow fight had become for them the reality of their fathers, a military game whose essence was competition for strength. Each boy's opponents were the youths who helped initiate the boy; homosexual contacts were appropriate only with them; and eventually he could seek a wife among their groups. Each of these spheres—ritualized fights, ritualized homosexual fellatio and initiation, and marriage—became a part of the contest for manhood.

Underlying each one of these activities is a stylized masculine protest: *"Mi aatmwunu tokwuno, mi aambelu-maiyo!"*—"I am a man, not a woman!" In such terms elders still coach the meaning of the warrior decorations first placed on boys at initiation. This returns us to the political context.

Despite this harsh declaration, the need of men to rationalize local war fatalities indicates that local groups sought to contain warfare. The presence of a local fightground was a key symbol of the regulation. The fightground parallels the confederacy danceground: they are only a few hundred yards apart in the Upper Sambia Valley. Both are signs of ritual relationship: neighboring hamlets were opponents, as well as some of them being in-laws. The men were initiated on the same danceground at the first-stage initiation and became members of an age-set. They had conflicting loyalties—first to their clansmen, then to in-laws, and usually last to their age-mates in other hamlets. Boys owed their primary allegiance to fellow clansmen. Fighting could take place between any of the hamlets, but the most frequent and deadly bow fights engaged nearby hamlets of different phratries.

Numerous marriage relationships between two hamlets create a political alliance between the in-laws. I mean by "alliance" nothing more than this: individual men aided and were indebted to their male-in-laws in those hamlets, so the more in-laws in two hamlets, the greater their reluctance to feud with each other. One norm prevailed in bow fighting: a man should not shoot an in-law. In-laws often help each other in battles, especially when their own hamlets were uncommitted third parties to fights elsewhere. In time marriage created kinship bonds (nieces, nephews, aunts, uncles, and cousins) that helped soften animosities when they flared up. But such alliances are unstable because bonds of blood are stronger than marital bonds for Sambia. Their weakness politically was the weakness of the confederacy itself. In the Sambia Valley these marital alliances—like the initiation confederacy alignments— crosscut phratry boundaries. Hamlets of the same phratry and confederacy were least likely to fight with bows. Conversely, hamlets of different phratries without in-law ties were most susceptible to fights. Finally, aligned hamlets were a potential refuge in case of attack or when fighting erupted inside the hamlet.

When a bow fight escalated into a broader engagement in the valley, Sambia called it a "big fight." Killings were more likely then. War leaders made plans for ambushes and raids. Shamans provided protection for warriors in nightly ceremonies and practiced lethal sorcery upon the enemies. Women and children were hidden in the hamlet stockade.

There were two reasons why a bow fight got out of hand, and both pertained to bloodshed. First, big fights nearly always sprang from a fatality. The slain warrior's group would demand blood revenge. Second, the scale of fighting broadened as both sides called on other hamlets for support. In the Sambia Valley big fights were (like confederacy initiations) invariably interphratry conflicts that evolved from bow fighting between two hamlets of different phratries. They too could begin over a variety of reasons, such as adultery, property disputes, or insulting conduct.

Even in the narrow sweep of the Sambia Valley, big fights were serious enough to provoke attacks on neighboring hamlets. Over the past 40 years, Nilangu hamlet has been besieged twice like this, whereas Pundei suffered at least half a dozen separate assaults. Killings from group attacks and individual ambushes did occur. Nilangu is nearly impenetrable because of its high and isolated location near forestland; its warriors also had the fiercest reputation in the area, were the most sought-after allies, and they successfully defended the hamlet—which has never been invaded. Pundei is less defensible, however, because of its broad ridge exposed on two sides and its vulnerable trails exposed to attack by the neighboring Wantukiu tribe. It has been invaded twice in recent memory. In seven drawn-out big fights between phratries, at least one man was killed in each, and sometimes as many as four or five persons were killed, including at least two known instances of women being killed. (This does not include other warriors who died later from wounds.) How long did such big fights last? They lasted from a week (one instance), to a few weeks (two instances), to several months (two instances), to over a year (one instance). Fighting did not occur every day but it could erupt at any time. This possibility kept men prepared.

Bow fights were historically common. Australian patrol officers noted that between around 1960 and 1964, at least a dozen reports of fights occurred, and this is surely an incomplete record. Intertribal raids were rarer. I do not have a complete total because they were also launched by different Sambia hamlets outside the valley, but my own local count indicates at least 10 major raids over the past 50 years.

After these big fights broke out, each side sought help from kin and in-laws in other hamlets. Men of ancestral phratries were brought in. Supporting war parties from the outside usually numbered no more than 15 to 25 men. These seem like small reinforcements, but remember that such forces still exceeded the warriorhood of many Sambia hamlets, who might count no more than 10 adult male fighters. The foreign and indigenous warriors fought together as a single line. The former usually stayed in the men's house of their kin. The men of one's phratry or ancestral phratry, therefore, were potential military reinforcements, and hamlets counted upon them at wartime. Phratry alignments in this sense served to check aggression by men of another phratry.

Yet, the involvement of alien warriors also escalated the conflict into a bigger fight. When one side called on its supporters, it compelled its opponents to do likewise. The escalation in the use of outsiders was more destructive because these men, as strangers fighting enemies, carried deadlier weapons. Why did imported war parties always carry stone clubs and axes, the armaments of deadly raids? A young warrior from an ancestral (outside) phratry, for example, could use the battle as a means of confirming his manhood following third-stage initiation. This is indeed how Sambia Valley men regarded their own war parties that supported external allies. Alien warriors, even though they were Sambia tribesmen, felt few compunctions about wounding fellow tribesmen to whom they were unrelated either as kin or age-mates, which increased the chance of killings. Only when the outside recruits left could the scale of fighting be reduced. External supporters were therefore a key source of military strength, but also a catalyst for the proliferation of intratribal warfare. One historical example will illustrate this process and serve also to clarify the behavioral environment of war.

Since earliest contact (c. 1957), Sambia were known as troublesome and warring, feared by surrounding tribes despite their small numbers. Like similar Anga groups on the Papuan Coast, they were feared because of their secretive and deadly guerrilla raids, after which they disappeared into forests, making it impossible to catch them. Australian patrol officers failed to hunt them out, since whole villages hid in the forest when the police forces appeared.

Eventually, after several years of contacts with neighboring tribes, the government decided to use dramatic displays to frighten the Upper Sambia hamlets. An Australian man—Patrol Officer D. K. Gordon—took it upon himself to personally stop the warfare among the Sambia. He began by jailing Kwol, a fierce Nilangu warrior captured in battle. Gordon wanted to intimidate Kwol's fellow warriors; so Kwol was jailed, the first Sambia to hold this dubious distinction. Even today Kwol still gripes over his treatment. Gordon's warning went unheeded, however. This led to the last big fight among Upper Sambia, which I will describe here because it was well documented by Gordon in 1964.

Fighting persisted among Sambia communities throughout 1963. Men did not fully comprehend the implications of Kwol's earlier jailing that year. By April 1964, Gordon learned of more fighting in the Sambia Valley. During a regular reconnaissance patrol, he accidentally stumbled on a raging battle (which began the day before his arrival). He wrote that there had been "four recent outbreaks" of warfare in the Sambia Valley during the weeks before his visit. He witnessed fighting in which the Seboolu phratry was pitted against the Wunyu-Sambia phratry. This interphratry conflict had occurred many times before. Gordon noted of one big fight, moreover, that Nilangu and its phratry sister hamlet were allied against Pundei and hers. Gordon personally counted 10 woundings in that battle. Again, he mentions that a "different battle" (but otherwise unexplained) had recently taken place between Wunjepti and Kwoli, two other nearby hamlets in the valley.

Gordon questioned the warriors about the cause of the Upper Sambia battle. Their reports left him incredulous. They spoke of a "theft of customs" and "washing with water," statements that puzzled him. Many years later I asked the parties involved how the war began. They say it originated from the imitation by the Pundei (Wunyu-Sambia phratry) men of their distant Great River Valley cousins (at Laki hamlet on the Great River Drainage Zone), who were taught to wash themselves with soap and water. Native evangelists working among the Laki at the time preached that to become like Europeans, they must learn to wash.[6] (Traditionally, Sambia did not bathe or wash with water, and older people and most women still do not do so.) The Seboolu people practice a traditional purificatory ritual requiring water to be briefly lapped on the body. They thus perceived the actions of the Wunyu-Sambia men as a serious infraction of the norm that groups may not perform the rituals of others. In addition, the Wunyu-Sambia men worsened the injury with insult by asserting that their washing made them "more manly" than the Seboolu. This bravado resulted in the violence. Meanwhile, Gordon devised a scheme: through a sequence of complex moves, he tricked the warriors into assembling and then he handcuffed them. This resulted in permanent peace; we shall return to that fateful peace and its extraordinary effects on masculine identity in the Epilogue.

A reconsideration of this 1964 report sheds light on the interplay of Sambia masculine values and warrior behavior some 20 years ago. The fight began over the "theft" of Seboolu phratry ritual custom by their opposing phratry. But Sambia on both sides now recognize that this big fight resulted from outright misunderstanding, exacerbated by boasting and pride.

To sum up the incident: the Wunyu-Sambia men (of Pundei hamlet) openly imitated their Laki hamlet kin in an aggressive way, taunting their neighbors. The Seboolu men responded to the perceived insult with a bow fight, mistakenly interpreting the washing behavior as a theft of their ritual rights—an understandable but sad comedy of errors. This escalated the fighting, pitting the phratries against each another. And to worsen the situation, the Wunyu-Sambia men castigated their Seboolu opponents as rubbish men. Such double insults drew a wide-scale call to arms. In their eyes, the Seboolu men felt that they had only one real choice: either they raised their bows, revenging their pride, or else they passively accepted public humiliation. They chose violence: 16 men were wounded in only a day of skirmishing. But rather open war, even death, than domination by their enemies.

The bloodshed of big fights wrought chaos in interhamlet relationships that only a truce ceremony could remedy. Truces were infrequent and usually short-lived. The ceremony is customarily held on the fightground, which suggests several things. Though men of nearby hamlets should avoid killing, deaths still occurred, which escalated the fighting. The parties could then use the truce to halt the fighting, restoring balance with compensation payments. The ceremony itself was simple enough: the war leaders and warriors on both sides shook hands, exchanged equivalent amounts of cowrie shells, and then spat ginger (mixed with yellow root) on one another's faces and torsos. This latter gesture dispelled the ghosts of slain warriors, since ghosts dislike the pungent smell of ginger; moreover, the ginger is here transmitted through the saliva of their own kinsmen, whom they would not strike. This implies, furthermore, a degree of mutual trust: one's saliva contains an aspect of one's

---

[6] Mountain District was restricted and outsiders were prohibited from entering the area; these New Guinean evangelists had surreptitiously entered from the Fore area, where they had worked for some years (see Lindenbaum 1979: 1–5).

soul substance, so there must not be lingering fears of retaliatory sorcery. In a more complex truce, ritual sacrifice using meat gifts was required. If the measure of human deaths was unequal, then compensation payments were paid. But the concept and practice of compensation among Sambia is poorly developed compared to that of the Hagen tribes of Western Highlands New Guinea (A. J. Strathern 1971). Compensation was, at any rate, a minor part of the Sambia warfare cycle. Groups were reluctant to stop fighting before blood revenge was exacted, for compensation was an unsatisfactory substitute for the slain, which often had to be accepted from a position of weakness: After fighting for long periods, food grew scarce because gardening had not been done. And no doubt the initial excitement of the conflict had gone.

The truce was a stylized armistice that contained an important message about local political cooperation. It laid to rest the open combat and destruction of warfare, even though some of the plotting and grievances would smolder on. Peace permitted the elders on both sides to cement marriage commitments or negotiate for future ones. Finally, large-scale war and peace had unforeseen effects on the collective organization of initiation by neighboring hamlets, since effective interphratry collective initiations required peace.

Lastly, and most deadly, there was intertribal warfare. The war parties of Sambia who journeyed to enemy tribes did so to kill and destroy. This brand of war was the most serious of all. It was waged against true enemies, called *iku-mamulu*, "man-eaters." Killings were an expected part of guerrilla raids. Enemy women were sometimes taken as captive brides. Other women and children were put to death in dawn massacres in enemy hamlets. Sambia marauded most of the tribes surrounding them and were attacked in retaliation. Thus, at various periods over the past 50 years, wars have been fought with the South Fore (west), the Baruya (northeast), the Amdi (east), the Yagwoia (southeast), the hinterland Papuans (south), and the Western Wantukiu (north). The conflict never really stopped, since no concept of truce applied beyond the valley. The most hated enemies were the Amdi, a Baruya-speaking tribe who were, legend says, cause of the original immigrations into the Sambia Valley; and the Fore, whom Sambia fear by association with sorcery and cannibalism (see Lindenbaum 1979). Here is a brief tale of one such raid.

Around 1938 a war party from the Sambia hamlets journeyed to the Moonagu hamlet area, in the Sambia River Delta. They were recruited to raid the Matnu hamlets, a distant Sambia-speaking phratry. The Moonagu men wanted revenge for the insults of some Matnu men. The Matnu called the Moonagu "boneless and spineless children." The two sides briefly lofted arrows at each other. Then the Matnu retreated a day or two downstream of the Lower Green River. The Moonagu then recruited about 20 men from half a dozen Sambia Valley hamlets (including six from Nilangu). The Sambia men assembled with Moonagu age-mates and distant in-laws in the hamlet of Yuvulu.

The next day this war party slipped into the mountains south and for two days walked downstream of the Lower Green River, a swamp-infested, desolate area famous for its severe walking, the worst of its kind in the district. They carried their food and slept without fire for fear of being detected. At dawn on the third day the warriors spotted a Matnu hamlet called Chegumulu. They dressed in full warrior regalia to "look like firelight" and strike terror in the unsuspecting villagers. The greater the element of surprise and fear, they felt, the likelier they were to succeed. Arrows were shot through the barricades. The warriors then swarmed inside and immediately bludgeoned several men. Then all of the houses (about 15 in total) were raided. Most of the people inside were killed. Two or three men and their families, however, managed to escape out the back. The men's house was surrounded, and the Sambia ambushed the occupants who tried to escape after it was set afire. The remaining men and initiate warriors were killed (they numbered 12 to 16 in all). Most of the women and children were killed. But 10 of the women (some of whom had babies) were taken prisoner. The bodies of the dead warriors were looted for decorations and weapons. Finally, the entire hamlet was burnt to the ground. Most of the party returned to the original Moonagu hamlets.

But a contingent of the warriors tracked the Matnu refugees. The reason is understandable: They wanted to finish the job they had started by doing away with the refugees, thus eliminating the possibility of their future reprisal attacks. They followed their trail over the mountains for a day, into the Lower Green Valley. The Matnu stragglers were there given shelter in a small and distantly related hamlet, Boolu, in exchange for giving two of their women as wives. When the enemy warriors approached Boolu, they were thus greeted with arrows. One of the attackers was wounded before they finally abandoned their efforts. Meanwhile, back at Yuvulu hamlet among the Moonagu, the captured Matnu women were divided as chattel among warriors of the participating groups. The Moonagu men took seven of the women, the remaining three went as wives to Sambia Valley men. One of these women went to the dead war leader, Mon, of Pundei hamlet, where she still lives, now an old widow.

Because of its mountainous isolation and relatively large population, Sambia Valley hamlets have suffered few tribal attacks from outside. Raids occurred during a long war with the Western Wantukiu phratry, fought intermittently between around 1943 and 1944. The war arose from a territorial boundary dispute, the Wantukiu claiming the southern slopes of the Papuan Divide that fall into the Sambia Valley. This huge territory is used for hunting and is still unoccupied. The Upper Sambia hamlets were aided by other Sambia phratries against these enemies. Sambia warriors have probably inflicted more damage on their neighbors than they have suffered. During the past two generations, other phraties have turned repeatedly to the Sambia Valley hamlets for assistance against enemy tribes. Thus, combined war parties from the Sambia Valley have aided, among others, the Great River Valley phratry against the Fore, the Yellow River phratry against Coastal Papuans, and the Green River phratries against the Amdi and Baruya. These were successful raids, though some warriors were killed.

This account of warfare is limited in explaining the causes and functions of violence in traditional Sambia society. Investigated after the fact, warfare descriptions confront an ethnographic dilemma: we cannot rely totally on Sambia explanations, but neither can we do without them (Hallpike 1973). One problem is that men can provide plausible reasons for certain conflicts but not others. When questioned, they revert back to particular behavioral contexts: slander, the garden ravagings of pigs, or the ravaging of women; or to a behavioral tradition: "We fought—over women and insults—like our fathers before us." That truth is too transparent: violent behavior, its extreme form being warfare, was a convention of Sambia society. We know that a great complex like warfare contains many causes. Masculine ethics, political gain, greed (for land), revenge, an absence of courts and counselors, power-hungry leaders, even boredom—the urge to escape monotonous routines—such motives figure into warfare, and each battle probably involved more than one of them.

In the Sambia Valley example described by Gordon, slander and ritual theft led to a big interphratry fight, and that war suggests a theme of aggressiveness and violent results that was common. *Jerungdu*—and everything it stood for in society and personality—led so quickly to dominating behavior. The insults of a handful escalated into a group confrontation. Misunderstanding and bravado were consequences of masculine values. Seen in historical perspective, this battle was no doubt similar to other battles: no land was gained, groups were not displaced, valuables and women were not looted—but men's prestige was much affected. Had the Australian Gordon not intervened and halted the fighting, it would have had a similar uncertain outcome in a few days or weeks: the sense of that particular incident is too much like many others reported. Of course adultery and wife-stealing occurred; pigs did destroy gardens; and men did feel that others had bewitched or insulted them. But it is the warrior ethos—the desire to be seen as strong not weak, the need to dominate and compete—which fires this masculine protest and fuels the social system.

Warfare, then, is an unfortunate outcome of a system of behavior that takes the *jerungdu* warrior ethos as its chief organizing principle. Though dominating behavior emerged in the long past of Sambia history, enabling certain communities to survive, it also devalued humans and wasted resources, creating greater and greater human problems.

This behavioral complex is not unique. Nor are Sambia alone, among the peoples of New Guinea, in having institutionalized values and relationships that engender dominance as characteristic of interpersonal relationships among groups. Here are other examples from the best-known anthropologists in New Guinea: Kenneth E. Read (1955: 272), writing of Eastern Highlands Gahuku-Gama, states that "The desire to dominate, to stand out from one's fellows, to receive their submission and their adulation, are among the most pronounced characteristics of Gahuku-Gama interpersonal and inter-group behavior. . . ." Marie Reay (1959: 22–23) notes of the Western Highlands Kuma that "It is a society dominated by men" and "male dominance is manifested in every institutional context." Lewis L. Langness (1972: 927), writing widely of New Guinea, argues:

> Physical power, both in individuals and groups, is respected, valued and admired. There is no notion of an underdog and no concept of fairplay. The expectation is to be dominated, if not destroyed, by the strong. A leader remains a leader only for so long as he can successfully dominate others, either through his ability to help them or maintain their respect.

Constant warfare exemplifies the behavioral environment reality of masculine life. Allies were unpredictable; political alignments were shaky. Oscillations of war and truce gave rise to inward-looking hamlets stockaded for defense, wherein one's blood kin and in-laws were a man's surest partners, forming a security circle of trust. These small, fragmented communities required aggressive warriors for survival. Yet the group is only as strong as its individual members, its soldiers; and simply being born male does not ensure that necessary masculinity. This is the perception that lies behind the protracted ritual initiations of Sambia that still channel boys into a warriorhood. Though Sambia were forcibly pacified 20 years ago, today, war is not dead. It lives on in the hearts and minds of the present adult generation. They will fiercely initiate boys as long as those memories remain, for to be strong, to stay in charge, is a principle they cannot relax.

3 / Ordinary people

What are the Sambia like as individual personalities? Even though this case study is focused on Sambia culture, we cannot ignore the distinctiveness of outstanding war leaders and shamans, or the ordinary virtues of mothers, sons, elders, and initiates. We saw how the environment and male ethos affected warfare, which in turn conditioned family life and gender. These factors take shape not only in the great institutions of Sambia society, but in the personalities of its citizens too. In this chapter I introduce you briefly to several long-time informants, friends, and neighbors. It is hard to describe their lives in a few pages, for no life can be summarized so briefly. Yet by reading these biographies you will better understand how Sambia culture shapes gender, and how its gender beliefs in turn shape these people.

Five people will be snapshotted. I have selected them to contrast key social status positions among Sambia. These include: the elder, Kanteilo; the leading woman shaman, Kaiyunango; my friend Weiyu, a married man; Sakulambei, a powerful shaman and a hermaphrodite; and Moondi, a close friend whom I observed as an initiate growing into the bachelor role. I will concentrate on the key social characteristics and psychological traits in each person's life, beginning with Moondi, since his biography reveals male gender development most clearly.

Moondi   Moondi is an intelligent and articulate young man of Nilangu. The eldest in a large family, he was born about 1960. His father is very mild, one of the so-called gentle men among Sambia. His mother, Kaiyunango, is an unusually strong and renowned shaman. Moondi's parents are a successful couple and theirs is a prominent marriage in the village. Moondi himself is a bit short (about 5'2"), stocky, and tough. He is personable but impetuous and hotheaded. I first met him in 1974 when he was a second-stage initiate. He became my main translator, helping me in my work with initiates, who distrust older Sambia men. As a sympathetic outsider, even though I was older, they entrusted me much more.

Moondi's is the last generation to have experienced warfare in their childhood. He still has vague memories of actual events (1960–1965), for instance, of his mother fleeing with him as a child into the forest when the village was attacked. These feelings do not go away; they are like scars on one's soul, scars later compounded by initiation. Yet Moondi thinks of his childhood as

59

having been relatively happy. His parents squabbled, and he sided with his mother mostly. This pattern is common. He was initiated with his peers into the ritual cult when he was about age eight. He was smaller than other boys and he says he was hazed and bullied more than others for this reason. Initiation was terrifying: the beatings, the nose-bleeding, the homosexual fellatio. This was a harder time for him than his childhood, he has always said; lonely and sad. He missed his mother and younger siblings and resented his parents' allowing him to be initiated. But eventually these feelings passed. He became an enthusiastic fellator and was sought out as a sexual partner by many bachelors. He lived in the men's house this way until late 1971.

Then Moondi left the valley and went to a small mission school a day's walk from home. He was among the first Sambia boys ever to be formally schooled. He became a nominal convert to the mission. This life was hard and lonely too; he was often hungry, without help from others. But he learned fast and was advanced. A year later he was transferred to a bigger school far away. At the end of that year he returned home for a visit. He became very ill, however, and had to drop out of grade school. So he fell back into village life because he was home, food was plentiful, and he was back with his own people. I arrived at this point. Moondi proved to be a gifted translator and field assistant, for he was among the few who could speak to me in Pidgin. I liked him and we became friends. We agreed that if he would assist me for a year, I would help him return to school. Then the 1975 initiations were held, and it was time for him to be elevated into bachelorhood, third-stage initiation. He resisted fiercely but finally gave into the pressure. That story is told below.

Moondi helped me until late 1975, when he did return to school. He was successful and graduated from government primary school at the Patrol Post in 1977. This was a high achievement. When I returned to the Sambia in 1979 he was back in the valley and he assisted me again. We were glad for each other's company, for many of his age-mates and my friends had left the area to work on coastal plantations. Moondi was betrothed to a woman during this time, a premenarchal girl. The marriage was arranged, but Moondi approved of it; he had seen her from a distance and liked her. He liked her family too. During this time he still engaged in homosexual activities with younger boys. But his thoughts turned more and more to girls, and in time he lost most interest in boys. He left the area in 1979 to live and work in Port Moresby. He married his betrothed in 1983 and took her to the city. They had their first child in 1985. There they remain today, busy with new lives and adult roles. Ten thousand years passed in half Moondi's lifetime— from stone-age war to city apartments. And the wonder is that so much change still lies ahead.

Kanteilo   My sponsor and supporter in the village is Kanteilo, a wiry old fox of about 60 years who is the leading elder. He speaks no Pidgin and has never been away from the Sambia world. He represents the old ways, tradition: what Moondi grew up with but which is now changing so fast. Kanteilo is a colorful and significant actor on the local scene. He was born in a now-defunct village not far from Nilangu that was one of the two original home-steaded villages in the whole valley. His father was a well-known war leader, though Kanteilo has surpassed him in reputation. Kanteilo remembers his father well because he has a superb memory. Indeed, he is my key genealogical informant, and he has recalled for me countless names spread over hundreds of genealogies. He takes pride in this phenomenal memory and he is known for his wide knowledge and interest in historical matters. His memories have always checked out, so his stories have helped me to reconstruct old wars and past events.

Kanteilo has been married five times. He presently lives with his last wife, a barren widow. They have a comfortable marriage. He has several children from his previous marriages, including two sons I know well. Neither of them, however, has Kanteilo's charisma or his charm. He loves to talk, to tell stories, to impress and cajole with jokes and flattery and little gifts of food. His nickname means "the good man," indicating his generosity and wisdom.

Yet, he was not always so. In his prime Kanteilo was a real fighter, a war leader, a womanizer, cunning and daring. He fought in many wars and battles and loves to pull back his bark cape to show the battle scars on his stomach. He was not above treachery; Kanteilo had to use his keen intelligence and guile to outlive his peers and survive the war raids that took him to distant lands. This hardens a man, whose vision grows sharper, pragmatic, cold. But he was no savage. We should not put him into the same heartless category as Mon, the great and rigid war hero in Pundei, Sakulambei's father. Indeed, Kanteilo's influence today surpasses that of other renown war leaders such as Mon, who lack qualities of compromise and wise rhetoric. You cannot be too bitter and strong and be an acknowledged elder among Sambia.

Kanteilo is a man with both a serious and a funny side, each developed in good measure. The seriousness was gained first through initiation into the warriorhood, and then in warfare itself. His marriages seasoned him too. Nowadays, Kanteilo is a defender of the old customs, especially traditional initiation and marriage. He rises to the occasion of ritual teaching with flurry and passion. He still commands respect and can hold audiences quiet. His calculating and planning organizes things, for example, he remembers the ritual magic spells. Yet his funny side constantly comes up. For instance, he loves to yodel—a social right of prominent men—at dawn. He loves to sing too. When I first lived in the village, Kanteilo often slept in my house, near the fire. He did this to keep me company, to gain prestige from association with me, to enjoy my food, and to teach me about the culture. He would arise at dawn and yodel loudly, waking everyone, which used to annoy and amuse me. Then he would chide us for sleeping past 5:00 A.M. Kanteilo is a character. But the side you will see below is the elder taking charge, affirming traditions and reminding others of their responsibilities.

Kaiyunango   The life of Sambia women is not easy, and yet Kaiyunango has shown what is possible given the will to gain esteem. A senior and highly respected woman of 40 or so and a remarkable shaman, Kaiyunango is in many respects atypical. Her influence and power stand her out from the crowd.

She is looked up to by younger women and listened to by elders. I knew her first as Moondi's mother, for I got to know his family well. She surprised me by seeming to run the show in their family, until I realized that she was the most powerful woman shaman, and that her husband, Moondi's father, is a mild man. Over the years I've gotten to know Kaiyunango in her own right and have interviewed her many times.

She was born in Nilangu, the daughter of the most important man in the village of the previous generation. He was a war leader and shaman, a founder of the village, and an age-mate of Kanteilo's. His adult children are now all prominent people: three are shamans—Kaiyunango, her sister, and a brother. But Kaiyunango's is acknowledged as the greatest power. Her shamanic traits first came to her in childhood. She had dreams that her father interpreted as signs of her calling to be a shaman (see Herdt 1977). Her mother, one of her father's three wives, was a minor shaman too, and she taught Kaiyunango magic. Kaiyunango saw her father do many healing ceremonies and says she wanted to do them too when she grew up. As a teenager a crisis befell her relatives, and only she was available to heal. This was her first shamanic performance and it was successful. From then on her skills increased and she became famous throughout the area.

She married Moondi's father in her late teens and was soon pregnant. Her husband fled ambush and fighting between relatives in his own village area on the other side of the valley. Kaiyunango's father and other men like Kanteilo suggested he settle in Nilangu. This allowed her to remain in her own village rather than move to her husband's. Consequently, she has family and friends to support and protect her, which I see reflected in her greater confidence and security compared to other women. She has had 10 children in succession, eight of whom are still living. And yet, even today, Kaiyunango remains youthful, vital, and striking—still attractive as the beauty she surely once was. Her youngest child is three years old. Lately, I have heard her say she is not too old to have more.

When ceremonies begin, Kaiyunango is usually to be seen. Like other women she provides food and female items expected of her. She is an excellent gardener and provider for her family. Moreover, she is extremely generous— a virtue Sambia expect from older women (they dislike it when they do not see it). Yet this alone does not stand her out from her woman age-mates. For that she has her shamanic role to thank and her reputation as a healer. At the women's ceremonies she takes a central place, teaching and talking. She helps as a midwife in the delivery of new mothers' babies as well. It is a tribute to the men's esteem that they allow Kaiyunango to do healing ceremonies with male shamans in a hut near the culthouse at the start of the initiation cycle. The men could not allow her to touch the initiates for fear of the usual pollution, or allow her into the culthouse itself for the same reason. That she can perform at all in the vicinity of male initiation is remarkable: Here we see an expression of her "strength" at work, an expression of a pattern Sambia would label masculine—and, therefore, an aspect of her womanly activity that transcends the usual male-female dichotomy in Sambia culture. In Chapter 6 we will return to this side of Kaiyunango's gender status.

Sakulambei   In a society that so much values masculine performances, in which ritual and myth give highest value to penis, semen, and many progeny as admission into adult masculine personhood, there could hardly be a condition more anomalous or sensitive than hermaphroditism. These are Sambia intersexed persons: biologically hermaphroditic males treated differently from birth, who have microscopic penes. Sakulambei is such a person. He was born about 1953 and warfare raged throughout his childhood. Though assigned to the male sex, he was labeled a hermaphrodite at birth because he had a tiny penis and an odd-looking scrotum. Like all Sambia male hermaphrodites he was assigned to the male sex because people knew that later sexual differentiation in the genitals would occur around puberty.

Hermaphroditism is a mystery to Sambia. That it has magical associations is understandable. When a people are so preoccupied with keeping the sexes apart, it is not surprising that sexual ambiguity would fascinate them, for it blurs sexual boundaries. But mysterious or magical, hermaphrodites are stigmatized. Saku, no different in appearance from other hermaphrodites at birth, has made himself different. He is at present the most powerful living shaman. I know of no other Sambia hermaphrodites, past or present, who became great shamans. Saku's achievement is unique (see Herdt and Stoller 1985).

Saku has a history sad and yet triumphant. His father rejected him in childhood because of the hermaphroditism. Life's cruel joke was for Saku to have been born the son of Mon, the terrible war leader of Pundei. At age five or so, Saku's mother died. His mother's brother, then the most powerful shaman and sorcerer in the valley, took him in and reared him as a son in another hamlet. He truly loved Saku. And when, like Kaiyunango, Saku had dreams and visions in childhood, his uncle knew that Saku would be a shaman. Shamanism is strong in Saku's family. As a child Saku says his first spirit familiar used to come and play with him out in the gardens. Perhaps this was like what psychologists would call a child's "imaginary companion," to replace his lost mother and father. Later Saku says he saw the familiar in dreams, and he still sees him, and other familiars, in his trance states. Children teased Saku. They made fun of his genitals and humiliated him, saying he was a girl, not a boy. Few of his childhood friends helped him. But Weiyu, his cousin, always defended him. (You will read about that more in Chapter 6.)

Saku's social development was otherwise normal until puberty. He was initiated with his age-mates. He was an active fellator for years. Second-stage initiation was normal too. But after that, the elders and his father passed him up. Their attitude was, "Why waste a good woman on *him*!" This hurt him deeply. They did not initiate him into the bachelorhood, so Saku persisted in the homosexual fellator role longer than normal. He became a shaman though, mainly through his uncle's influence. In 1975 he arranged his own third-stage initiation, years behind his mates. His uncle also got him a wife. During this initiation he was also formally installed as a full shaman, and thereafter he quickly became more powerful. He has managed to hold onto his wife in spite of many problems associated with his stigmatized sexual condition. His uncle died in the late 1970s, leaving Saku the most powerful man shaman. He often performs healing ceremonies together with Kaiyunango.

The masculinity and identity of Saku are therefore complex. His shamanic powers have been thoroughly blended into his identity, such that it is hard to separate the one from the other. His sense of himself is neither absolutely masculine nor feminine, but rather hermaphroditic. His courage in earning the status of shaman and in overcoming his childhood difficulties rings clear in his proud bearing and defiance of others who gossip about his inadequacies. His feeling of power thus derives from the conviction that "I am the shaman Saku, whose identity is strong." In this sense, then, Saku has *created* his own self. This is, in all of us, a necessary part of development, but in Saku's case it was an act of heroism against great odds. We will see more of him later.

Weiyu   My older translator, who is my age, is Weiyu. He is my best Sambia friend. I've known and worked with him since 1974.

Weiyu was among the first people I got to know well. His marriage ceremony occurred only a month after my arrival in the village. He stood out from his peers: he was taller, more verbal, gregarious, and (by Sambia standards and my own) handsome. He liked to show off, to be seen as acculturated when it counted; but when dressed in warrior garb (which was rare, for he usually wore Western clothes), he cut a dashing figure. Women liked him and he knew it; he is still a lady's man, a Don Juan. He liked sex with boys too—in fact, he likes sex in general. He's more blatant about that than other Sambia men; his coastal experience was a big factor in making him more sexually aggressive. Weiyu and his cohort of fellow initiates invited me (in December 1974) to join in their initiation shortly after my arrival. I was honored; the experience made me, by age (I was 25, about their age), by subsequent identification by other villagers, and by common interests (being bachelors), their age-mate.

Weiyu's childhood was unusual. His true father was a renowned and feared shaman of Pundei village (Nilangu's sister hamlet). He was said to have been a physically powerful man too—tall and strong, impressive and reckless (Weiyu doesn't remember him). Some 20 years ago he was murdered by his own clan brothers in an infamous massacre that set off a war between Pundei and Nilangu. Weiyu's father was simply too brazen and reckless: he openly flirted with women, let it be known that he was having affairs with other men's wives, using his powerful sorcery knowledge to keep men afraid of him, and—the unbearable and insane sin—he claimed responsibility for the (sorcery) deaths of several people. He was disposed of in an ambush, hacked to death by a gang of warriors. One of them was Mon, Saku's father. His widow fled with her two children, Weiyu and his older sister, to Nilangu, where they were given shelter by their in-laws. A Nilangu big man, Chemgalo, who was himself an older widower, took Weiyu's mother as his wife. He adopted Weiyu and, with unusual kindness for that day, gave Weiyu the advantage of full social rights in the village. Shortly before his initiation, Weiyu's mother died.

He has been cared for since by Chemgalo's eldest daughter (his step-sister) and Chemgalo himself, who never remarried.

The wound opened by Weiyu's father's murder has never healed. His father's only biological brother (himself a powerful shaman) also fled Pundei and never returned. This man still mutters that the murderers will pay eventually through his sorcery powers. Sambia is a society that honors blood revenge, yet Weiyu's father has never been revenged. So Weiyu grew up with a fantasy, sometimes quietly expressed today, that *he*, the son, carries the burden of knowing that there has as yet been no revenge. This awareness—and a quiet, romantic identification with an amazing father cut down and never known—is burned into Weiyu's masculinity.

Weiyu's marriage following social change was also odd. He and his wife were the first couple (to my knowledge) to have chosen each other. They were mutually attracted and went against others' wishes in marrying. There is also a sense that Weiyu's wife is socially inappropriate for him, because they are too closely related through marriage. They have been at each other's throats for years. Both are jealous. Weiyu is flirtatious and an exuberant fornicator whenever possible. (As a bachelor he frequently had sex with boys and was even sometimes unscrupulous, having sex with male cousins such as Moondi, who are supposed to be tabooed, Moondi says.) He outgrew boys and concentrated on women, whom he prefers. Weiyu is, nonetheless, misogynous. He has had many fights with his wife. (I know he beats his wife, but I have never seen him do it. She has also beaten him.) Though they have a house, gardens, and two children, their marriage is not successful or satisfying. Weiyu's mother-in-law didn't want them to marry. She seems to feel that their chaos is the result of marriage inspired by romance, not by custom. Though other men share feelings of misogyny with Weiyu, and they may sometimes fight, they do not—nor do most other couples—persist in the vicious combat that characterizes Weiyu's marriage. One is tempted to suggest that their romantic beginning is the cause of their conflict, but that is too simple.

Weiyu represents, in a paradoxical way, old-fashioned phallic masculinity. It is paradoxical because he has had outside life experience other men lack. Yet his sense of self is so much more like Kanteilo's than Moondi's. The elder, like Weiyu, is an old-fashioned warrior, the kind of men made famous by Sambia.

In the following pages these people will appear as key actors. Now that you know about their lives, you will be better able to understand their motives and behavior when you see them involved in the initiation ceremonies. Their involvement places them in the center of their society, along with their fellows and kin. And now that you have met them you must be aware that they are not ordinary people at all; they are the inheritors of a rich cultural tradition that they are adapting to, and in some cases changing, which makes them not so different from the remarkable ordinary people you know at home.

4/Gender and socialization

How are the biological facts of an individual's temperament and gender identity shaped by culture and adapted to fit the particular society's behavioral environment? This chapter addresses this problem. We shall see how Sambia male (*aatmwol*) and female (*aambelu*) infants are changed into the cultural beings labelled "boy" and "girl," "man" and "woman." "Sex" will here refer to biological factors, whereas "gender" will indicate those shared and learned ideas and feelings a group has regarding the *ways to be* (identity) and the *ways to act* (role), male or female, masculine or feminine.

Socialization is a concept used by anthropologists to mean the teaching that prepares the young to be competent members of their society. Training children to fit gender roles and to internalize the beliefs and values appropriate to performing their roles in all situations and social institutions is a primary job of socializers the world over. The training may not always be intentional, however. Some gender socialization may be unconscious, for example, when parents or the media communicate that certain roles are sex-restricted ("boys are doctors, girls are nurses"). Some cultures are also more restrictive than others: social and economic roles and cultural and sexual rules restrict people's activities and behaviors according to their sex. Sambia culture, like that of many New Guinea societies, is highly restrictive in this way.

Since Margaret Mead's classic study *Sex and Temperament* (1935)—a field study of three New Guinea cultures—anthropologists and others have argued the extent to which culture can shape gender and sexual temperament. We will enter into this debate by learning how socialization shapes gender roles in childhood; by understanding that boys are placed in a sort of double bind since Sambia have two cultural worlds—the male and the female—and boys are developmentally adjusted earlier to the female one; by seeing (in Chapter 5) that ritual initiation is the key social mechanism for changing boys' gender roles and internal gender identity; and finally, by evaluating the overall effect of this developmental history on Sambia sexual orientations and sexual behavior later in life. We will see, therefore, how there are really two broad socialization contexts for gender roles—childhood and initiation—a duality made necessary by the very different cultural worlds of childhood and the men's house.

Photo 6. Tali's small son

CONCEPTS

Several concepts will help facilitate your reading. First, there is the above distinction between sex and gender, in which sex is normally determined at birth by external genitals, but it can also be verified at the genetic, chromosomal, and reproductive-tract levels. Thus, we may say that John is a member of the male sex with an anatomically normal penis, scrotum, and postpubertal secondary sex traits like muscled arms and facial hair. *Gender* refers to learned behaviors, skills, ideas, and feelings, relatively independent of biological sex. So we can argue that there are male and female *gender roles*: typical behavioral patterns expected of biological men or women. The inner sense of these roles is called male or female *gender identity*: the sense of belonging to the male or female sex, which includes appropriate life goals, beliefs, and so forth. Fundamental to experiencing this is *core gender identity*, the sense of one's existence, body image, and the conviction of selfhood that is tied either to maleness or femaleness.

In any society, people are explicitly trained to perform in this or that gender role; subjectively, however, these people's experiences are actually a composite of *masculine* (associated with the male gender role) and *feminine* (associated with the female gender role) traits. Masculinity and femininity are also directed by the cultural code of a society, over and above any individual participant. Consequently, one has a biological sex, a gender role, and a gender identity, reflected in masculine or feminine behaviors, roughly correlated with social status and gender role. Sexual behavior and sexual orientation, though, are only roughly correlated with gender. *Sexual behavior* means any sexual act, whereas *erotic* refers to any stimuli that arouse sexual desire. *Sexual orientation* implies a habitualized and enduring preference for a certain kind of *sexual object choice*, male or female, perhaps with preferences for the type of sexual contact (anal/genital) and the emotional quality implied (for example, authoritarian/reciprocal, promiscuous), though the latter are of secondary importance.

You will see later that Sambia initiates are biological males believed to be unmasculinized until ritual, which places them into normative gender roles with only masculine traits and behaviors permitted. However, they retain feminine *identifications* in their secret identities, and they have, for the first 10 or 15 years of their lives, an exclusive homosexual sexual orientation. Women, on the other hand, are assigned to the female sex and reared as competent persons in feminine gender roles, with few ritual aids needed to assist in their attainment of reproductive competence (at menarche). Their sexual orientation is always heterosexual. In other words, maleness is cultural and bisexual, and femaleness is natural and heterosexual in the Sambia social design.

GENDER AS A SOCIAL PRINCIPLE

There are many ways to organize a society. *Class* is an economic principle that culturally restricts group rights and privileges according to one's income and social position. *Caste* functions likewise in the economic and religious spheres. *Age* is a way of ranking and regulating people by absolute birth-order or by relative generation. *Sex* is a way of restricting access to certain jobs, social statuses, and income opportunities, as is *race*, another widely used principle in human societies. Of these possibilities, age and sex are the most important social organization principles in New Guinea societies. In spite of their age-ranked religious system and its gerontocracy (like Australian Aboriginal cultures: see Hart and Pilling 1979, on the Tiwi), however, sex is the more central factor in understanding Sambia society.

But it is not absolute biological sex so much as learned gender rules that operate in regulating Sambia social behavior. Sex at birth is crucial in determining social position. These status distinctions, rights, and duties are hard and fast. Women are not allowed to be warriors or hunters; men cannot babysit or clean offspring; and women are as forbidden to enter the men's house as are the men to enter the menstrual hut. Thus biological sex alone does not account for all the restrictions on people; here, culture goes far beyond nature. Cultural belief, social value, and collective and private fantasy restrict masculinity and femininity in social behavior. We saw in Chapter 1, for example, how species in nature are genderized, according to Sambia ideas. These classifications of animals and plants reveal the widespread tendency of Sambia to apply their gender ideas to everything.

Males and females are thought to have the same origin: mother's womb. Yet even inside of the womb the sexes differ somewhat, as we will see. After birth, the sexes develop in increasingly different ways. This differentiation reaches its peak in adult Sambia life, where there are major oppositions between men and women in politics and economics, in religion and ritual. Let us now examine how these differences get worked out in everyday life and in the socialization of children.

HAMLET SECURITY CIRCLE

Every society must weigh the dangers of its behavioral environment for children. A boundary of security must be drawn around them. Peter Lawrence (1966) has coined the term *security circle* to indicate the widest area within which the New Guinean felt free and safe to move about. For Sambia this was usually the hamlet, as the perceived dangers beyond the hamlet were great. But what we must not forget is that inside the village too there were insecurities.

Several factors color the nature of the hamlet security circle. First, war was going on, and people got killed. Second, women were imported from potential enemy groups, so the insecurity of having such "aliens" around permeated village life. Third, the hamlet was a small place, a fact that made living in close quarters harder when conflict broke out. Fourth, everyone knew everyone else and much of their private business, yet ritual secrecy created gaps and fears in women's and children's lives. Fifth, there is a high infant mortality rate and much sickness in the area (and there was no modern medicine till recently). Sixth, biological maturation is extremely slow in the region, supporting ritual beliefs about gender.

The Sambia social world is very small. In the valley with its population of about a thousand, everyone knows almost everyone else, for everyone is named and present. These people have grown up in villages with each other their whole lives. They know one another intimately, and what is hidden emerges in gossip or in the shaman's visions. Members of the group are all around; neighbors are known too. Only children do not know everyone directly, so for them we may say that the people of distant hamlets form a group of vicarious others. For children, the ancestors' identities are like this too. Some of their exploits are known from myths, like those surrounding Numboolyu and his wife Chemchi, the great busybodies of Sambia mythology. The greatest war leaders, shamans, and gardeners are known to everyone throughout a region.

Neighboring hamlets harbor stereotypes about others, stereotypes symbolized by clan totems. Thus, Nilangu men are fierce fighters with claws like the harpy eagle, their totem. Pundei are sorcerers and shamans, to be feared like their totem, the blood plant. These animosities and stereotypes may remind us of legendary hillbilly feuds between the McCoys and the Hatfields in the United States.[1] The point is that hamlets were like tiny islands, with overlapping social relationships of marriage and politics and ritual, everyone assigned to definite roles.

The feeling of security in the hamlet is real. It is hard to convey this feeling to Western city dwellers. Yet, if I could transport you for a moment to the village on a warm, dry-season night with a full moon, you would see what security and happiness truly look like when they are *lived*. You would see the naked children laughing in the extraordinary silver light as they dash through the hamlet playing tag. You would see the orange glow of fireplaces through friendly and wide-open doors. Dogs bark and cicadas sing; the old people gab. Kanteilo draws chuckles of amazement when he announces, at his advanced age, that he will set off tomorrow to trade bark capes way over in Wantukiu tribal country. Smoking and betel-chewing relax people, who turn to gossip, to local news, to stories—the old men always ready to spin tales about war and adventures of the past, the children always ready to hear the ghost stories that make them wide-eyed and giggly with excitement. Maybe there will be a songfest, for Sambia love to sing. Everything is not ideal: the sexes remain divided, and there is perhaps a marital spat mixed into the evening's events. But these are usually temporary and soon forgotten. It is the feeling of being at home and being safe that pervades and warms.

We should recall the physical setting of the hamlet: a narrow stockade containing a few huts encircling a tiny plaza on a narrow mountain terrace. The hamlet site is lush and green and fertile, but tidy in a way that sets it apart from the encroaching forest. The family houses are built in line formation, the men's house being situated at the higher end of the sloping ridge. This spot affords the warriors the widest surveillance during wartime. By placing the clubhouse at the top of the residential zone, nearest the forest, men also reduce the possibilities of female contact and pollution. Women are told not to walk above the clubhouse, which would contaminate the initiates, war weapons, and ritual paraphernalia. "Women belong down below, men on top," my age-mate Weiyu likes to say. This pat statement, which downgrades women because of their polluting vaginas, rationalizes living arrangements.

An invisible tapestry of spatial taboos and architectural designs separates women from men inside the hamlet, its narrow confines segregated into men's and women's spaces. Zones of female movement are polluted, according to male dogma; since no area is immune to this contagion, everyone is restricted by taboos. A startling assortment of such taboos and avoidance rules curtail the movements of women, initiates, and men. No part of the hamlet is perceived as being unrestricted by sex-related taboos, except for the dusty central plaza (and even this is not neutral during ceremonies). Interpersonal heterosexual behavior is therefore rigidly structured. Women are not at all free to

---

[1] The analogy cannot be taken too far. Meggitt (1977), one of the world's great authorities on Melanesia, has said recently that he was wrong to characterize fighting as "feuding" among the Mae Enga tribe of the Western Highlands. He believes "warfare" is the more apt concept to describe their sustained violence.

move about as they wish, and initiates are even more hemmed in. Men believe that women may pollute them merely by stepping over, above, or beside them, or by touching their persons, food, or possessions. During menstrual periods women retire to the menstrual hut, which is below the hamlet. Men and initiates completely avoid this area. Likewise, women must not walk near the men's clubhouse or ever look inside.

SECRECY

Because gender roles are so strongly related to secret ritual initiations, we must expect the mechanism of secrecy itself to play a large part in hamlet life. Secrecy divides men and initiated boys from women and children. Secrecy also supports gender-role segregation and opposition. Since ritual knowledge is so important in Sambia culture, and because this information is gained only by age-graded entry into the men's or women's secret ceremonies, secret knowledge is a key cultural barrier that always separates the sexes. Secrecy is essential to the very operation of Sambia society, and one marvels at the incredible lengths to which it has been carried here. To illustrate: many things have secret names, the list of which in plants, animals, and folklore numbers in the hundreds. Since secrecy creates unequal power, it creates distrust between the sexes. To understand how important secrecy is, let us study how it influences communication.

Inside the hamlet people operate and behave in three types of social situations: public, secret, and private. The secret life is established by ritual, whereas the private is defined by each person. These situations occur in various institutional settings basic to Sambia society. Social action in each situation corresponds to one of three different types of talk: public talk (*iyungacheru yungalu*, lit. "free talk"), secret talk (*ioolu yungalu*, lit. "hidden talk"), and private talk (no marked category). These styles are related to social rules and standards that organize men's and women's experiences, motivations, and fantasies—their gender identities.

Public discourse is the most common form of speech. It is associated with domestic situations in women's houses, casual gatherings on the plaza of a hamlet, work teams, and formal public meetings. Local meetings shape how Sambia now use the Pidgin concepts *tok publik* (public talk) and *tok hait* (secret talk), because all ritual is *tok hait*. Warfare and village disputes are public talk. Mixed audiences of men, women, and children thus define the public situation: public affairs.

Secret talk is hushed and sexually segregated. Talk concerning ritual secrets forbidden to the uninitiated characterizes this mode. It can occur in three main situations: the clubhouse (but even there it is whispered and more common at night), the forest (when men are alone), and in culthouses on the rare occasions of initiation, when ritual teaching occurs formally. Men and women have their own secret domains, the details of which the opposite sex is supposed to be ignorant. Secret ritual knowledge is organized by age and ritual grade in both sexes. All male initiates first learn of homosexuality and the secret of the flutes and bullroarer through initiation teachings. After third- and fourth-stage initiation, adolescents learn more advanced secrets about heterosexual purification rites. By final initiation, young men know the entire body of initiation teachings, special ritual foods, semen-replenishing techniques, and the sacred myth of parthenogenesis (see Chapter 5). Yet they still do not know all. The elders retain sacred knowledge of the most secret spells, sorcery magic, and ritual paraphernalia, which gives them absolute authority over younger men. Secret talk can emerge anywhere, wedged in between public and private talk, which is why the anthropologist can spend years decoding euphemisms, metaphors, and double entendres that hide the meanings or names of secret ritual things.

Several examples of men's secret talk, disguised in public symbols to hide their true meanings, will alert you to this issue. Men taboo cassowary meat to all females. So when men snare one, they cook and eat it in the forest, not sharing with women. They alert others by saying, "Let's go fetch nuts in the forest," or "I just found some nice new mushrooms; let's go collect them." When youths jealously fight over boy-fellators, they must of course disguise their conflict in front of women. A common ploy when women ask what is wrong is to say the youths are fighting over a "stolen betel nut." Lying and subterfuge are thus common in hamlet life and influence gender identity, as we will see more in Chapter 6.

Private talk concerns a person's innermost thoughts and desires, some of which may be idiosyncratic and forbidden. Valuable magical knowledge passed from parent to child (about gardening, hunting, and sorcery) is private talk. More significant because it is more frequent and intimate: all sexual experience is treated as private talk, for Sambia are a prudish people who value virginity and have intense feelings of shame regarding coitus. Children hide their sex play and adults hide coition. Even dream reports are affected, for though Sambia share dreams with each other, many sexual dreams and especially wet dreams are not shared. Homosexual intercourse is both secret and private. Adultery is so strongly condemned that when rumors turn into scandalous public accusations, one or both parties may attempt suicide by hanging. In past cases some of them have tragically succeeded; so relatives watch the shamed parties closely for days afterward. People thus hide thoughts and monitor their speech, as reflected in the Sambia concept of *hidden thought*, which refers to the individual's idiosyncratic wishes and secret feelings.

Institutionalized secrecy associated with sex segregation creates unusual effects in New Guinea cultures like that of Sambia. Each of these modes of talking—with their rules and expectations—reinforces sex-related information in gender-role behavior and gender identity. By contrast, in Western culture we have only two speech modes, public and private discourse. Secret societies add a third domain of experience: collective ritual secrets, which functions as a screen for the individual's unconscious. Therefore, secrecy provides a symbolic way to rope off childhood experience and keep adult male identity separate from females. We will return to this idea in later chapters.

PUBLIC MORALITY

I must not go too far in painting a negative picture of hamlet life. It is true that the past lives in the present, that warfare was violent and some violence persists. But nowadays the Sambia are, by and large, a warm and gregarious people who, in spite of their differences, live a peaceful life. Traditionally, their violence was directed primarily at their neighbors. Inside the security circle of the clan-hamlet, however, sociable relations prevailed, notwithstanding that some wives hailed from enemy groups.

Sambia have, in a sense, two very different sides to their personality. The one side faces village life. In spite of the divisive ritual cult, Sambia are a sociable people with strong moral ideas about what constitutes good (*singundu*) and bad (*maatnu-maatnu*) conduct in village life. For children and adults alike, these moral norms are simple and sensible: one should be hospitable and share food (or consumables like tobacco); one should not steal or destroy others' property; one should not physically harm others or needlessly shame them; one should provide for self and family and not be lazy; and one should converse with others, follow parents' instructions, be true to one's word, and not meddle too much in others' affairs. For adults, morality includes more serious injunctions about not defiling rituals, not fighting with or killing (except in self-defense) one's kin or in-laws, and never engaging in heterosexual adultery.

The other side of their personality faces outsiders. All of the above norms apply only to one's known social world, the village and outside relatives. By marking the boundary this way, enemies are not considered human. Therefore killing, raping, and looting among enemies are not moral violations, as we saw in the war-raid example from Chapter 2. All Sambia share in these morals; that is what makes their culture distinctive. In childhood before initiation, boys are exposed to this moral system. It takes root and binds them. As we will see, the men's ritual rhetoric plays down these shared roots—planted in the same soil of public life with the women—but it cannot erase them.

One of the problems of Sambia culture is that while it is secret ritual that is used to socialize boys into adult gender roles, the main context for their adult behavior is public interaction. Thus, there always remains tensions between secret and public experience and activity for men.

The full adult person is defined in public culture against the norms of esteemed village family life. Full masculine persons are those who have been through all initiations, are married, and have at least two children. Men must participate in war raids, be good hunters, and provide well for their families through ample gardens. They should be involved in ritual activities and not spend too much time with women and children. As elders, men are the prime negotiators in marriage, ritual, and land-tenure matters; they should stand up to be counted through sensible public rhetoric when necessary. Full feminine persons should have attained menarche and been initiated, married, and have at least two children. Women should be successful gardeners and be generous in giving others food and consumables. They should also maintain appropriate contacts with their relatives in other hamlets. This allows them to make use of their own clan's resources, and yet it lays them open to the sorcery suspicions noted above. As elders, women should be involved in female ritual activities and instruct younger women in matters of sex and marriage. These normative models of persons provide powerful rules and images of how children ought to behave and what they should strive toward being.

Yet, at the same time, Sambia, like other Highlanders, are rugged individualists. They recognize both moral and personal differences among individuals. This recognition can be found in spontaneous remarks that so-and-so is a good storyteller or a sayer of funny things; that some men are great hunters and fearless warriors, while others are rubbishy; or that some women are industrious gardeners and generous with their food, while others are lazy or stingy. So the ideals of personhood find exceptions. Why are people this way? Eccentricity, biological inheritance, ritual teachings, clan differences, malevolent spirit influences: accounts may vary, but the principles refer back to beliefs about sexual temperament. Let us look at how such beliefs structure male and female experience and development.

BELIEFS ABOUT SEXUAL DIFFERENTIATION

Sambia see the biological development of the sexes as being strikingly different in most regards. They know that both males and females start life in the womb, and they use anatomical differences at birth to make the sex assignment of the infant. Mothers say boys and girls develop differently soon after birth. Boys fuss more, sleep more poorly than girls, and are more prone to illness, whereas girls nurse more and grow faster. Baby girls babble and toddle before boys, Sambia say. As times goes on, this biological leap continues, girls achieving reproductive competence in adulthood easily, naturally. Boys have it harder. They mature slower and have to be socially aided by rituals to achieve adult fertility. What an ironic view in a warrior culture whose men so much pride themselves on their superiority to women!

New Guinea cultures—like our own in the Middle Ages when we believed in dragons and wizards' alchemy—are animistic, so in their world view they perceive a *structure of essences* that governs all life. We have already seen examples of this biological *essentialist* view in Sambia ideas about nature. Now we need to focus on how the same structure of thought is applied to blood and semen as essences of the body. Remember that Sambia have a simple technology and no science as we know it, so their ideas are a mix of fact and fantasy, unchecked by our sophisticated experimental sciences. The point is that Sambia see blood and semen as the crucial fluids in the working of maleness and femaleness.

Femaleness is vital and fast-growing, whereas maleness is slower in gaining maturation. Maleness is believed to depend on the acquisition of semen— the essence of biological maleness—for precipitating male anatomy *and* masculine behavioral traits. Femaleness rests on the creation and circulation of blood. This essence is held, in turn, to stimulate the production of menstrual blood, menarche, and adult reproductive competence. A girl's menarche is celebrated by women in secret events that socially recognize her "natural" achievements. In girls, who possess a self-activating and functional menstrual-blood organ *(tingu)*, maturation is viewed as an unbroken process leading from birth and maternal bonding into adulthood and motherhood. In boys, however, two obstacles block male growth. The first is their mother's pollution, food, and overall caretaking, which nurtures them but then stifles their growth. The second is their lack of semen, because the semen organ *(kereku-kereku)* can only store, not manufacture, semen—the key to manly reproductive competence. In this model, therefore, femaleness is a natural development leading to feminine adulthood; maleness is not a naturally driven process but rather a personal achievement that men wrest control of through ritual initiations to ensure that they attain adult masculinity. Here we will examine ideas about the essence of blood. In Chapter 5 we will see how boys learn the function of semen in promoting masculine gender. Beliefs about both fluids are a basic part of the experience of gender identity in growing up.

Blood is identified by all Sambia with the vitality and longevity of women and their femaleness. Females, unlike males, are thought to be gifted with an innate means of producing blood that hastens the development of growth, menarche, and regular menses. Menstrual blood is also the provider of womb life for the fetus. The male and female parts in reproduction are clearly defined. A man's semen enters the womb and becomes a "pool" that eventually coagulates into fetal skin and bone tissue, which grows inside the female womb. Fetal or womb blood, supplied only by the mother's womb, later becomes part of the circulatory blood needed by all children and adults.

This circulatory blood is thought to be a true stimulator—with certain limits for males—that promotes body functioning and growth and the ability to withstand sickness. The limitations on this idea are centered in concepts through which Sambia define blood itself. First, there is the distinction between circulatory blood and menstrual-womb blood. Both males and females possess circulatory blood *(menjaaku)*; but only females have menstrual blood *(chenchi)*, which is categorized with all other contaminating female fluids. Second, Sambia speak of reproductively competent humans (as well as trees and animals) as being fluid or wet, not dry (that is, either sexually immature or old and used up). In females, fluidity stems from having plentiful circulatory and menstrual blood, vaginal fluids, and that part of her husband's semen a woman "ingests" through sexual intercourse. Males, by contrast, are "drier" because of less fluid; only through their original circulatory blood and later through (artificially ingested) semen are they fluid. Children and old people are most dry; girls are more fluid than boys. Adults—unless sickly or sexually depleted—are generally believed to be fluid. Third, blood is said to be "cold" whereas semen is "hot." Since Sambia see sickness and plagues as active and animated agents (like spirit beings) attracted to heat and repelled by cold, this temperature difference is important in body functioning: the more blood, the less sickness; the more semen, the greater the chance of illness and degeneration. So men are prone to be ill and women healthy. Menstrual periods are compared to a periodic natural defense that rids female bodies of excess menstrual blood and any sickness that manages to penetrate them. Ironically, then, women bounce back from their periods with even greater vitality because of this natural function. The female capacity to create and discharge blood is thus perceived as a sign by the society of the structure and functioning of women's bodies, the fertile powers of birth-giving, procreative sexuality, and health, so men reckon this is why women typically outlive men.

What matters for masculinity is that menstrual-womb blood, though a life-giving female stimulator, also represents after childhood the most dangerous essence for male body functioning. All male circulatory blood originates from the mother's womb, so in later initiation nose-bleedings men attempt to get rid of it. Other female substances—such as skin flakes, saliva, sweat, and especially vaginal fluid—are also classified as polluting and dangerous to men. Male illness resulting from female sorcery, for example, usually hinges on the fear that a man has been slipped menstrual or vaginal fluids in his food, though menstrual blood is dreaded most. Children cannot help but take in these substances through birth and their mother's feeding and handling. Here are the men's main worries that lead to sexual antagonism. But women have similar concerns. They are careful not to contaminate themselves or others, especially their children, during their periods. Neither women's public statements nor activities, however, reveal anything approaching the intense anxiety aroused in men. Men can be directly harmed since menstrual blood, they believe, can penetrate the urethra during genital-to-genital sex, bringing sickness and thus destroying the manliness that has been so hard won. For this reason, men say, they must also be wary of contact with their own children, who may accidentally transmit and infect men with the traces of their mother's body products.[2]

The structure of maleness is relayed through three organs: the semen organ, semen-feeder ducts, and the penis. Together with semen, their essence, they form a physiological system.

All males possess a functional semen organ. Lower mammals, such as dogs and pigs, have the same organ. Females are said to have a semen organ, but its form and function differ from that of males. Here is a remark from Weiyu depicting an image of fetal development:

Semen makes all the infant: bone, skin, brain [including the spinal column]. . . . One thing only—blood—your momma gives to you. Momma gives you blood; [but] everything else, only semen makes. The woman is filled up with blood—the *tingu* makes it and fills it up.

[2] For recent comparative studies on pollution beliefs in Melanesia, see Anna Meigs's (1984) and Fitz John Poole's (1981, 1982) important work, and my own essay on semen as a commodity (Herdt 1984).

Both semen and blood are involved in sexual differentiation. Semen is the more substantial component, even though blood overwhelms it internally by "filling up" the insides.

The immature male semen organ is "solid and dry" and only changes after the ingestion of semen through homosexual contacts. Boys do not inherit semen from their fathers or mothers. By contrast, the *tingu*, initially holding only a smear of blood, gradually grows, engorged by its own blood, which also fills up the girl's womb. The semen organ in a boy is an empty container. It cannot manufacture the essence; it only accumulates what semen is swallowed. Orally ingested semen modifies the organ's form. A pubescent semen organ is called "soft," because the orally ingested semen, by opening and swelling the organ, softens it from inside.

Women's semen organs are filled by blood or vaginal fluid or both, but not by semen. The male *tingu*, by contrast, is not functional: "Of you and me [men] too—we have a *tingu*. But it is hard and dry. . . . Women also have a *kereku-kereku* . . . but theirs is filled with vaginal fluid." Tali the ritual expert said this. The prepubescent boy's semen organ is empty, as is his *tingu* organ, Tali has also suggested. No semen or maleness there; so manhood is not possible until homosexual inseminations begin.

How does this bodily change take place? The semen organ is joined by "feeder tubes" to the mouth, navel, and penis. There are two such tubes. One, the esophagus, is shared by all humans. The esophagus transports semen in both women and boys, but to different places. Some (perhaps most) swallowed semen is siphoned off by the "breast ducts" of women and converted into milk before it reaches the stomach or womb. Slight amounts of it may get into a woman's womb. None of it goes to her semen organ since she lacks the internal tubes associated with a penis. This is consistent with the men's view that orally ingested semen goes to "strengthen" a woman or provide milk, while semen "fed" into the vagina goes into the womb for fetal growth. Women, however, generally believe that their own bodies make them strong. Boys lack a vulva, birth canal, and womb; their ingested semen goes first to "strengthen" them by becoming a liquid pool accumulating in the semen organ. Like food and water, semen can be swallowed; but unlike those substances, it is thought to be funneled undiluted into the semen organ through a feeder tube only males possess. This organ, the "semen tube," directly connects the navel with the penis and testes, and thus with the semen organ. The tubes extend from that organ (in the upper abdominal region) upwards to the navel, and downwards to the stem of the penis. (Another, separate organ, the "urine tube," connects the bladder with the urethra.) Tali has said this: "Both the semen tube and urine tube are joined at the base of the penis, so semen is ejaculated through the urine tube during intercourse." In boys, these semen-related tubes and organs are "closed, hard, and dry" at birth and into childhood, until ritual fellatio matures them.

The prepubescent boy's penis is sexually and reproductively immature, for the boy's body lacks semen. His penis is puny, like a "little leech," men say. It lacks the mature glans penis and foreskin, male biological signs greatly stressed by Sambia. Men and initiates jokingly refer to the adult glans penis as that "ugly nose" and as that "face within the penis [pubic] hair." Such idioms characteristically distinguish the sexually immature from the mature male. Semen has the biological power to change this immaturity. Here is Weiyu on the subject:

> Now when we [males] drink the milk of a man or that of a tree it goes down and paints the *kereku-kereku*. It paints it and it [semen organ] comes up white. And so it makes semen. The penis alone contains nothing . . . it remains empty. But only the tube—it joins the penis—it shakes it, and it expels semen [at ejaculation].

Later you will learn how only adult men drink certain white tree saps to replace their semen. That too is a male secret.

To reach this point of having a potent ejaculation requires years of semen ingestion and appropriate rituals. What matters, to sum up, is that this result is not natural or inevitable; instead, it comes from strict adherence to the male cult's formula.

A harmful effect of women's verbal behavior during childhood is pinpointed on the boy's nose which is, next to the mouth, the body's main port of entry, and which receives ritual treatment. Here, mother's speech and harangues have a lethal power. A woman's airstream emitted while speaking is thought to emerge from her blood-filled caverns. If it is directed—particularly at close range during anger—toward a boy, the latter is harmed: simply by inhaling her insults and air he is defiled. The nose absorbs and stores her contaminants, thereafter blocking the free movement of circulatory blood and other fluids from the nose throughout his body. Likewise, men say women pollute boys simply by lifting their legs in proximity to them, emitting vaginal smells that boys can breathe in. For this reason, men keep their noses secretly plugged during coitus, avoiding incorporation of the vaginal smell they describe as harmfully foul. Women, incidentally, reject some of these male ideas. Particularly today, younger women say that this is more men's idle talk than reality. We will see in Chapter 5 that ritual nose-bleeding is *the* critical means of expelling these harmful female materials from the male body, since Sambia practice no other form of ceremonial bloodletting.

These sexual development beliefs provide a framework for cultural institutions and for individual behavior. For boys and girls, these beliefs underlie the normative gender roles they must adapt to and perform as they reach adulthood. The beliefs also provide a structure for experiencing the self as being either male or female. Here, the individual differentiates him- or herself internally in response to such questions as, "Am I male?" "Am I feminine?" "Should I act in such-and-such way to seem more masculine?" These feelings relate to the person's identification with gender roles and social status positions like those of the hunter, the shaman, and the war leader. Beliefs about sexual differentiation provide guidelines for acting masculine or feminine, which merge into gender beliefs, ideas about *being* male or female, in accord with the society's cultural code of evaluative standards. When there is only one world view—one code for appropriate gender behavior—there may be no great difficulties in learning gender beliefs and in acting upon them in one's life. But what happens when there are two world views, each having different ideas and standards?

THE TWO WORLDS

We have seen that "male" and "female" not only are two sexes but are, for Sambia, two different principles of biological essence, related to two different ways of being social, to the extent that they regard the sexes as different species in many respects. It is only another step—a conceptual leap but an important one—to recognize that this dichotomy creates two distinct symbolic worlds: that of adult men and women. Many New Guinea ethnographers have seen in warfare (the men's aggressive ethos) and the patterning of sexual antagonism the bases for opposition and conflict between the sexes. But how do these factors actually affect child socialization?

Cultures are systems of symbols and behaviors. Sambia men and women clearly have alternative standards in this regard. They do not share all of the same beliefs, they are not guided entirely by the same values, and they disagree on certain fundamentals: Should women have a choice in marriage? Are women as polluting to themselves and to men to the extent men believe? Do women experience orgasm? Should men not bear a larger share of garden work, especially now that warfare is over? Should men not be closer to children and do more caretaking of infants? These issues spark conflict between the sexes and suggest basic gender-role differences, fundamental controversies between the worlds of men and women.

Ritual training and secrecy further accentuate polarity between the two camps. Historically, warfare made men distrust imported wives. They could be spies or they might pollute, sorcerize, or undermine their husbands so their own fathers and brothers could succeed. Fathers worried over the allegiance of their sons. Would they be warriors faithful to themselves or to their mothers? And remember that the sexes had alternative and secret initiations and cults. Women's secret ritual knowledge was different from men's. And neither sex was supposed to share its ritual secrets with the other. Here lies the soil for the growth of two unintegrated world views. We will now consider how they affected gender socialization.

Usually we Westerners think of socialization as a way to produce continuities in the social development of children. Boys and girls learn cultural concepts and rules from parents and others. Their morality develops hand in hand. Later in adolescence, social training simply builds on this early core. We expect adult behavior to be the culmination of what went before, which can be seen in miniature or unfinished ways in children. Likewise, we could think of moral and personality development in tribal societies as also being a steady development of social accomplishments from childhood into adulthood. In this view, then, even groups with ritual initiation such as Sambia are no exception to this image; the initiation simply breaks up the developmental pattern into age-graded periods of new learning episodes. But no matter how persuasive this view is for our own culture, I do not think it truly represents the Sambia developmental cycle.

Social and psychological development for Sambia is marked by dramatic discontinuity because of the initiation rites. We can label this change in the individual's gender identity and role as radical *resocialization*. We will examine this idea closely in the following chapter. What matters here is that the two worlds of men and women represent different evaluative systems for socializing boys and girls. When these standards are at odds, as among the Sambia, gender socialization will involve internal psychological conflicts and social difficulties in adapting to society's roles. Conflict can make it hard for people to conform to their given social roles, for it forces them to choose between two competing sets of standards. Should a boy cry like mother or hold in his crying like father? Perhaps this is why situational, rather than abstract universalistic, morality pervades New Guinea cultures (Read 1955). Contradictions develop in people's lives over whether to follow one value standard or another. The situational demands of home life or the ritual cult point up the discrepancies. Ritual obedience partially resolves this personal difficulty by forcing conformity to ritual standards, leaving no choice for the individual. Yet paradoxes remain in male gender identity and morality, as Chapter 6 reveals.

Socializers' perceptions of dangers in the behavioral environment influence Sambia socialization patterns throughout childhood and early adolescence. A society's investment of scarce resources in a socialization regime such as initiation is a long-term selective index of these dangers. The degree of the parents' active commitment to particular socializing processes—namely teaching, enforcing, and monitoring—is the form this social investment takes at the individual level. For example, only knowledgeable socializers are permitted to teach critical skills, such as war leaders being the primary trainers of young male initiates in the warriorhood role. And only elders are allowed to instruct in certain domains of ritual socialization, to be sure the correct knowledge is passed on.

What happens when socializers train children according to standards that conflict with those of other socializers'? For instance: mothers allow boys to be affectionate and cry, whereas fathers frown on this. Women tend to do the disciplining at home, not men. So there is a striking difference in parents' roles. The village always had to think of training new warrior recruits to replace those who died or were too old. Here warfare was instrumental in creating conflict between the worlds of men and women. When no deviations from norms are allowed, reactive socialization responses are particularly acute and sanctioned. This is the case in initiation, because every Sambia boy is initiated without exception into the warriorhood. Boys who are not aggressive enough are teased, then shamed. They become fair game for hazing and later in life for being dominated by war leaders. The dangers of war led people to stigmatize unaggressive boys. The ones who are disruptive may be punished, exiled, or in extreme cases eliminated altogether—as we saw with Weiyu's father. We can expect peer groups, likewise, to ostracize and sanction deviants among their age-mates in crucial situations of cooperation requiring conformity to warriorhood norms, examples of which we will see in later chapters.

THE FAMILY SYSTEM

Every society has a form of the nuclear family as well as a cultural code that sets the wider context for parents and children to act and experience themselves as part of an extended family system. This context therefore implies a level of consciousness about what one can or even must do to be esteemed, to be accepted, to survive. Family *system* means that all parts of the family—its parents, children, habitation, economy, gender roles, and so forth—are interrelated, each part affecting the other. Change one part and you change the whole. In this sense, children *learn in a context*: the family. Their learning is, consequently, context-dependent: certain feelings, sensations, ideas, identifications, occur in relation to loved ones. Growth or *un*learning, too, later occurs through these same contextual relationships or through adult ones that replaced them. This may be the reason we say, in our culture, that by being parents we become children again. Or, to put it differently, that adults never fully mature until they themselves become parents who re-experience being children through the role of being loving parents. The key word here is *loving*. There are different styles of lovingness correlated with culture and family system types. Some styles are based on warmer and more emotionally flexible relationships; others show rigid or unemotional ties. These differences in style influence gender development in socialization.

The nuclear family is part of a broader unit among Sambia: the clan-based extended family in the hamlet. The hamlet provides the alternate caretakers of grandparents, parents, aunts and uncles, and cousins for children growing up. How could children be isolated or alone? They live in such a people-filled world.

Gender roles and the development of heterosexuality (in gender identity and later in sexual behavior) evolve as a function of this broader familial system. Parents usually live together with uninitiated children in a small, igloo-shaped hut. Yet the ritual and sexual taboos apply to this domestic abode as much as anywhere else, and men's fear of pollution extends into the family home. For example, male and female compartments are marked off by sticks laid across the floor in the family hut. Everything—food, utensils, tools, people—belongs either in its proper "male" or "female" place. In these circumstances it is problematic for children (boys especially) to feel fully involved with both their purposely separate mother and father. Moreover, father's secret ritual world intrudes constantly because he spends so much time in the clubhouse. It is thus not simply a matter of whether children identify with their father or mother or with their parents' gender roles. Gender differentiation is conditioned by the *consciousness of the family relationships* that govern children's attempts to be like their parents. Children pay attention to the *quality* of their parents' relationship. For example, they can subconsciously identify with father's aloofness or mother's warmth in their parents' interactions. This affects their own ability to have fulfilling relationships with the opposite sex (Lidz 1976). We will return to these ideas in the conclusion.

PREGNANCY AND BIRTH

What do Sambia believe about human birth? Their ideas are a mixture of fact and folklore. Let us here study their beliefs, for these will help us understand the cultural context of early child-rearing.

Pregnancy brings visible changes in a young woman. The Sambia woman has been "fed" enough semen by her husband to enlarge her breasts. They become full, with black nipples—a result of coitus, men say. Weiyu says, "Fellatio doesn't make black nipples, only genital intercourse does." The breasts are now filled with milk and change to a darker skin tone. Sambia say the limbs and face, on the other hand, turn dull yellow and the stomach develops a red hue, and the overall effect is a nice vibrant glow in the pregnant mother.

The fetus inside the womb is thought to be blood red. At birth, the womb blood is expelled. (Until then, the full womb keeps the mother's milk from flowing.) It is this mass of blood, surrounding the fetus, that gives the stomach its red glow. What do these skin coloration changes mean? Here is Tali's sharp answer to my question:

> This is to produce a baby [*kwulai'u imutnundikeinun-tokeno*]. The woman carries a belly, has a child [*kwulai'u imutnyi*]; she can develop loose [and yellow] skin. It's the same as pandanus—we've told you many times.

Here we have a good example of how Sambia compare the birth-giving process in women to related changes in the "female" species of nature. Birth in women corresponds to the growth of a nut pod in female pandanus trees. Both in women and trees, "pregnancy" is identified with a slackness of skin, a darkening of breasts—or of the nut pod—and a yellowing of the overall body or the pandanus foliage.

Genital-to-genital sex between spouses should continue until a woman feels the fetus moving inside her (near the sixth month of pregnancy) because these last few months of accumulating semen are believed critical to the baby's health. Not only does the father's sperm complete fetal development, but Sambia believe it also lends more milk to the mother for postpartum breastfeeding. After the seventh month, however, all sexual intercourse must stop, since "blocking the birth canal" is felt to threaten the fetus and to agitate birth labor.

Sambia women consider birth painful and dangerous, particularly the first birth. The expectant mother is removed to the menstrual hut. There are two reasons for this. First, birth is secret and, like the menses, it carries some shame for women. Second, the birth-giving process is highly polluting to others. Consequently, the infant's sex assignment is done in private and it is always solely the province of women. A secret myth of the men says that women originally hid their first birth, so now men hide homosexuality. A woman's body and her innards are naked and exposed as well, so only women should witness labor. Children are also kept out. Elder women ease the labor by serving as midwives. A difficult birth requires a woman shaman such as Kaiyunango, whose healing spells, as she massages the abdomen, address the fetus as a slippery eel—so as to coax it from its dark, cavernous hiding place. When the newborn finally emerges, it is laid on freshly cut banana leaves. The infant looks "completely red and bloodied" from the birth sac, women say, and the mass of female fluids becomes the greatest pool of pollution Sambia know.

This is why men perceive birth to be deeply contaminating and dangerous to themselves. Indeed, the menstrual hut is temporarily referred to as a "birth house," wherein the blood and the afterbirth are contained. The mother uses her own grass skirt to clean the infant. The umbilical cord (cut with a bamboo knife) is buried in the earth near the hut.

Immediately upon birth, women hastily clean the infant so as to determine its sex. The genitals are the only certain clue and, as I said, only women examine them. There they pronounce the infant's sex, which is stamped forever. Instantly, word of the birth and the baby's sex spreads like wildfire among the villagers. It is remarkable how, in a day or so, an entire region seems to know about the birth of a boy or a girl. Men, especially the new father, will not be allowed to see the infant for weeks and even months to come.

The traditional norm was that the first child should be a male. This ideal is expressed by parents and is reflected in custom and myth. First-born sons administer their father's estate and take his name and name-song after his death. The preference for sons hinges on their providing the main manpower for the village in warfare, hunting, and gardening. The second born could be either a boy or girl, but most parents favor later births to be girls. Too many sons would "fight over land," they say. And girls are needed for providing women to exchange as wives for their brothers, as well as for helping their mothers. There could never be too many daughters, it seems, for they produce food and provide wives and babies for the nuclear family and the clan.

Mothers take great care to protect their infants at all times, suckling them whenever they cry. Babies are soothed usually by being offered the breast. The mother takes the infant everywhere and sleeps with it every night. Newborns are seldom entrusted to other women, and then only for brief periods. Mothers say that babies are too prone to get ill and die, so they do not want to risk using babysitters. Young mothers are more anxious than older, experienced ones, who seem more secure. Without doubt the mother's security has to do with feeling somewhat alone and estranged in her husband's hamlet, where she is under suspicion. She keeps the baby closer as a result.

There are three primary risks to the infant at birth, and each should be mentioned for they affect gender socialization. First, the entire Sambia region shows high infant mortality. Second, men fear male infanticide practiced secretly by women. Third, parents wonder whether the newborn will be a hermaphrodite, though fathers seem the most concerned, for reasons you will see.

The risk of infant mortality is real. In the mid-1970s, before Western medical care was introduced, infant mortality was high. Since then it has declined, yet even in 1981 my census showed a tragically high 50 percent infant mortality rate in my village (eight out of 16 infants died between 1980 and 1981) due to an epidemic of malaria compounded by pneumonia.

Male infanticide is another risk and one over which men, who oppose the practice, have no control. It is odd to think of a warrior society practicing male infanticide. Yet this practice is known elsewhere in New Guinea as well (Herdt 1981). It was hard for me to collect information on infanticide for the government outlawed it and Sambia know that Westerners condemn the practice. Women themselves felt conflict and remorse over the practice, even when it was reportedly done by neighboring mothers. Sambia love children, and it is hard to imagine that infanticide was done except in desperate circumstances. Where a mother discussed it with me, she made it plain that she felt she already had many children, including sons, and she feared another son (whom she put to death at birth) would create fighting among them over property later in adulthood. Men believe women secretly suffocated the baby at birth and then reported that it had been stillborn. "How can we know for sure?" they would ask. "We weren't there."

Male infanticide is understandable from another standpoint: male overpopulation. Throughout New Guinea, males outnumber females at birth, often in high ratios (see Malcolm 1970; Herdt 1984). For Sambia, the birthrate ratio is 120 male births to 100 female births. The sex-ratio imbalance continues into marriageable age. In the Sambia Valley, for example, 32 percent of all marriageable-aged males are single, whereas only 24 percent of all marriageable-aged females are single. Bachelorhood for males can thus be stretched out for years. In some New Guinea regions *permanent bachelors*, those who cannot find wives, are a significant social factor in the population pool (Bowers 1965).

And what of hermaphroditism?* It is remarkable how men express concern to one another that their infant sons could turn out to be male pseudohermaphrodites. When they discuss the problems of masculinizing their tiny sons, their wives' pollution, the boys' "weakness," and hermaphroditism are all mentioned. Sometimes in idle moments (Tali, for instance, communicated this to me) men worry that a baby son might "change into a girl." As we saw in Sakulambei's biography, Sambia know of cases of boys who have femalelike genitals at birth. At puberty these males' bodies become further masculinized due to androgens (male sex hormones) naturally released at the

---

* There are several types of biologically determined hermaphroditism in humans, but that found among Sambia should technically be called pseudo-hermaphroditism, which afflicts only males.

time. Sambia assume only that the child's penis may be absent or very small. Part of the men's concern is caused by the fact that they avoid the mother and child, so the infant remains virtually an appendage of the mother's body, due to postpartum sex taboos and sexual antagonism between spouses.

Most of the male pseudo-hermaphrodites probably suffer from androgen hormone–processing deficiency. Of a dozen or so instances of persons class-ified as hermaphrodites (only several of whom are now living), most were assigned to the male sex and were reared and initiated as men. This genetically high ratio of pseudo-hermaphroditism in the Sambia population (it is many times higher than in our society) provides a means of understanding why hermaphroditism is a focus of men's concerns. The phrase "changing into a man" has recently entered public talk because of the infamous case of a Sambia person who was reared as a female, then married (as a woman), and was discovered by her husband to have a penis. Government medical officers verified this in 1975. This case may have resulted from a possibility that men do not themselves consider: a pseudo-hermaphrodite with an undersized penis at birth can be assigned to the female sex. Having ambiguous genitals, her-maphrodites are both pitied and ridiculed, as we saw with Sakulambei. Like anomalous persons everywhere, their mystery makes them suspect. Hence these "male-females" come closest to occupying a true pariah category among Sambia. Understandably, in a society where sexual differentiation counts so heavily, men fear lest their sons suffer the same fate.

Genital sexual intercourse between spouses is forbidden by postpartum sex taboos until the child is weaned. Oral sex (the wife fellating her husband) is acceptable, but many women dislike it, especially when they are older. Other kinds of social interaction are also highly restricted. The mother keeps the infant with her at all times during the first months of life. Women hide infants from their fathers until later (traditionally several months), when it is felt the baby is healthy and will look pleasing to the father. Fathers avoid the mother-infant pair too. Ideally, they should go on long hunting, war-raiding, or trading trips away from their families during this period. For all these reasons, the baby is not named until months after birth. Until then, personal pronouns are used in speaking to the infant. (Even after bestowing a name, Sambia still use personal pronouns instead of names, I have found, more often than do many American mothers.) Women say they resist naming the infant earlier because they grow so attached, and if the baby dies they will "cry for it too much." The high infant mortality rate gives credence to their view. The child, until then, is like a part of the mother, without a self of its own. The bestowal of a childhood name recognizes the increasing separateness of the infant from skin contact with the body from which it emerged. In this sense, the baby is not considered a person until after it survives its first months.

Children have two names: this childhood name and an adult name conferred on them at birth by the mother's kin but not used until many years later. Boys lose their childhood name at first initiation, when they are formally addressed by their adult name; informally, age-mates refer to them with a nickname. Thereafter, the childhood name (and name-song) is taboo for both girls and boys, but especially for the boys: that piece of early identity must be forgotten. Indeed, it is a violent insult to call a man by his childhood name. Women receive their adult names and lose their childhood names much later in life, at the first menses.

The infant's soul is felt to be present in his or her body at this time, as revealed by an increasing capacity to verbalize and reason. The soul arises in the womb and accompanies the healthy baby into childhood and adulthood. This is a significant acceptance of the mother's influence on the child's spiritual essence, which seems at variance with male beliefs governing men's social behavior. Like the female guardian spirits of the men's cult, we will later see that such symbols suggest a stronger female power than the men say.

CHILDHOOD GENDER SOCIALIZATION

Let us now outline the development of gender and the accumulating impact of cultural beliefs on the child's growing identity and behavior. Scientists today see the first five years of life as being highly significant for development. In fact, experts believe we should think of these sensitive years as a "critical learning period" in early gender development (reviewed in Herdt 1981; Luria 1979). "Critical learning" has been compared by analogy with early language acquisition. It is believed that the child's mind and brain are more psychoneurologically flexible and receptive to language learning now than later in life. Perhaps *core* gender identity—one's awareness of existence, sense of maleness or femaleness (in the self and in body image), and one's life goals are conditioned and strongly reinforced early on. For Sambia, the conditions of early gender socialization are typical of a range of New Guinea societies. These conditions structure the conscious and unconscious "learning" of core gender identity, and underline the difficulties of "unlearning" this in later life.

First we can map the critical events in the baby's growth and separation from its mother. Close proximity to mother marks the initial phase. Being shown to the father at the age of three or four months opens the next phase. Afterward, the father may hold the baby for short periods, which expands the base of adult caretakers beyond mother. When the baby begins to crawl, other women and older children are used as babysitters for brief periods (an hour or two). By the time it starts taking solid foods at six to eight months, the baby spends more hours with substitute caretakers. Toddlers are allowed to go beyond the hut as long as they remain in sight of mother or someone else. Most mothers take their infants with them wherever they go, so children spend long hours with them in gardens. After the child is walking, the father takes him or her for periods of an hour or two in the hamlet. Fathers favor sons in this respect.

Breast-weaning is the next critical juncture. Until then, the baby always sleeps in mother's bed. This is an essential part of the mother's protectiveness.

Weaning—which occurs around two and a half years of age—changes sleeping arrangements. Children now sleep in separate beds but still near their mother in the female space of the hut. The child plays and interacts with siblings and peers, and siblings may also act as babysitters. By age five or so, boys are encouraged, and then forced, to shift their beds to the male space in the hut, where their fathers sleep. Girls always sleep in the female space of their mothers. Hereafter, boys are often with playmates, older brothers, and their fathers.

Early toilet training is casual, but this changes. Sambia are highly conscious of bodily hygiene. Being prudish, they are uncomfortable handling feces, and they are extremely shamed and irritated when seen defecating. Yet in spite of all this, infants are treated easily when they relieve themselves. By the time of their weaning, most children know to go off to the toilet or into the bushes to relieve themselves. Children are shamed for excreting in public by age four or five. This stress on the privacy of toilet functions continues throughout life.

It bothers men that girls physically grow faster than boys, as suggested by their common saying *nuno-wuluwut'nji*—meaning, a girl "can win over you," outgrow you. This biological race refers to more than their occupations; girls are more dependable than their brothers, who dislike gardening and throw tantrums. Before initiation, when boys are playing games or catching tadpoles, girls have regular garden chores and babysitting responsibilities. "What happens in this land," Moondi said, "is that girls win over boys in growth size." Why this matters is a subject of endless preaching to boys. Here again Moondi comments: "If a woman outgrows you, another [older] youth can steal her, your [betrothed] woman. Where can you get a woman then? Men can take two or three wives. Some steal women. Where can you obtain another woman from?" In short, it spells trouble if a girl reaches maturity before the boy assigned for her in marriage.

The concern about physical growth raises the question of the causes of Sambia gender beliefs. I have stressed the real-life environment and dangers of Sambia as factors influencing child-rearing practices. Some anthropologists have argued that men grow jealous of their sons' attachments to their wives. In this view, men are unconsciously motivated to use initiation to separate mother from son. Initiation thus inhibits potential incest desires and also expresses the father's envy of his son's special position in his wife's affections (Whiting et al. 1958). While I do not completely accept this explanation, it does have the merit of calling our attention to the prolonged closeness between mothers and sons as a foundation for Sambia beliefs. This addresses the classical Oedipus complex (Spiro 1982). Oedipal rivalry between fathers and sons does emerge later in initiation. But there is another developmental factor. Malcolm (1968) has shown that Sambia and people of their cultural population have the slowest physical maturation in the world. Children here mature very slowly and puberty is late. This medical study supports the Sambias' own belief that children grow slowly. Still, it does not explain why boys are singled out for ritual treatment early, why male initiations are so harsh, or why girls

Photo 7. Three small boys of Nilangu village

are left to grow up without ritual until they are adults, questions examined in Chapter 6.

Boys are increasingly pressured to spend time with father and other males after age five. They are expected to shift informally into the men's world. At first, many boys may resist this shift. They cry and are teased or shamed into complying. Even then, however, upon awakening at night they crawl over to the female space, or if frightened by a nightmare or some nocturnal experience, they go to their mothers for comfort. And rarely are frightened children refused the breast—security—even up to age five or six. Yes, contacts with father increase, both in quality and in time. But boys continue to be more with their mothers, siblings, and playmates, not with their fathers. This is especially true when ritual or hunting draw the men away for weeks at a time. Not until first-stage initiation, between ages seven and ten, is there a *formal* change in boys' sleeping arrangements when they are taken into the men's house.

A powerful factor in early child development here is the father's aloofness. Adult gender norms dictate emotional and behavioral patterns of avoidance for men. Too much contact with children is as potentially polluting as being with their mother. Moreover, it is unmanly. Men typically spend so much time away from home, hunting and in the men's house, which sets up a barrier in interactions with their children. Ritual teaches men to be tough. Here is my friend Tali, the ritual expert, commenting on the commandment to be aloof:

Suppose you see your woman carrying firewood, a pile of food, and she complains. [Her husband may be carrying nothing.] The man [still] mustn't carry the baby. The man will say: "I've made that baby in you—it's something belonging to you. I've given it over to you." If a man carries a child, his skin will slacken, he can become weak, age quickly. You [father] won't produce another baby. . . . So you mustn't carry a child for her; if she gets angry, that's her worry. And when a couple go to the forest, that time, too, you shouldn't carry the baby. The woman can cry—let her: "I've come to hunt possum—why should I carry your baby?"

Men are arrogant and avoid femininity. They fear their manhood is always being tested. But in judging their aloofness, remember that they are warriors who are trained to kill, if necessary, to protect the village. They never forget what they have been taught: to survive.

The acquisition of speech affords parents more opportunities to train for and reinforce children's verbal understanding of gender norms and rules. Training for social roles may begin implicitly. Children learn by watching. Cultural transmission is later more explicit, as in instruction about economic duties (gardening) or training for domestic tasks (cooking). Both types of learning experiences convey to children basic attitudes about appropriate sex-related behavior patterns and tasks. Thus, boys should climb trees and girls should weed in gardens. Children learn, in other words, sex-typing: the polarity of everyday life into the two worlds of men and women. Certainly in New Guinea societies, sex-typing and training for gender-appropriate activities and values point children in the direction of expected normative adult social roles. Oral traditions—such as ghost stories or folktales—implicitly reinforce moral images of appropriate gender and social behavior. Many folktales, for instance, show children the nasty consequences of adultery: the adulterers terrorized or killed by ghosts or betrayed by their own lover. The moral is to be a faithful spouse.

Speech highlights the more emotional versus the more cognitive dimensions of childhood socialization. How much control can a culture exercise over the formation of personality and gender? Age is certainly an important factor in the child's readiness to receive and understand messages. In the preverbal stage, infants and toddlers cannot fully comprehend cultural rules or norms, which are cognitively based. Symbolic sex-typing—such as labelling items or activities men's things or women's things—though noticed by children, are not cognitively internalized in their entirety until later, perhaps in middle to late childhood. Boys sense the abstract identification between masculinity and ritual, for example, but they do not fully comprehend this symbolic identification or what it means for being a male person.

Emotional patterns, however, seem to be shaped earlier and more fully. Crying and smiling, touching or avoiding can be trained and controlled well before the child fully knows what these feelings mean in society, or why adults shape them this way. Children learn to emotionally respond in normative ways consistent with cultural values and ethos. Training boys to be aggressive and girls to be submissive are examples. Reactive socialization episodes also occur: for instance, when a toddler falls and cries and is immediately offered the breast, food, and soothing words—or instead is shunned—basic emotional patterns are communicated. These parental responses communicate feelings about dependency, independence, interpersonal availability, the possibility of spontaneous emotional expression, trust, and so forth. Children's games, gender-appropriate routines, and the stories they are later told all reinforce the expected emotional responses. In short, early training for emotion is a systematic coding of the cultural world view of the parents and other social-izers. Children acquire explicit and implicit goals, particularly concerning the emotional quality of gender relationships, through these interactions. This consolidates core gender identity by reinforcing the emotional basis of gender beliefs, which increasingly "make sense" in the whole scheme of things.

A powerful message Sambia children receive about the quality of gender relationships concerns the avoidance of touching members of the opposite sex. It is striking how men and women avoid physical contact in public: they never sit close, hold hands, touch, fondle, or lie together. This is morally wrong and culturally distasteful. Kissing is unknown, and those Sambia who have seen other New Guineans kiss consider it shocking. The thought of mixing saliva with a woman is utterly disgusting to men. Sexual intercourse only occurs in private, preferably in the forest, so foreplay leading up to this is never observed by others. Though men walk hand in hand as an expression of friendship, and women do the same with each other, it is unthinkable for the sexes to do so together. This is why we may refer to Sambia as prudish and sexually restrictive as a culture. Rumor has it that the missionaries (an American couple with children) sleep in the same bed, which Sambia find truly astonishing. Elders have warned the male missionary to avoid this contact or else he will age and die young. Although I worked with Sambia for over 10 years, with nearly three years spent among friends in their villages, never once did I see a man and woman purposely touch each other in public.

This avoidance is, of course, a result of sexual antagonism and men's aloof-ness. Can we imagine that this behavioral pattern does not profoundly shape children's feelings about their mothers and fathers, about the sex they belong to and their sense of themselves? Will such children not feel the strain and tension of always physically avoiding the opposite sex, especially when contact with their own sex is so permissible, warm, and comfortable? Will years of such patterning not influence the boy's sexual orientation, making homosexual activity more understandable? Of course it will. Later we shall see how these behavioral trends are exploited by the symbolism of the men's secret society to motivate boys to "change their childhood ways."

AGGRESSIVITY, SHAMING, AND CONTROL

Until male initiation, the daily routines of boys and girls are quite different. Parents are unable to discipline or exercise control over boys. Older unini-tiated boys love to make mischief, and they have a social freedom unique in Sambia life. They are too small and untrained to be involved in warfare, so

Photo 8. Three initiates of Nilangu village

they are left in the women's care. They are well protected and fed, inside the security circle of the hamlet; hence, life's hardships fall on adults. Boys enjoy their games and explorations in the adjacent gardens and edgeland forest, though the forest is too dangerous for them to hunt in yet. Sometimes they can be dragged into doing garden chores by their mothers, or be persuaded to fetch water or betel nuts by their fathers. They are notoriously bad babysitters. Girls are much better garden producers and far better babysitters. Indeed, it is a chore to get boys to do the little they do, and they are undependable in getting it done. Only when older, near initiation, do they contribute much to their families' resources by helping to weed and by trapping rats, frogs, and tadpoles, which are female foods initiates and young men cannot eat. Yet even then they are hard to control: boys disobey orders, sass their mothers, and quarrel with smaller children. They make fun of the men's cult, for instance, by imitating the sounds of the secret flutes, which annoys the elders, who pay them back later in initiation rites. They take food, spoil men's hunting traps in the forest, and reveal a genius for finding exciting ways to have fun at the expense of adults.

Physical punishment of children is culturally disapproved by Sambia. Mothers more than fathers must discipline children, since women are usually the caretakers. Fathers are lax in this way. Mothers scold their children if necessary and sometimes they holler. Physical discipline, however, is highly unusual. Shaming is used informally to control children. Children are told not to "act like babies," and parents refer to others watching the children and thinking they are "foolish" and "childish." In my experience, though, shaming is more effective with girls, who cry more easily than boys. This is understandable, for girls are trained to be more dependent and responsive to others' needs. But boys too will cry if parents persist. Teasing and threats are also used: "Don't act like a ghost"; "I won't give you any food tonight unless you . . ."; "It's almost dark; don't go far or the ghosts will get you"; etc., etc.

Disciplining children is a real problem for Sambia. Both sexes believe that physical punishment "stunts children's growth." Parents will take an extraordinary amount of abuse from children before they will discipline. They threaten verbally but are short on action. Only rarely, when they lose their tempers, will mothers hit a child. The men say women are more quick to punish than themselves; even verbal reprimands are frowned upon by fathers. (We will see in Chapter 5 how men castigate mothers bitterly for such cursing of boys.) So emotional are they, in fact, that one suspects the men are still angry at some childhood hurt that has never healed. Occasionally when this subject came up, my friends pointed out how "mean" the missionaries are, for in spite of white men's Christian teachings, they actually spank their own children! Kanteilo's attitude in this regard always is: "Let the boys go. They'll be initiated soon enough, they'll feel what real pain is, and there'll be no more trouble with discipline." Another reason for not directly disciplining children is the idea that children have "no thought," that they are really incapable of taking responsibility in many areas. So before initiation it is cruel and foolish to punish them for their misbehavior.

The problem of discipline gets mixed in with sex-role affiliations in the Sambia family. Children know how to manipulate their parents. Fathers get pitted against mothers over the need for controlling children. A mother will scold a boy during some conflict, while the father tends to side with him. The parents then argue, so the child ends up being undisciplined or overindulged. Many parental spats start this way. Children are clever at this manipulating, and adults (who were, after all, once children themselves) know that it goes on. But nothing changes. These conflicts confirm rivalries between parents and alliances between children and parents. Such parent-child alliances draw on the love of Sambia for their children, as well as the kinship and family dynamics of identification between children and parents. Mothers and daughters garden together and share in the women's secret life. Boys and their fathers will always belong to the same clan and act to promote its interests. Boys are the mediators in these conflicts because as children they do not fit into either their mother's or father's world fully. They can use either parent against the other and avoid responsibilities. Boys have an ambivalent relationship to their parents as authority figures, but they are closest of all to their mothers. Perhaps this is inevitable in a culture that institutionalizes sexual antagonism, by placing fathers in secret rituals and making them aloof from sons.

Boys use the temper tantrum to get what they want or to take revenge. It is quite effective. They howl and bawl, scream and roll in the dirt sometimes for hours until they get their way or exhaust themselves, in which case they resort to sulking. They often do this when left by their parents, who wish to be alone in the garden for sex. One sees disguised in adult men the same sulking behavior when they do not get their way in some matter—only they withdraw and become aloof and silent, rather than bawl or roll on the ground. Adults hate for children to cry—among other things, it is socially embarrassing to themselves—so they often give in to a child's demands, shoving food their way to quiet them. Tantrums thus implicitly reinforce boys for hotheaded and stubborn masculinity.

Finally, there is the additional fact that some mothers pamper and favor their sons over their daughters. The chief reason for this is the reality-oriented attitude that one day sons will replace husbands as their main economic supporters in old age. Here again a rivalry is set up, since men feel their wives will outlive them. In Chapters 5 and 6 we will study this family conflict, which is played out at length in the dramas of ritual initiation. Shakespeare often wrote of these timeless human problems in his tragic plays that deal with Oedipal desires *(Hamlet)*, family treachery *(Macbeth)*, and the ingratitude of children *(King Lear)*; but his brilliant portrait of the mother-indulged *Coriolanus*, the pampered and tempestuous favored son, is an image Sambia would recognize best.

There is one area, however, in which Sambia adults cooperate and are extraordinarily stern and unbending: control of sexuality. Children are kept sexually ignorant and all sexual experimentation is suppressed.

Prudishness is socialized in childhood, since men and women alike feel that children are best kept ignorant of all sexual matters. People are careful to cover their genitals and to avoid reference to them in heterosexual company. Coitus and fellatio activities (among spouses) belong only to the forest. Heterosexual intercourse should always be hidden from children and should not (but occasionally does) occur at night within houses after they are asleep. Women are shy about their menstruations and conceal them from children; menstruation is never discussed. Boys are first prevented (at around three years of age) from accompanying their mothers to the menstrual hut through the admonishment that contact with the menses may block their growth. Both mothers and fathers say this. Raucous humor or lewd stories are bluntly discouraged in the presence of children, and adults are self-conscious about risque behavior. Both men and women use euphemisms for erotic matters in the presence of children: "water" substitutes for semen, "bamboo" for vagina, and "stick" for penis.

Boys go about naked till they are three or four years of age. Girls, however, are from birth completely covered from the waist down by grass skirts, whereas even until initiation boys wear only a pubic cover (their buttocks remain exposed), a contrast that reinforces the taboo on female virginity. Boys are also teased and playfully taunted about their genitals in a way that is never done to girls. Clearly, girls are expected to hide their genitals, to protect their virginity and behave decorously, whereas before initiation boys can act very differently. Here is one of the small details of socialization that lead, no doubt, to the origins of sexual excitement: hiding one's body purposely (to be feminine) and being allowed to exhibit (to be masculine) lead eventually to sexual "hiding" and sexual "looking" in adult heterosexuality.

Following infancy, boys and girls are encouraged to play apart and all sex play is forbidden. Parents fear that casual sexual experimentation would make children prone to adultery in later life. All this is necessary, men say, because if boys and girls could "sexually play among themselves" they "would have no thought of being warriors or of making gardens." This taboo seems successful; most males I interviewed denied any knowledge of semen or erotic intercourse until they were initiated. Men avoid mentioning heterosexual intercourse around initiates or women, and women do likewise with girls.

These sexual restrictions are associated with the patterning of Sambia socialization we have surveyed, gender-role training in particular. Sexually restrictive cultures generally suppress erotic experimentation among children. Taboos and rules are firmly placed, and shaming is a powerful tool for sexual repression. Children are made to be sensitive to social expectations and taboos. This is true in spite of boys' independence. Sexual play is one deviation that parents punish physically.

The Sambia have, in other words, a shame culture; their most powerful constraints operate to make people fear shame. So much do they fear it that a person may commit suicide to escape the great shame of adultery. It is no mystery why shame should be a powerful control mechanism in a small village where everyone knows everyone else. Shame reflects not only on the self, but also upon parents and family. By contrast, our own society has been seen as a guilt culture, in which the individual's conscience and self-control keep him or her in check. Ours is a mass society; we may barely know neighbors, fellow students, and others. Our shame is mild compared to that of Sambia. Consequently, we are less restricted than they are, and our sexuality is affected accordingly. Sex, shame, and social control are thus interwoven, a theme we will analyze in the conclusion.

The workings of a culture are usually meaningful and often adaptive, so we would expect this emphasis on shame—as a counterbalance to the lack of childhood discipline—to have a functional effect on later adult life too. We can see this in relation to the men's aggressive ethos. On the one hand there is the assertiveness of men in their warriorhood; while on the other the impulsiveness of boys is implicitly reinforced by their lack of discipline, social freedom, and temper tantrums. What needs to be questioned is how these boys are kept under control when they become men. What keeps them from committing antisocial acts like violence on their own people? Warriorhood training through initiation is the main institutional control. Initiation uses fear and then shame to make boys obedient to the male elders. Here is the key to their impulse control. Later we will see how elders train boys to be aggressive—but only toward their wives and enemies in war.

LATER SOCIALIZATION

Gender-role training becomes increasingly explicit after age five. Boys are trained to be assertive and independent, whereas girls are reinforced for being compliant and submissive. Fathers expect sons to acquire adult masculine gender behaviors. They give their boys miniature bows and arrows to hunt birds and mice. Boys start to learn how to climb pandanus trees to fetch their nuts or fruit. Though they help their parents in gardening chores, boys pick up their fathers' feeling that digging and planting are dull, dirty, feminine activities. Likewise, boys dislike babysitting. As children mature, boys are discouraged from playing with girls, and girls are expected to do more garden work under their mothers' supervision. Girls are discouraged from climbing trees, damming creeks to catch tadpoles or fish (like boys), and going into the forest. They never hunt, except for frogs or insects late at night by the river with their mothers. Play groups are made up of the same sex. So the general pattern of sex segregation takes form from middle childhood onward. Later, initiation removes any question of personal choice and rules out heterosexual playfulness through sex avoidance.

Girls remain in their parents' households until they are married. They stay out of public affairs and decision-making beyond their immediate family. Girls learn gardening techniques and mothering. They are liked for being hardworking and are shamed for being unable or unwilling to work. Women themselves scoff at others who are unsuccessful gardeners. Girls also have considerable freedom in their everyday activities until puberty (about age 15 onward). Unlike initiates, they are not directly accountable to anyone beyond their family. After puberty, though, they are monitored carefully lest they be tempted to engage in sexual activity with older males, because now the taboo on their virginity is actively enforced. Women are suspiciously watched after marriage by their husbands, mothers-, and sisters-in-law for any hint of sorcery, sexual pollution, or adultery that might harm or shame their husbands. In menarche ceremonies, women are praised for being industrious gardeners and faithful wives; Kaiyunango stresses this when she does ritual teaching for girls. Menarche, marriage, and sex are thus highly interrelated for Sambia. The powerful restrictions on virginity make premarital sex a serious moral violation. So strong is the norm of sex in marriage that bastard children are not culturally recognized with any category term. Menarche occurs very late. Malcolm's (1968) careful medical study shows that the mean age of first menstruation is 19.2 years in the region. Marriage can thus occur formally before menarche, but not genital-to-genital intercourse. When an pre-menarchal female is married, she lives with her parents or in-laws, while her husband remains in the men's house. The girl is secretly instructed in modes of sexual intercourse by female elders. During this time the newlyweds can quietly go to gardens together where, nearby in the forest, it is permissible to have fellatio, with the young woman sucking her husband's penis to ejaculation. The semen is always swallowed for this, the men believe, aids women's growth. Women, however, often dispute this view: another sign of conflict between the two world views. These initial sexual contacts are fraught with anxiety for both sexes. Only later, after her first period, can the woman and her husband engage in genital sex (in the "missionary position," the man on top of his wife, who lies on her back). After the birth of a child, fellatio is permitted a few months later, though women usually dislike it. After the infant is weaned, most sexual activity is genital-to-genital intercourse, into old age.

SUMMARY: THE TWO WORLDS AND TWO CONTEXTS OF SOCIALIZATION

Sambia society has internal divisions based on patterns of warfare, ritual, and sexual antagonism. Gender roles are oriented both to public social life and to ritual secrets. But ritual secrecy is the more powerful controlling force. I have argued that there are two separate worlds, the feminine and masculine, which have somewhat different rules, values, and norms (world views) associated with secret knowledge. That complementary areas exist between the sexes and that their cultural knowledge overlaps should not blind us to the facts of antagonism dividing them.

Boys and girls are primarily attached to their mothers in infancy. Even in late childhood mother is the more central figure in their day-to-day living. Mothers socialize children in line with their own female concerns and daily routines. It is true that they treat boys somewhat differently than girls, as we have seen in the boys' temper tantrums. Nonetheless, a boy is not a man; he is perceived as being "unfinished" and is mostly ignored by men until initiation.

The uninitiated boy is problematic. He is male but not biologically, socially, or psychologically masculine. Although an object of paternal pride and a valuable maternal asset, a boy is a consumer, not a producer, and he is useless for village defense. He does not contribute economically as much as his sisters do. And unlike girls, the men's hard work through initiation is required to ensure a boy's achievement of adult reproductive competence. Since boys are lumped together with women in many ways and run virtually free through the hamlet (excepting the men's clubhouse), they are innocent transmitters of female contaminants. They cannot be trusted to help preserve masculine ritual purity. The older boys pose threats to the men's maintenance of authority over both public affairs and ritual secrets. The unmanageability of a whole gang of boys eventually plays a role in the village's decision to stage a new initiation. Initiation can be viewed as a collective measure to place boys under ritual control, structurally removing them from the public domain—the social hierarchy of which they increasingly threaten as they age and sexually mature, becoming social agents dangerously unrestricted by adult morals.

Viewed this way, then, there are two global contexts for gender socialization: early childhood and ritual initiation. These contexts are associated with the changing focus of the two worlds in boys' development: women are their first main influence, men are the later exclusive socializers. To fully recognize these differences we must distinguish early from late training. In some ways these socialization regimes conflict, while in others they are complementary. Yet these phases are, for Sambia, done by different subgroups of their society: women, then men. We may label these "primary" and "secondary" socialization groups.

The primary socialization group includes mother (or her substitutes) and any others socially responsible for protection, care, and training of the infant. In many Western countries, the primary socialization group is the nuclear family. Others beyond this unit—grandparents, babysitters, friends, or extended family members—may be involved in early training, depending on such factors as geography, class, and ethnic identity. The biological parents normally have sole responsibility for care and training. They are given wide authority by our society for the cultural transmission of rules and goals. As the child matures, though, other primary socializers such as grandparents are important for socialization. So long as these persons do not violate socially accepted standards of behavior (e.g., as in child abuse), other agents beyond the primary group will not interfere.

The secondary group includes all trainers responsible for teaching, evaluating, monitoring, and enforcing the child's later incorporation into adult institutions and roles. The transition from primary to secondary socialization groups is necessary for the child to achieve cultural goals and assume social status positions in the wider society. To become a lawyer or king or teacher or priestess requires social training beyond the family. Secondary social groups such as age-sets, school playmates, castes, religious organizations, and so forth become new reference groups for the trainee. In Western society school for formal education is crucial. In these transitions, too, the child moves from being defined as a nonresponsible dependent of his or her primary group, to being an independent social, economic, and moral agent in the society as a whole. Thus, children are also transformed from being consumers to producers. Secondary socializers include trainers and enforcers, especially teachers and the police in Western countries, elders, shamans, and ritual experts in non-Western groups. Persons in primary groups may be socializers in secondary groups too, as when one's father is a shaman. What matters are the wide teaching and enforcing powers of secondary socializers: they are given authority to reward achievements and punish violations in adolescents and adults.

By contrasting early and later socialization we can see that learning how to be a *socializer*, by teaching norms and rules, is itself a final stage of socialization. Some teaching, such as the elders' ritual instruction to boys, reveals how society requires accumulated knowledge to be allowed to socialize in such areas. Active teaching and evaluating are involved in sophisticated tasks such as performing sacred myths or ceremonies. The rule that only elders be allowed to train for these traditions suggests that wisdom, age, and little innovation are expected of the performers. To put it differently, these elders are the closest to being like the culture heroes of myths and legends in idealizing the desired characteristics and the gender role models of a culture. Children are reinforced to emulate them. And when the elders' teaching occurs in secret, ritual boundaries mark off their knowledge and power to socialize initiates into sacred traditions.

Primary versus secondary groups and learning versus performing raise the general issue of the continuity between childhood and adulthood. In what ways are adults different than children? We have seen significant differences between the thought worlds of the men and women. Boys and girls adjust to these differences, but boys must move on: What are the boys' discontinuities? On the eve of initiation, boys are made very aware of their masculine inadequacies, of the fact that they do not fit in.

Boys are in between the women's and men's worlds: they must be changed and incorporated into the secret society. Men constantly point to the fine and shining example of older initiates while lecturing boys. These cult members are strong and virile, good warriors and hunters who help the village in economic tasks and follow their elders' directives—as can be seen from how fast they have grown and how healthy they are—despite the dangers of war, sickness, the forest, and the seductive and contaminating presence of women. What better reason for the boys' radical resocialization?

5/The men's secret society

Many warrior societies throughout history have used initiation rites to recruit and train males. This is common in New Guinea, and Sambia are no exception. Indeed, their local warriorhoods exemplify the strong link between war and initiation.

What shall we call the unit that initiates boys? I mean here not the confederacy as described before, because that is the political union of neighboring hamlets who do collective initiations (called *iku mokeiyu*) together. I mean rather the social and psychological bond that connects men of different villages, their sharing in secret rites—in spite of their warring with one another. We could speak of their being members of a military club, since initiation aimed to produce warriors. The initiation system also created age-graded and ritual-ranked status positions, akin to generals, lieutenants, and soldiers: members of a military order. And we could think of this initiating group as a religious cult, for the clubhouse has the blessings of spirit beings, mystical powers associated with magical formulas, and it conducts fantastic ceremonies—public, private, and secret—which perpetuate the sacred core of Sambia society. Whether we choose to think of it as a military club or cult, initiation is the most colorful and powerful institution in Sambia society. Let us call it a secret society.

This secret club instills the warrior ethos in boys and transmits to them the power called *jerungdu*. Sambia men associate this power with homosexual intercourse and the use of phallic symbols, especially the ritual flutes, that represent the cult and masculinity. The men's club honors the old men and denigrates women, so we may refer to it also as a phallic cult. Much of its power derives from its secrecy; or, to be more precise, from the way the men use secrecy to accomplish military, ritual, and sexual aims. I want to impress upon you that in spite of how exotic and almost archaic this secret society may seem, the account you will read represents not the dead past but the present. The phallic cult of Sambia is alive today.

INITIATION FOR STRENGTH

The main goal of initiation is to make boys big and strong, to make them aggressive warriors. This requires changing them: where they sleep and eat,

Photo 9. Two shamans purify first-stage initiate (Sambia Valley initiation, 1975)

how they act, whom they interact with, look up to, and obey. This is no easy change. They must be removed, by force if necessary, from the women's domain and placed in the culthouse. This changes them dramatically, for they lose their childhood freedom and must conform to rigid roles. Pre-initiates are seen as boys, not men, for they show feminine traits such as shyness and crying, and they engage in female tasks and routines such as babysitting and weeding. In this sense they belong to the female world, though they are not female. Though they must become participants in the men's secret society, they are too "feminine" in the above ways to be admitted without change— radical change. They must learn new things, but they must also *un*learn old traits and ideas, so that they can truly feel in their gender identity: "I am *not* feminine; I *am* masculine." Such marked change we call *radical resocialization.*

The change from boyhood to manhood is tough and men do not spare boys the ordeals of initiations. To the elders, this is necessary. Warfare was the number-one reality to be reckoned with, and the men still prepare for it. *A war is going on:* this is the old idea that underlies initiation. The whole secret society is oriented toward the constant struggle to survive war.

How are boys to acquire the strength to be warriors? Here the dilemma in Sambia thinking about *jerungdu* is twofold. First, the male body is believed incapable of manufacturing semen, so it must be externally acquired. This means that *jerungdu* itself is not an intrinsic capacity of male functioning but must be artificially created, as we have seen. Second, semen can be "lost" (ejaculated), and, along with it, the *jerungdu* that it sustains. Therefore, ritual measures must be taken to artificially replace what essence is lost in order to prevent weakness and death. No semen, no *jerungdu*, no masculinity. Overcoming these masculine challenges is the long-term goal of Sambia secret initiations. This entire process I call *ritualized masculinization.* Oral ingestion of semen—ritualized fellatio—is critical to the development of *jerungdu* in boys. Only after years of ritualized homosexuality and body treatment do the key sexual signs of strength take physical form. Initiation is thus a means of simulating maleness and masculinity. Be clear about what this means: *jerungdu* is felt to be a real force, not a metaphor or symbol. Fellatio behavior is a concrete means of attaining it. Men are absolutely convinced of their innate lack of semen and of the need for their rituals, and they transmit their convictions to boys in ritual teaching.

Men likewise stress the cultural values of strength, equivalence, and weakness, which are vague in childhood but made explicit in ritual initiation. *Jerungdu* motivates aggressiveness and assertive protests. Equivalence places initiates in age-mate relationships that require them to match their peers' achievements. The unmanly label *wogaanyu* makes boys conform to masculine standards that despise weakness and passivity in all actions. And females—the softness of femininity—represent a lower and weaker condition. Through initiation boys are radically resocialized to change their cultural orientations, like a sort of brain-washing that traumatically modifies their thought. The effect is to end their attachments to their mothers and to create new aggressive and sexual impulses, thereby directing boys along the lines of culturally standardized male gender role and identity.

Initiation is the true funnel into the warriorhood. It has the pomp and ceremony of a festival and is also sacred, so its secret parts are solemn and dramatic. Initiation occurs at the harvest season, when men recognize the bounty of nature's fertility. Organized by one's fathers, brothers, and clan elders, the ritual is done by the most loved and admired people in society. Even one's mother takes pride in the event and in her son's accomplishment. For despite her husband's demands, her workload, the heavy gardening responsibilities expected to ensure the success of the event, her other babies' needs and her own—and notwithstanding her ambivalence in losing a son's companionship and help, or her occasional opposition to the idea of initiation, which sometimes provokes nasty quarrels with her husband—a mother surely recognizes that this is the course a son must take, that the hamlet needs her boy as a defender. Where mother loses a son, father gains a comrade. This is so for all of one's playmates, too, the lads who become age-mates, members of the village warrior class.

The pre-initiated boy, then, is seen as a small person with a penis who is polluted, weak, and not yet manly. He is still polluted from the womb, and has taken in mother's food and saliva. He has been constantly in touch with the contaminated skin of her breasts and body. He is entirely too dependent on her for protection and warmth; her body remains too much of a haven for him. There is more than a hint of femininity about him; he even wears the same type of grass apron as females. He is undisciplined and bawls and throws tantrums when unable to get what he wants. At such times men are openly hostile to boys, taunting them till they cry, saying "Go back to your mother where you belong!" The boy sometimes disobeys his parents and talks back to them. Men cannot forget that their sons are carriers of feminine pollution, so they watch them lest they pollute men, their weapons, or their food. Boys are, of course, kept ignorant of ritual secrets and chased away when these are discussed. Such considerations come to mind when men discuss the need to initiate their maturing sons.

Another urgent thought is that masculinization is literally a matter of life and death. A boy's body has female contaminants inside it that retard masculine development. His body is male: he has male genitals and his *tingu* contains no blood, nor will it activate. Yet for boys to reach puberty requires semen. Milk "nurtures the boy"; sweet potatoes and other "female" foods provide "stomach nourishment" and become only feces, not semen. Women's own bodies internally produce menstruation, the hallmark of reproductive maturity. No comparable mechanism is active in boys to stimulate their biological secondary sex traits. Only semen can do that and only men have semen—boys have none.

What is left to do, then, but initiate boys and thereby masculinize them? Only through initiation can men collectively and immediately put a halt to what they perceive as the stultifying effects of mothering upon their sons. The mother's blood and womb and care, which gave life to and nourished the lad, are finally seen by the secret society as symbols of antilife. To undo these feminizing effects, boys must be drastically detached from women and then ritually treated. Thereafter boys avoid women until marriage, by which time the idealized masculine behaviors of initiation have remade the boy into the image of a warrior.

THE ECOLOGY OF INITIATION

The Sambia calendrical system is based on the sun's yearly cycle and seasonal climatic changes. The sun's fertility effects are especially important to the Sambia. They credit the sun with many of their harvest blessings because the sun is another power in nature that has *jerungdu*. So in their own native "cognized model" (Rappaport 1968), magical beliefs about the sun are woven into harvest rites and initiation. The initiation cycle performed every three to four years during the dry season celebrates these fertility effects in the earth and in humans.

The sun comes at a period of natural abundance. It signals, for Sambia, the impending maturation of special root crops (yams and taro) as well as other foods like sugar cane and banana, planted in the preceding agricultural season to be used in initiation. Most crops such as sugar cane are then at their peak. Certain ritual trees and plants are also in bloom and these are used for ritual decoration. More important, the pandanus trees—first the fruit tree species and then the nut tree species—reproduce and ripen, becoming available for harvesting in response to the sun's natural warmth. Both types of pandanus are crucial for initiation rites. Possum appear in greater numbers and are most easily hunted in the dry season—a fact essential to the success of all Sambia initiations, for possum are consumed in all feasts and ceremonial exchanges. So this is a time of plenty, of fertility and renewal, of success in hunting.

The sun is experienced sensually: not as an abstract planetary body or as a meteorological force of physics, and not only as a pleasant change into dry weather, but as a vital being, a masculine power that unites nature and society. The old-fashioned term for this idea in anthropology is *animism* (from Latin, *anima*, "soul"), which is appropriate so long as we stress the natives' view that this force has regulative control over human existence. Sambia elders refer to the power with sayings such as "The sun gives us everything" and "The sun is our father." Indeed, the archaic word *akumu* ("father sun") is sometimes used in this metaphoric kinship sense. Its imaginative association with the native word for the sun season, *atamdu*, seems certain. In myth, the sun is depicted as male and is masculinized. The moon is sometimes said to be male, but it is androgynous too and is spoken of as "the mate of the sun." Furthermore, the myth of pandanus fruit tells how the sun provided this red phallic fruit and war weapons at the very founding of Sambia society (a tale symbolically reflected in second-stage initiation). When need be, men refer to the qualities of the sun's power with the term *jerungdu*.

When the dry-season sun finally comes, cutting through the clouds after months, its achievement is grand. People go outdoors and lie in the sun: "It burns our skins, we become like men again." "The sun clears the fur away, making us men again, not like possums." This outlook is a result of living on mile-high mountains where clouds are literally breathed in. Being so fogbound for months on end changes one's existence. At dawn in the dry season the light—high in the tropics at the summer solstice—must be experienced to be believed: it is so bright and sweeps across the countryside, vanquishing the fog, bathing the hamlet and gardens, clean and horizontal, whitewashing everything in its path down toward the Papuan coastal ranges, 50 miles south. The whiteness catches the bone-bleached dead trees in nearby gardens, brilliant ivory against the green slopes, like a graveyard of great tusks lifelessly guarding the entangled undergrowth threatening to reclaim man's timid outpost of neat cultivation. "The sun paints the sky," Sambia say. At noon there is a remarkable corona of light around the sun (an event our smoggy cities have stolen from us). Later, the sun strikes across the valley in broad afternoon, its golden rays looking so much like yellow shafts that men call them "the sun's arrows," which shoot into the emerald mountainsides. And the sunsets: red, orange, yellow, white, even green and violet, sharp and dazzling as Monet watercolors. Even at night, when the stars are like beacons, the full moon has a golden lunar corona. This is when the Sambia love to do their sensational nighttime rituals.

Let me stress that Sambia themselves are moved and thrilled by such sights, and initiation symbols derive some of their power from such experiences. Sambia ritual symbolism draws from the aesthetics of the sun's dry season: the lunar and solar bodies, their colors and dimensions, solar and lunar coronas, sunset and sunrise colors, stars and configurations, even thunder and lightning. These are not the only objects reflected in ritual symbols, but they do stand for feminine and masculine qualities of virility, longevity, and fertility, which Sambia associate with the harvest period of their tropical dry season.[1]

The collective rites reflect this environmental milieu and embody men's attempts to use the sun's power to create *jerungdu* in boys' growing bodies. Natural resources like pandanus trees are perceived as being under the sun's control. Even the root crops and animal migrations are thought to result from sunlight, rain, and the earth's seasons. During good times—periods without famine—initiation feast crop gardens are planted a year in advance. In the following calendar year, the new sunny period begins with the ritual culthouse-raising ceremonies described below. These ceremonies are immediately followed by a long possum hunt to get meat for third-stage initiation feasts. Soon after, when the pandanus fruit ripen and are harvested, second-stage initiation is performed. Lastly, as the yams and taro reach maturity, more possum are hunted and the first-stage initiation is held. The last ritual uses the pandanus nuts, which are by then at their full ripeness. Initiations await the full moon, which lights the nighttime events. Sambia have built the entire cycle around sun images, including the eventual war-raiding party. Sambia thus utilize the sun and harvest images as a generalized background for their symbolism. Yet the cosmology does not aim as much to "control" these seasonal cycles as to take advantage of and tap into the diffuse power, *jerungdu*, believed manifest in everything the sun touches. This men try to magically absorb and insert into boys through the proper rites.

Finally, the initiations represent a message that the communities involved (the local confederacy) are healthy and thriving. Staging the collective rites means that during the preceding year a political agreement among hamlet leaders had been reached to initiate; so either peace was at hand or a truce was imminent. The same understanding also made it possible for initiates to travel to other villages for the purpose of homosexual contacts: boys were supposed to enjoy safe passage back to their village during war. Planting the gardens was the first step in planning. Ecological conditions must be good for crops, since abnormally wet or dry years deplete the harvest; during bad years, initiations done in the following year were meager. Sambia believe that local droughts affected past ritual cycles, though no one could recall one that was postponed due to food shortages. (Warfare, on the other hand, clearly has interrupted past initiation plans.) Nonetheless, after the initiations I observed a mild famine did occur in the Lower Sambia Valley in 1976, and food was scarce throughout the area. Hamlet leaders blamed the situation on the

---

[1] There are special conditions of cloudiness and light in the Highlands, since, as Brookfield (1964: 25) noted of the atmosphere: "The air is different, with less water vapor and solid particles, and hence more rapid heating and cooling" (see also Brookfield and Hart 1971: 17). Bowra (1957: 23), in a classical work on Attic Greek poetry, made a more romantic point: "What matters above all is the quality of the light . . . even in winter the light is unlike that of any other European country, brighter, cleaner, stronger. . . . The beauty of the Greek landscape depends primarily on the light, and this had a powerful influence on the Greek vision of the world."

TABLE 2 INITIATION AND THE MEN'S SECRET SOCIETY

Age in Years		Initiation	Ritual Grade	Status Rank	Sexual Behavior	Categories Used in This Case Study
0–6				child	neuter	child
7–10	collective	First-Stage (choowinuku)	kuwatni'u	initiate	homosexual	initiate
11–14	collective	Second-Stage (imbutu)	kuwatni'u	initiate	homosexual	initiate
15–18	collective	Third-Stage (ipmangwi)	nungenyu	bachelor	homosexual	bachelor
17+	individualized	Fourth-Stage (nuposhu)	aatmwol-chenchorai	newlywed	homosexual	bachelor
Late teens	individualized	Fifth-Stage (taiketnyi)	aatmwol-chenchorai	newlywed	bisexual	married man
Early 20's	individualized	Sixth-Stage (moondangu)	aatmwunu	adult	heterosexual	married man
Mid 30's+			aatmangootu	big man	heterosexual	elder

1975 initiations, saying that sponsoring the feasts had exhausted gardens and prevented them from planting enough new crops before the monsoons began, indications that initiation has a significant economic impact.

Everything is under the direction of elders and ritual leaders, who retain control of the events and their timing, which will be known only to them. And everyone—including clan groups, initiates, and women—is assigned a job to help successfully stage the rituals. It is this investment of productive resources and political aims that matters most, for the boys' initiations stand for the security of a new set of warriors, the defense of the communities, and interhamlet political cooperation in military and marriage affairs within the confederacy.

THE INITIATION CYCLE

The men's secret society regulates psychosocial and sexual development in males from middle childhood through old age. Without exception, every male is initiated. The first initiation places one in a fixed age-set for life. It also creates age-mate ties to males throughout the valley. There are six initiations in all, leading to full manhood. These initiations and age-mate bonds get intermixed with kinship and political relationships, as shown in Table 2.

The initiation system has two distinct segments. The first segment consists of *collective* initiations done by the hamlets acting together. This involves first-, second-, and third-stage initiations, bachelorhood ceremonies. They

occur following the communal constructing of a great culthouse, whose name—
moo-angu—incorporates ideas about the feeding process (*monjapi'u*) and the
word for breast milk (*aammoonalyu*). The reasons have to do with ritual
homosexuality and they will be obvious later. Fourth-, fifth-, and sixth-stage
initiations comprise the second segment, which begins in adolescence and
extends to adulthood. These are *individualized* rites, done by each hamlet
separately. Unlike the collective rituals, they are not done simultaneously,
but rather are strung out over the years and performed as necessary for
individuals.

The initial phases of collective initiations are held in a fixed sequence in
the early dry season. First the culthouse is built. Then third-stage (*ipmangwi*)
initiation is performed for youths aged 15 to 18. These boys are thus elevated
from second-stage status. Please note: *they are initiated first to help older men
in hunting and in initiating boys*. A few weeks later the second-stage (*imbutu*)
initiation is held for boys aged 11 to 14. They too assist third-stage bachelors
in helping initiate the youngest boys. The first-stage initiation (*choowinuku*)
is then held last, for boys aged seven to 10. It must be done soon after the
imbutu, Sambia believe, for that second-stage initiation leaves no members
of the first-stage grade, which people feel is bad. Each successive initiation
builds up a larger pool of cult members, adds to the local warriorhoods, and
contributes to the mounting drama of first-stage ceremonies—which climaxes
in great feasts, dancing ceremonies, and competitive songfests between villages on the initiation danceground.

Following collective initiation there is a period of several months' living in
forest houses for the new initiates of all ages. A makeshift hut is constructed
for them. This is called the "rat house," because first-stage novices hunt forest
rats to smoke and present as return food gifts to elders, who earlier hunted
possum for the boys' feasts. Boys are strictly forbidden during this period
from seeing or interacting with women or children, who, in turn, are tabooed
from entering this area of the forest. Homosexual activity is at a peak here,
as is the hazing of younger boys. Thereafter, the boys return to the clubhouse
of their own hamlet. They reside there for years, until they marry and build
a new house with their wife.

The second segement of initiations may begin some months up to several
years after the third-stage collective rite. It depends on a youth's maturity
and the elders having obtained a woman for him, which is often several years
after his third-stage initiation. Then, the youth's own clan-hamlet will hold a
marriage ceremony (*nuposha*) for him. This is a lavish affair, however, so the
village likes to have several age-mates married at the same ceremony (see
below). The public sees the grooms in their elaborate ceremonial dress, as
shown in Photo 29. Then, off in the forest, the men do secret ceremonies on
the youths, while far away, women hold their own secret ceremony for the
brides in the menstrual hut. After the brides' menarche, which can be several
years later, the spouses have genital intercourse. Menarche triggers a man's
fifth-stage initiation (*taiketnyi*), which is held in secret again. After the birth
of the first child, sixth-stage initiation (*moondangu*, "new birth") is held for

the man. Both fifth- and sixth-stage initiations are done only for the individual man undergoing status changes, due to the "life crisis" events his wife is undergoing. Each of the fourth-, fifth-, and sixth-stage ceremonies is preceded again by long possum hunts, some lasting months in the high forest. Age-mates are expected to help each other secure meat gifts, preferably by capturing possum by hand, for this too is a test of manhood. After menarche, a couple cohabit alone in their own hut, which concludes the clubhouse residence for the man. After two children are born, no further initiations are done on him or his wife because they have attained full adulthood (*aatm-wunu*).

Initiation thus perpetuates a ranked set of ritual categories of male persons involving differential social statuses, roles, and their rights and duties in male-male relationships. At the most basic level of cultural contrast, these categories distinguish all males from all females. There are four marked categories of ritual-based male personhood. (1) All first-stage and second-stage initiates are categorized as *kuwatni'u*, or "initiate." These initiates are subordinates of all older males, who exercise political and sexual control over them. Within the age-mate group, though, initiates are both peers and competitors. (2) Third-stage initiates are classed as bachelor youths, *aatmwol nungenyu* (literally "male bamboo," a euphemism for the mature penis). They are prototypic bachelors because they are sexually mature inserters who are seen as being nearly eligible for marriage. Fourth-stage initiates are "in-between men," Sambia say, for they are married but not yet living with their wives (they still reside in the clubhouse and engage in homosexual practices). So they are referred to as *nuposha* (named after the marriage ceremony), their ritual status title. (3) However, they are sometimes lumped together with fifth-stage and sixth-stage initiates as *aatmwol chenchorai*, or "newlywed." (4) The final category is *aatmwunu* or "adult," a term of respect for men who have fathered children and who exercise legal and moral authority over all younger initiates, women and children. In the rituals below married men are called adults, fourth- and fifth-stage youths are newlyweds, third-stage youths are bachelors, and younger initiates are called initiates.

Each of these ritual categories can be visibly recognized by distinctive gender signs in Sambia culture. A gender sign is an emblem or mark that denotes one's masculinity or femininity. In this case, the signs are mainly body decorations, such as noseplugs, which differentiate males into higher or lower types of social status and biological development (see Figure 1). Small children do not wear noseplugs, but in late childhood the nasal septum in boys and girls is pierced. After initiation, all males wear the noseplug of their ritual status. In the youngest initiate category, small sugar cane stems are used (see Figure 1, types E and F). This is the sign of lowest masculine development. Next are second-stage initiates, who wear cassowary quill-bones, noseplug type D. (Nubile women also wear quill-bone noseplugs: see below.) Third-stage initiates can wear type C noseplugs. Category 3 men, newlyweds and young men, may wear type B. But only fully initiated older men and elders can wear type A, *sogamdu*—the famous pig's tusk—the hallmark of

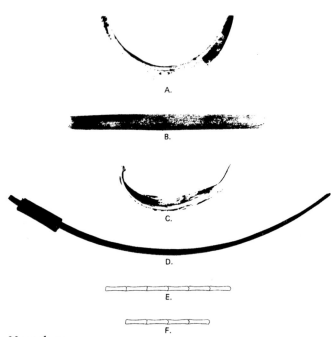

Figure 1. Noseplugs

proud and aggressive maleness. (see Mon in Photo 3, p. 39.) Normally the tusks are worn with the points down. But in initiation and in warfare, they are pointed up, "like an erect penis," men say.

BOYS' CONSCIOUSNESS AT INITIATION

First come piercing cries, mysteriously, as if from nowhere: everyone knows the initiations are approaching. From within the men's house, later near the danceground where a new culthouse is going up, and eventually at the edge-land forest, the haunting sounds increase in tempo. Children are told the cries come from old female hamlet spirits. Somehow—never fully explained—the men's secret society has power over these spirits. Their music alerts women of the coming preparations. Boys may be curious or fearful. They are teased with remarks like "The spirit wants to get you, she wants to kill and eat you!" Then mother or father may smile or laugh or be quiet, responses that heighten the mounting tension that intrudes on the household of a boy whose time has come. "The female spirit protects the clubhouse; she's aged, we keep her hidden in an old net bag," fathers tell sons. Boys' responses differ according to their age and personality. Yet they all experience discomfort that in some of them turns into panic at initiation. Unknown to the boys, the ritual flutes (*namboolu aambelu*, "female frog") create this mysterious sound that triggers the boys' fear, signalling an unalterable transition into warrior life.

Several factors dovetail and contribute to the boys' anxiety near initiation time. These are: the mysteriousness and secrecy of fathers and the men; the fact that there are no exits—no escaping initiation; no exceptions are made to being initiated; boys' fear of physical punishment in the rites; the treatment of the boys as a batch-living group, not as individuals; and the feeling that there is "no going back" once initiation starts. Let us briefly examine these elements of the boys' consciousness before observing the initiation itself.

Boys are kept in the dark about initiation. Many are never told they will be taken, though most can guess it. Their parents prepare ritual decorations for the boy, sometimes in secret. Boys hear that a new culthouse is going up, yet secrecy surrounds the plans. Some boys ask if they will be initiated; some parents, knowing boys' opposition, deceive them: "Oh, not this time, the next." Such tricks add to boys' later feelings that they are dupes—that parents, especially mothers, betray them—or that adults are to be distrusted. Many mothers comfort and cry over their sons, however; they say they can do nothing to stop the rites. They know initiation will be filled with glory and pride, and that only through this ceremony can they "grow up." But remember that Sambia boys are only seven to 10 years old, and that they have heard rumors that the rituals are filled with frightening ordeals.

Boys cannot escape initiation. Where can they go? Traditionally their world was small, bordered by enemies on all sides. Only the hamlet offered safety. Yet many tales tell how boys ran away into the forest to escape initiation. To stay boys? No, these are more than "Peter Pan" stories. I have twice seen boys flee into the forest at initiation. In the 1975 rites, described below, three boys (two of them from one hamlet, a third from another) ran and hid to escape. Search parties were sent to find them; they were brought back, and in retaliation they were more severely handled during the rites. In the summer of 1983 another boy tried to escape initiation in the valley while I was there: there are still no exits for them. Why? Because everything that matters most— village survival through the cult and warriorhood—depends on initiation. The elders still insist on this. This feeling that there are no exits is laced into Sambia consciousness of ritual.

The lack of exits is reinforced by the fact that no exceptions are permitted to the norm that *all* males be initiated. Only very sick children at the time are allowed to postpone initiation, but this is considered "bad" in many ways. No Sambia man exists who is uninitiated. In the valley, for instance, a mentally retarded man and another who is viewed as permanently insane are both initiated. "Even they have kept the secrets," my friends say with a gleam in their eyes. A bigger challenge, however, is presented by the male hermaphrodites. How does the phallic cult regard these biologically abnormal children with microscopic penes? They initiate them without exception, and in this way treat them no differently than normal males. They also take pride in their bravery as they face the ordeals (see Chapter 6). Once I even encountered a blind 10-year-old boy who was initiated in the Blue Valley. Though blind at birth, he was still cared for. The men said: "He is a man: we have to initiate him!"

For years boys are threatened with impending initiation whenever they misbehave. Sambia boys are ingenious at pranks, such as making mock traps to fool the men or blowing reeds to sound like the secret flutes. (Do they know the flutes are not spirits? When asked later, following initiation, they say no. But perhaps their knowledge is not conscious; like their mothers they sense things that cannot be confirmed due to the men's threats and secrecy.) "Wait till we get you in the culthouse! You'll see! You'll be sorry," older brothers say. Mothers, too, sometimes use this threat to get boys to obey them. Boys fear the physical punishment and ordeals of ritual. No wonder: there is plenty of it. The thrashing rites of collective initiation are public, so in early childhood they have witnessed these painful ordeals on older brothers and male cousins.

Boys lose their individuality in initiation they are handled as a batch, an age-set. This group treatment comforts them in the sense that they are not singled out for ordeals. But it threatens them too, for they become aware that no exceptions can be made for the individual boy; not even father can halt the process. The boy child, in other words, experiences the loss of parental protection and security, while being forced into the broader social group of the secret society wherein he has to make his own way. This secondary socialization group has its own agenda (to initiate boys) and it will not pamper them as did their parents.

Finally, there is the feeling that once initiated, a boy "cannot go back" to his childhood home. He must live in the clubhouse. Yet this feeling extends far beyond his living arrangements. I mentioned above the loss of parental security. More than this, however, boys totally "lose" their mothers, as it were. They are detached from mother, whom they can never again be with—touch, hold, talk to, eat with, or look at directly. She is off-limits. And what this taboo of detachment represents symbolically is the way the female world becomes generally forbidden. These changes cannot be halted or reversed. Once told the ritual secrets, a boy can never be trusted to be close to his mother again for fear he might reveal these secrets. This dimension of secret knowledge gives the boy a secret identity, shared with father and age-mates. The feeling of loss of mother is compounded, then, by the sense that he can never return to the innocence of childhood.

ORGANIZERS AND SPECTATORS

Who is involved in this unfolding drama? The answer is virtually everyone in the valley. The roles played by elders, war leaders and shamans, bachelors, women, and the initiates are very different. So we should expect that their experiences will differ too.

The elders are in command of the initiation process. This is as it has always been, for Sambia is a headless society, without kings or chiefs, courts or councils. Political power rests primarily in the elders' hands. During warfare, though, young war leaders take charge, whereas at other times the elders—

former war leaders, for the most part—do so. As a warrior culture, power in Sambia men is vested in a principle expressed by the Latin phrase *primus inter pares*: first among equals. Elders lead by force of personality, by ritual knowledge, by social connections, and by show. Look around at the streaming initiation events and you see a flurry of activity. Young war leaders parade around and older ritual experts shout orders directing the crowds or "stage-sets" for the pomp of ceremonies. But these are not the true organizers. They are puppets of the elders in the sense that the old men decide what rites to perform, by whom, in what order, and with what magic. Their vast magical knowledge, required in mixing feast foods and in saying spells over rituals, is the ultimate source of elders' authority. The hurried younger men are not "calling the shots" in initiation; the elders do this, far removed from the public eye, off in a little hut somewhere, muttering about what to do next. At the critical moment in ritual teaching, when sage words are needed, when authority figures are required to impress on initiates the secret society's power over the sacred, the elders will appear.[2]

The elders' control should not surprise us, for Sambia is an age-graded society. It is not far wrong to call their political system a form of gerontocracy. People's social status generally rises with age. Merely outliving others is an accomplishment, though not enough of one to bestow leadership in itself. For that the elder must organize, make his presence felt in ceremonies, and be able to orate in public. The old men are committed to advancing their own village. This makes them rivals with their elderly age-mates in other villages. Yet, for the purposes of collective initiation, they forget their differences and join together to stage a grand event.

Adult men provide the real manpower for the rites, however. They hunt and build the culthouse, harvest the feast gardens, stage key events by placing themselves in long rows as fearsome warriors, and collect food from women to feed initiates and make feasts. The bachelors assist them. In traditional times, they later went together as a war party, after the collective cycle of rites was done. In the meantime, men's sexual life changes. While preparing for initiation, all heterosexual activity is forbidden. Men cannot copulate with their wives since female pollution is transmitted, via the person of the man, to the boys, whose "growth" would be thwarted or whose faces would turn "ugly and black." For weeks, then, spouses have no sex. Bachelors have homosexual contacts with younger initiates, but the men—married with children—are not supposed to, and most do not. A few break the rules. Other men break the heterosexual taboos, or so it is rumored. When the moonlight dances begin and the crowds assemble, people say there is illicit heterosexual play and even adultery going on in the shadows. It is a time of sexual license, a bacchanalian time, when the normally prudish Sambia momentarily escape their strict sexual code.

How do mothers and fathers respond? The rituals tend to obscure the role

---

[2] Donald Tuzin has vividly portrayed this power of the elders' presence as ritual authorities in his stunning work, *The Voice of the Tamberan* (1980), on the Ilahita Arapesh ritual cult in the Sepik River area of Papua New Guinea.

of individual parents. What emerges instead is a collective image of the men versus the women. The antagonism between the sexes is exaggerated by the ritual cycle. For, after all, hostile hamlets are brought together in the same place, the women rejoined with people of their own villages, the men of each village competing with others to see which group is strongest in ritual and dancing performances. Since the parents must be separated during the hunting and initiation activities, their relationship is more polarized, and it is obvious to the initiate that the distance between his parents is greater than ever. A woman is acting both as the boy's mother and as his father's wife. A man is both the lad's father—an initiator—and his mother's husband. What men do toward boys may be interpreted as well as an action against the boy's mother. This is why men forcibly separate boys from their mothers at the very start. Women's responses, likewise, seem to be partially aimed at their husbands and partially at their sons.

The attitude of women about their sons is ambivalent. Women resist the separation. At the Yulami initiation below we will see the ceremonial wailing of the initiates' mothers opening the rituals. Later they aggressively reclaim their sons for the frog-feeding on the danceground. And yet women chastise boys for their laziness as economic providers. Finally, the women identify the boys with their hostile fathers, just as the men identify their polluting wives with their sons. The boys are caught between the two worlds.

Women thus play a definite role, though men think of them mainly as spectators. Women have interpersonal influence in the domestic sphere, extending even to a say over how much time their husbands spend gardening or hunting. In public affairs, however, women have little formal power. The exception, as we shall see in Chapter 6, is a fascinating one: women shamans, an oddity in such a warrior culture. Women contribute food and handcrafted items such as net bags and grass sporrans for the initiates and other kinsmen involved in the rites. Their labor is also crucial at the start when they supply piles of grass thatching for the culthouse roof. These are customary female tasks that prepare for initiation. Women dance on the danceground in the opening public ceremonies and play other minor parts too. But the fact that they are always there, always an audience for whom the men stage the public displays, adds force to the idea that spectators really have more power than we think. (The late anthropologist George Devereux reminded me of this point by noting that women spectators in Ancient Greece were always an important audience, except at the Olympics, where the "homo-social" atmosphere made men uneasy about having women around.)

The final category of organizers is the boy's ritual guardian or sponsor. He is called "mother's brother." Not all ritual guardians are actual mother's brothers, though many are. For the others, the title is honorific. At Yulami village, only about a third of the guardians were actual or classificatory mother's brothers. Nonetheless, the warmth in the maternal uncle-nephew relationship is obviously being highlighted. The sponsor's job is to protect the initiate from being beaten too much and to teach him about ritual lore, especially the need to ingest semen. Guardians physically carry initiates through the ordeals of initiation, physical contact and mutual experiencing of emotionally dramatic events that create a bond between them which lasts throughout life. The sponsor serves as a boy's supervisor and mentor at first-, second-, and third-stage initiations, wherein he is ceremonially treated or thrashed along with a boy whom he carries. He also instructs and ritually decorates the boy. Later, at fourth-, fifth-, and sixth-stage rites (if alive and active), the sponsor participates and takes pride in his ward's achievement of advanced masculine status.

The guardian is usually selected by the boy's father, an important fact in appreciating his social ties to the family. A man may earn this guardianship right by giving an *ichinyu* possum food gift to celebrate the birth of a child by another man's wife. These men should not be blood kin, which means only men of other clans can bestow the gift. If a female child is born, the possum gift obliges the family to give her to the donor for a delayed-exchange marriage to his own son years later. A male infant's birth creates a different opportunity, because a male infant eventually needs initiating, and the gift of possum provides a right to serve as his sponsor. Here, the boy's mother will also have a say in the matter. The father remunerates the sponsor for his services with possum, vegetal salt, bark capes, and the like. The initiate, moreover, later gives gifts to his sponsor over the years, and also receives food from him. Another mode of selection is for adult age-mates (of different clans) to act as the sponsors for each other's sons. This arrangement precludes the exchange of gifts between them, and Sambia dislike this method because they feel such fathers are simply stingy or unwilling to hunt or trap for meat gifts. In either case, such fathers are labelled *wogaanyu*, unmanly. More rarely, a father names his trade partner as a sponsor. These men reside in distant hamlets of other phratries or the Wantuki'u tribe. Such trade bonds are special, can be inherited by sons, and the parties involved help each other in times of war. Though these long-distance ties make travel and communication cumbersome, they provide a useful excuse for trade expeditions, which are a pleasant change of pace. In short, the sponsor is well known to the novice's father and they are comrades. Most boys no doubt see this, which is perhaps why boys often identify their guardians with their fathers.

Yet, ironically, the cultural norms governing the initiate guardian relationship suggest that, symbolically, the sponsor is like a surrogate mother. Initiates are at first respectful and fond of their sponsors. Later, as they mature, they develop a joking relationship. The initiate is, however, bound by strong taboos toward his sponsor that match those toward his mother and women to a surprising degree. He should not, for example, ever say his sponsor's name, a taboo that also applies to spouses. Not until he is an adult can he eat food or drink in front of his sponsor, which applies to women as well. The sponsor holds primary responsibility for motivating a lad to engage in homosexual activity, but they are absolutely forbidden to have sex between themselves. Later, when the initiate marries, his mentor will pass on the magic of heterosexual-purification techniques and his wisdom regarding the "proper" way to handle a wife.

THE INITIATIONS BEGIN

The planning of the Sambia Valley initiations was set with the planting of feast gardens in 1974. Some of these gardens were being planted when I arrived in October 1974. The culthouse was built in early 1975. From April to mid-July there were intermittent months of possum hunting that secured the meat for initiation feasts. Throughout the whole Sambia tribe, several different initiation cycles were done in this period by different confederacies.

I spent 62 days and nights attending the rites for these initiations. I could provide you with an idealized or formal account of the rites, which would tend to standardize the details and be impersonal. Instead, I will concentrate on my eyewitness observations of the events. Initiation ceremonies are very elaborate, so we can only examine a few key rituals, touching on the main happenings while skimming the surface of others. My selection of ethnographic data will illustrate the main events and the overall theme of initiation. We will begin with the culthouse scene, followed by short sections on third- and second-stage initiation. The bulk of our study highlights the first-stage rites, though, for there one can see the very beginnings of male ritual resocialization, and thereby understand how initiation turns boys into men.

All Sambia initiations have a political dimension, as I have said, but the first-stage rites described below occurred in a most highly charged political climate. The Sambia Valley confederacy of hamlets and its men's society crosscut phratry boundaries. In the Upper Valley the opposing phratries have long performed joint initiations, over 20 of them since 1900. Yet warfare has sometimes disrupted this alliance between hamlets and phratries. The ritual cycle performance of 1975 was influenced by historical events in the previous generation, and the initiation itself represented a change in local politics. Only once before (c. 1953) had the particular surrounding hamlets participated in collective initiation. This meant that some of their rituals were still unknown to the opposing phratries. Warfare and sorcery accusations had plagued the relationships between the Yulami hamlet, their Moonagu phratry allies, and the Upper Sambia phratries. This political antagonism did not, however, cause a breakdown in the initiation plans. Indeed, the sheer fact of the performance showed that leaders of both sides recognized peace and the end of war, as seen in men's rhetoric during the ceremonies. In still another way, this initiation shows the general acceptance by Sambia of the political realities of increasing social change in the area.

On the night that ushers in the construction of the culthouse, men of nearby hamlets gather in the clubhouse of the host hamlet. They have an all-night songfest and make plans for events of the coming days. There is the usual singing, smoking, and betel-nut chewing of all-male songfests. But the war songs and blowing of long bamboo flutes distinguish this songfest from ordinary ones. Local shamans perform a collective ceremony and divinate for omens revealing the success or failure of the impending rites. Despite preparations and rumors, the actual day the rites will begin remains unknown to women and children. The urgent, mysterious power of the flutes announces the beginning of the ritual cycle that night. Initiates have told me how the flute sound alerted them of their inevitable initiation and made them worry about what was to come.

Transition Rites   A characteristic *structure of transitions* can be seen in Sambia initiation rites. It will help you to follow these events if you understand the early insights of the French anthropologist Van Gennep (1909). In his *Rites of Passage*, Van Gennep discovered a set of changes associated with life-crisis events in many societies. He found that people involved in initiations, puberty rites, marriage, and other ceremonies undergo similar status changes. First, they are separated from the group. Usually they are secluded or otherwise treated as ritually special, as if they were more powerful or sacred than normal. Then they are endowed with the status of true marginal beings, who are "betwixt and between" normal states of social living, on the margins of the group. We refer to this special marginal status as *liminal* due to its ritual power.[3] This is a momentous and dangerous condition. Society itself can undergo change here because the initiates are between different social roles, reflecting on their own identities, and realizing new things about their bodies, their past experience, and future social positions. This is why they are confined and kept removed from society. Finally, following these changes, the initiates are re-aggregated into society and returned to normal social relationships. But not as before: their ritual experience has made them different, both in their outward social roles and in their inner identities. By experiencing these transitions together as a group, Sambia initiates develop affectionate friends as well as age-mate bonds, which we shall examine later.

THE CULTHOUSE SCENE

Early in the morning, a large group leaves our hamlet for the culthouse and danceground on the other side of the valley. They include Kanteilo, my elder sponsor, Weiyu, Moondi, and younger friends, males at all ages from the village. I am among them. We take up quarters near the culthouse. Other men, some women and children, follow. Soon hundreds of visitors are settling all around us. Tonight the first moonlight rituals and dancing begin. Everyone is beautifully garbed and decorated. Weiyu and Moondi show me around. We see throngs of people from all over, even from other valleys.

A long sequence of nighttime ceremonies is held that first night. The next night these are duplicated, with the third-stage initiates taking prominence. On the third day things calm a bit. That afternoon I went to the culthouse and was amazed to see open homosexual play, which I had not seen before.

How did the men accept me in this scene? This question is basic to all

---

[3] Liminality is taken from the Latin term *limen*, meaning threshold. Victor Turner (1967: 93–94) states: "If our basic model of society is that of a structure of positions, we must regard the period of margin or 'liminality' as an interstructural situation." This notion depends on Van Gennep's scheme of the *marginal* period of *rites de passage*, when "the state of the ritual subject (the *passanger*) is ambiguous" (Turner 1967: 94).

anthropological research. Yet in sensitive settings like this one it is essential
to know how and why people accepted an outsider, how he or she influenced
their behavior, and whether they kept secrets. Remember that I had already
been in the village eight months. I had lived in the men's house, where
homosexual activities were at first hidden from me. I had friends, and several
informants had stayed in my house and I ate with them. We had often travelled
together. But after four months it was still a scandal when my friend Nilutwo
told them he had told me about the secret homosexuality. The men were
furious with him. Things were tense for days. What could I do? I waited, and
gradually their anger passed. They made me promise I would not tell women
and children the secret. As time passed and I was good to my word, they
trusted me more. When the initiations rolled around, my friends never doubted
I would go to see the secret ceremonies. The men of other hamlets asked
about me too. Could I be trusted? A few tried to get me to leave or tried to
trick me into missing the ceremonies; but they were exceptional. Most of the
people accepted me, for the men with whom I worked always stood up to
speak in my behalf. They still do. I was involved in their cult in this sense; I
saw the rites and was there when it all happened. Yet I tried to stay off to
the sidelines, not wanting to attract undue attention. Some things, like the
harsh beatings in initiation, were hard for me to witness. I tried always to
describe my own reactions to things too. Thus, I was a participant-observer
of the rites, though I did not directly join in or accept as a part of my own
personal style all that I saw.

The emotional and sexual tenor of the culthouse scene reveals that Sambia
society is temporarily in a state very different from everyday life. Norms and
rules are turned on their head. Some anthropologists have referred to this as
"ritual time": a time with the license to act out normally forbidden impulses,
a sort of free "play" within ritual. Turner (1971) has referred to this as a
period of "anti-structure" in society, when relationships are open to recon-
stitution of ideals and exploration of tabooed feelings. We will see the individual counterpart of anti-structure in the liminal experience of initiates later.

The danceground comes alive at dusk. The weather is cool and clear. Men
and initiates are everywhere, though the area is uncrowded. From somewhere,
out of sight, flutes can be heard, a part of the male camaraderie celebrating
the complete absence of women and children. Homosexual contacts are rampant here. People are open and unabashed, though they do honor certain
taboos. Homosexual activity is governed by rules that match incest taboos:
all kinsmen and distant relatives are tabooed sexual partners, as are boys'
age-mates and ritual guardians. Brothers-in-law may be acceptable homosexual partners, depending on their exact relation to the boy. The mood is
festive and light, initiates running around, laughing and clowning, an atmosphere as different from the heavy solemnity characterizing formal rituals as
is the night from the day. The following are my very first observations of
homosexual play in the danceground context. Similar things happened in later
initiations too.

The culthouse is darkening and noisy, a mass of bodies and movement and laughter. There are two dozen initiates and older bachelors. None of the new *ipmangwi* bachelors are here; they are in ritual seclusion. The elders have absented themselves. Sambia males feel that it is in bad taste for initiates to engage in homoerotic play in the presence of elders. (Homosexual jokes or innuendos, however, alluded to by elders vis-à-vis their peers, are appropriate in front of initiates.) So boys usually refrain from homosexual play when near elders or their fathers. In situations like this one, where elders know what to expect, they conveniently disappear. Several men have built a small fire in the hearth. Some adults who are forbidden to engage in homosexual activities are present. They sit detachedly chatting, incongruously calm in the center of a storm. All but one of them can sustain this composure—which feels artificial—as seen by his fascination in watching the homoerotic play. The boys are openly initiating foreplay here. Several sitting near the fire are flirting and hanging onto bachelors. Allusions are made to me watching, but no one seems to mind.

Outside on the danceground three boys are hanging on to Sonoko, a bachelor who seems to be in demand. He is talking loudly. A short, strange little Wantuki'u tribesman, who is older but still unmarried, is glued to the second-stage initiate Sollu, a pubescent boy from our hamlet. I am amazed to see Sollu, who is surly, hugging him, their arms locked, faces cheek to cheek. The boy actually nuzzles the man's neck, but there is no kissing. (Sambia do not kiss mouth-to-mouth.) Nearby, several small boys reach underneath the older bachelors' grass aprons to arouse them. A tiny initiate says impatiently to Sonoko: "Come on, shoot me." Occasionally the smiling youths halfheartedly protest that the initiates are pulling on them too hard. In the shadows of the house are several male couples rolling around in the grass. One of them is older, married, and a father—which makes his behavior immoral by ritual convention, but no one pays attention.

Most of the new third-stage initiates are milling around outside. I walk over to join them. Several feet away is their ritual seclusion hut, filled with elders and off-limits to the younger initiates. Some of these youths flirt with initiates, though the youths are forbidden to inseminate them until they complete their own initiation. Some smaller initiates look nervous in anticipation of the night events. Moondi is among this mob but he appears calm. It is not clear exactly which youths will be initiated; several of them are strangers from outside the Sambia Valley. Two Sambia boys from the village talk with me. Someone hands us baked taro, our first food.

I turn back to the shadowy danceground where sexual exploits and their risque sounds are even more outrageous than those in the culthouse, which seems to excite the crowd. There is still a faint light outside and I am conspicuous. Several times I hear allusions with mild hostility to my presence, but I try to ignore them. A little later, in response to one of these mutterings, I heard my friend Sonoko say: "That's nothing. . . . He knows." Here— witnessing open homoerotic activities and standing alone, tall, white, Western-clothed—I feel awkward and out of place, more like a voyeur than I ever did, peeping in on a private show. I clutched my pipe nervously and smoked more than usual. There seemed nothing else for me to do if I was to remain and yet ease my tension.

Some two dozen men, bachelors, and initiates are now milling around the danceground, scattered on the great empty space here and there. Some walk in pairs, others in small clusters of bodies, all restlessly flowing clockwise round the circular ground, as if keeping time with some slow, silent hymn (and there was no singing). Initiates are also horsing around among themselves, playing tag, running back and forth, pushing, pulling, and shoving. In the center are several married men who are oddly detached, circling idly among the others. But there are no initiates with them. Nearby are several young and recently married men (without children yet), including my friends Erujundei, Sonoko, Ooterum, and Aatwo (the latter a hard-bitten man in his early twenties whose father is a war leader). Each of them has one or two initiates; Aatwo is with a boy whom he has long favored. Sonoko has three initiates, who come and go, while I stay on the danceground over the next two hours. The atmosphere remains edgy and exciting. There is rampant sexual foreplay, initiates even competing to hold a man's genitals. From time to time, these couples exit the danceground, into the grass close by, for fellatio; Sambia never permit sex in public. When they reappear minutes later, most walk over and sit inside the culthouse.

There is variation in this sexual behavior but two general patterns emerged. First, most of the couples returned to the culthouse afterward, some—in blatant public "statements"—entering together, while still physically touching, arm in arm. Others, out of embarrassment (as noted by waiting on purpose, then nervously talking to friends), enter separately, moments apart. Second, a few couples would return to the danceground together, but then separate. In some instances the initiate would go to another man, leaving his bachelor on his own or with another boy. Generally, in ordinary life, homosexual partners will split up after sexual intercourse and go in different directions to avoid notice. Several Wantuki'u men joined in, initiates trailing after them. And so did Chemona later on. Like Sonoko, he is very popular with the initiates.

It is the older second-stage initiates, especially the ones recently initiated, who are the most aggressive at this sexual play. Nilangu's own initiates are prominent here: Kambo, Buvuluruton, Sollu, and Dangetnyu. But there were others too. For instance, Merolkopi (Tulutwo's younger blood brother) literally hung on to Nolerutwo, smiling and petting him. Around 7:00 P.M. I heard the youth say matter of factly to the younger Merolkopi (who stood with two other initiates who wanted to be inseminated, all pleading "Me! Me!"): "All right, I mark you to shoot." The initiate lit up in a wide smile. Two other initiates keep teasing and pulling Sonoko's genitals, trying to get him aroused. But twice he said loudly: "Stop it, I've already slept [had sex]!"

Thus it went into the night. On the next night it was the same. And again, at the start of each successive initiation, this free and orgiastic carnival atmosphere was repeated. Never before or since have I seen public erotic behavior of this sort or on this scale. Homosexual play does occur in other secret situations: at night in the clubhouses, and in the forest or hunting lodges. But it is never this blatant, with open foreplay, and it certainly never occurs on such a wide scale within a large group. The closest situation is that of the rat-hunting lodge, which follows first-stage initiation in the forest. Indeed, the repressive nature of Sambia society makes it seem impossible to casual observers that such frenetic energy could be so easily unleashed in males who, except for these several nights—two or possibly three times in their lives at initiations—are renowned for their reserved, straitlaced behavior, abhorring public eroticism. Yet, my most singular memory of that night was the *openness* of sexual play—which shocked me—for it meant there were similar past experiences locked inside the adult men I thought I knew before but would never have imagined out in that crowd. Yet, the anthropologist knows that some of the most profound experiences in a society are those that are normally taken for granted or hidden, except on occasions such as this. Participant-observation is thus a valuable "corrective" method in studying people, for in spite of its shortcomings, it can reveal a fuller picture of how they live their lives.

MOONDI'S DECISION

There are several hours till nightfall—and the formal seclusion of the third-stage initiation candidates. My friend and younger interpreter Moondi is one of them. This is a momentous time, when the older second-stage initiates who have reached puberty are expected by elders to voluntarily enter the culthouse. Though they are nearly independent, they are still not adults. Social change in recent years has made this a key "pressure point" on youths. Beginning in the late 1960s, bachelors began leaving Sambia to work on coastal plantations far away. They would walk to the patrol post and be flown out. We saw in Chapter 3 as well that Moondi started school in 1970. He saw this schooling as preparing him for an alternative life-style, though elders and parents rejected this idea. Moondi had been to a mission school on the patrol post for two years. Then his circumstances and sickness forced him to return to the valley. Eventually he worked as my key interpreter and we became good friends. When the initiations approached, Moondi was dead set against them as he wanted to continue his schooling. The elders are still doing everything in their power to pressure youths like Moondi to be initiated. Here the issue of there being "no exits" from initiation remains relevant in the face of change. Moondi's generation is at a historic turning point. His situation will introduce the initiations in the context of the changing behavioral environment as it is today.

Moondi appears around noon with his age-mate, Tulutwo, at the dance-ground. Both youths are expected to be initiated but they are defiant. As the danceground quiets down in the afternoon, the men's talk turns to the subject of these new bachelors, the men intent on having their will done, and proper induction of the whole set of youths that night. So far I have managed to

remain neutral in this conflict over Moondi's initiation without making enemies or compromising my integrity. I want to keep it that way; I am no
ombudsman. Moondi's intentions are muddy: he says initiation is not for him,
yet at the critical moment he has publicly appeared again. He is a complex
young man, intelligent, vocal, headstrong. Sometimes he is torn between two
worlds: the village and the dream of a different life far off in Port Moresby,
New Guinea's capital. He is of two minds, not knowing what he wants or
what he can have. This day he will decide. The men pressure him. Sitting
with Moondi and the men, it is hard for me to silently watch the age-old
dilemmas of tradition versus change, of group needs pitted against the individual's will played out again, my friend the pawn, myself an audience. I feel
painfully helpless. After some minutes of interrogation, in which Moondi
stays silent, I rise to leave. Then so does everyone else.

Down the hill we walk to a hut where I am staying and the drama continues.
(Looking back now, I see that Moondi's only real—and final—defense against
being initiated was the "authority" of my presence. But he knew I could not
stop the men.) Moondi stayed physically close to me; his friend Tulutwo
stayed close to him; my friend Weiyu, as if defending *me*, walked on my other
side. And a mob of men are on our heels.

Suddenly I realized that Moondi was actually afraid the men would abduct
him and force him into the culthouse. Were a scuffle to ensue, trouble could
errupt. What were we to do?

Moondi's father (who is characteristically soft-spoken) pursues us, implor-
ing his son to talk. Oolerum, whom Moondi favors as a mother's brother,
speeds along asking me if Moondi would be initiated. The men assume I
know what he is up to, but they are wrong. "This is your matter and Moondi's
own choice," I said. When they told me that Moondi said I asked him to go
to my house and fetch some things for me, I halted. Now I understood.
Unknown to me, Moondi had been using this lie as an excuse. I could neither
betray him nor lie. Caught between Moondi and his fate, I sputtered: "That's
Moondi's affair; I don't need anything urgently. But if he does go, well—he
can bring back my tennis shoes. *If* he comes back." The men look perplexed.
Moondi sped up (as we all did), actually running just ahead of us, as if the
men might still grab hold of him to prevent his escape. The tension is not
over.

The hut I am staying in fills up with the whole mob of men. We are an
hour's walk from our own village. The men corner Moondi again, repeatedly
asking him if he plans to run away, to leave for the coast and work. He keeps
saying no. Some of Tulutwo's clansmen appear too. They press in on both
youths, whom everyone suspects to be in league. I am silent. Even Tulutwo
is scared, and this surprises me, because he is built like a boxer and the little
likable fellow always acts so tough around the younger initiates. Finally, the
men allow the two youths to go back briefly to village Nilangu, on condition
that Oolerum, a young married man well trusted by all, accompanies them.
They depart, and I am left still wondering about their initiation. Will they
return?

An hour passes in relative peace and I breathe a sigh of relief. Doolu, Moondi's father, never budges. But otherwise I am left alone to have a cup of soup and write field notes. In walk Kanteilo and Weiyu: "Is Moondi going to run off?" More veiled exchanges like before. Kanteilo knows I am sympathetic both to Moondi *and* to him. The old man—to whom I owe so much for his social support, who was a great warrior and is still a great fox—plays on my sympathies, saying he is very ill (he has a large tropical sore). He is forever using this ploy to have his way.

Moondi suddenly reappears. Doolu rises. He stands 10 feet from his son but only half looks at him, saying "Moondi, what are you doing?" Quietly but firm. "What about your initiation decorations? They are ready." Kanteilo keeps hammering away that Moondi's ritual sponsor, a Wantuki'u tribesman and Doolu's trading partner, has arrived. He was Moondi's first ritual sponsor years ago. Moondi, who barely knows him, does not feel close to him.

Kanteilo refers to his open tropical sore, baring his abdomen so we can see it, appealing to Moondi to listen to him. "I am old and sick," he says to a silent Moondi. When his father appeals again, Moondi angrily snaps back, "*Koonanu!* [Lies!] No." His face and voice are tense. The others then leave. Doolu stands alone and sad in the thankful darkness of the room. I feel awful. They have come close to cursing each other—a fatal turn in a father-son relationship that would never be forgotten, even if forgiven. Never once did Moondi look at his father, as is common in such arguments. He wanders off. His father leaves and I am alone.

Moondi returns shortly and for a moment we are in private. I ask why he came back if he does not want to be initiated. "I had no choice: Oolerum was with us." (He did bring my tennis shoes!) "So what now?" I ask. "I don't want to be made a bachelor yet. Very much not! I'm afraid of the great pain— I know what they'll do. . . ." I sense that he fears another nose-bleeding. I could only nod in agreement, adding that they will soon force him to decide.

How strikingly Moondi's feelings have changed back and forth over the past few days. A week ago he repeatedly said he disliked initiation because it would block his thinking: he never would get back to school, never learn, or never learn as fast again. He had seen this "blocking" occur in several other youths and wanted no part of it. He is too young to be married yet, he says. Later, he admitted something else: he didn't want to be shamed at school. "Why shamed?" I asked. Third-stage initiation "says" you are grown, that you have pubic hair, semen, sexual urges (that is, have reached puberty), and that a female will be assigned in marriage for you, he argues. The schoolboys make fun of these things; they laugh at the initiated bachelors among them, who are in turn shamed. I believe him, for he has been in school and Sambians have a terrible fear of being shamed. But now, right down to the wire, as it were, Moondi reveals his *fears* about initiation ordeals: beatings, nose-bleeding, and who knows what else. Moondi later added a more personal fear: that he must now stop consuming men's semen, and through sex give semen to younger boys. "When I think about that, I'm afraid, afraid to be a bachelor! What if I don't grow big quickly? I won't be able to eat more 'milk' [semen] later." Here, Moondi referred to the fact that bachelors can never reverse sexual roles once initiated: they can only give, not receive, semen. Powerful fears these were. But the social pressures were more powerful.

Enter Kanteilo again, who plunges ahead: he says Moondi must be crazy (*abrumbru*) to be acting like this. What will Moondi do? Kanteilo lectures him: "Your body isn't the same as a white man's. Nor is your food . . . you've got to be initiated to stay as strong as your age-mates and marry." Here, Kanteilo hints that I have exercised a bad influence on Moondi through sharing my food and my Western ways. At one point Moondi scoffs that the old man's talk was all *koonanu* (a lie or a joke). "*Koonanu!* Boy, what do *you* know? Do *you* understand these matters?" The elder's voice raises and his chestnut-colored face turns red with anger. Weiyu, as if to calm him down, chimes in, agreeing with Kanteilo. They glance at one another, but Moondi keeps looking away.

Chemona comes by a bit later, word of the ruckus having spread quickly. He is Moondi's older friend.[4] He says nothing after eyeing us except "Wait," in response to something from Doolu. Chemona consoles Moondi; they talk quietly. He persuades the youth to come and eat with him. A minute later I went to Chemona's hut, where they continued talking privately. Here Chemona gently coaxes Moondi, trying to make him give in. He refuses. We all eat Chemona's taro. Meanwhile, Oolerum comes by and joins in, and together they try again. Soon they break off in whispers among themselves. This is remarkable: Sambia never whisper in front of close company. Moondi stops them, afraid of their intrigues. Then a plan emerges, a bargain: Oolerum will "stand in" as a special ritual sponsor for Moondi, saying he won't let Moondi be really "killed" with pain. I took this to mean they would not let Moondi be nose-bled, though their meaning was only hinted. (Later, I discovered that this is indeed what they had agreed upon.) Their promise calms Moondi, who finally relents. He seems satisfied. They all leave for the danceground.

Moondi's decision has been made, there is no further personal drama for him. On the danceground the men too do an about-face: no one reproaches or questions him, they are all smiles. His presence speaks for itself. After a moment he blends into the crowd and is absorbed by his age-mates.

THIRD-STAGE INITIATION

The third-stage initiates are led from the men's house to the culthouse, where they are left in seclusion until dark. Moondi is with them. Now they

---

[4] By his own reckoning, Moondi says he has slept promiscuously with more than two-score bachelors and men over the past seven years. He has had sex with over 20 of them at least twice. Besides Erujundei (a young man), Chemona has been Moondi's favorite bachelor, to whom he was attached for a few weeks four years ago. During that period they had fellatio (he served as Chemona's fellator) at least once a day. With Erujundei, however, he has continued to have homosexual contacts sporadically over the past four years, the most recent having been 10 days ago, at the time of the culthouse-raising ceremonies. (Unlike Chemona, who prefers smaller boys, Erujundei openly favors older boys who are masculine and even pubescent.)

fall under the burden of many ritual taboos. They cannot drink water or take food. It is forbidden to talk under pain of harsh punishment. Nor can they move about or sleep. In this motionless state, they can reflect on themselves and the momentous changes they are experiencing. Their ritual decorations, some originally selected by their parents years ago at first-stage initiation and other new decorations, are prepared and placed on them by their ritual guardians. An all-night songfest is held. Early in the morning ritual experts lead the youths to the forest for purification ceremonies using ritually sacred trees, such as the giant redwood (selected for its qualities of sturdiness and longevity). These rites are done to remove any feminine residues from youths and masculinize them. The sequence takes hours. Afterward, the bachelors remain under the seclusion taboos. Hungry, thirsty, tired from lack of sleep, and worn out from the long trek to the high forest, they return at nightfall for still more moonlight dancing. What an endurance test! They dine very late at night on cold taro.

In the morning the youths undergo more forest purification rites, followed by severe thrashings with cassowary quill-bones. Both these rites strengthen and stimulate the growth and aggressive characteristics of youths. The most violent Sambia rite—the nose-bleeding—follows this. These occur throughout the male life cycle, coordinated with initiation: at first-, third-, fifth-, sixth-stage initiation rites, and always thereafter when a man's wife has her monthly period. (Because of its importance and the difficulty of describing all types of nose-bleedings, we will return to a full discussion of this ritual behavior below, under first-stage initiation.) The nose-bleedings, done violently and by surprise, re-introduce the ritual flutes to bachelors, who learned of them originally in their first-stage rites years ago. Then they are decorated for dancing again. Later, for the first time in days, they are allowed a night's sleep.

The final events of third-stage initiation lead the men back to the forest, to a special ceremony that identifies the bachelors with the strong, "masculine" black palm tree. This also reveals how much they share (as a male group) in the passions of secret collective rituals (Herdt 1981).

At the very last, their new warrior armbands are placed on their forearms: they are young men now, and the armband is the key gender sign of puberty in males. New shell noseplugs are also placed on them. The youths scatter to their respective hamlets, where they again reside in their clubhouses. Soon, though, they are called upon to leave with adult men for the high forest to hunt possum again—this time as feast gifts for the second-stage initiates, for whom they too will serve as initiators.

SECOND-STAGE INITIATION

Several weeks later, the old first-stage initiates are elevated to *imbutu* status in the second-stage rites. These are the simplest of all collective ceremonies, though they still stretch over several days and are colorful, with red pandanus fruit and red decorations being the focus of decoration. The initiates are collected as an age-set from all the neighboring hamlets and are placed in the culthouse. Now the new third-stage bachelors are key actors in organizing the main events.

The second-stage boys are still very young: 10, 11, 12, a few a bit older, the latter with peach-fuzz facial hair showing. These second-stage initiates are more confident than the younger boys at first-stage initiation, though they are not as hardened as the older third-stage youths. For one thing, they have never been on a war raid, and most of them have never fought in a real battle. When they dress up in the warrior garb befitting their status, however, they make a handsome and proud lot.

These second-stage initiates, too, assume heavy food and behavioral taboos. For some days they cannot eat, sleep, or drink; they must not speak at all: which is no different than the preceding initiation. The same taboos are applicable to them. These are taught in the initiations and enforced for the duration of their being in this ritual position. First-stage initiates, for instance, have many food taboos, which include all red and blue foods (identified with women), such as red pandanus fruit oil, red and blue yams, and many red-colored leaves. The feasting in second-stage rites ends these particular taboos. This is the trend throughout ritual life: initiates begin with a very few acceptable foods and a great long list of food taboos. By final initiation few taboos remain, and by old age all the food taboos are gone because Sambia see the elderly as being relatively genderless. Food is identified with sexual potency and gender, as is most everything in the Sambia world, so food intake is ritually restricted to ensure health, long life, and fertility.

The forest purificatory rites are colorful and dramatic in second-stage initiation. Tali and several ritual experts took boys out at dawn each morning to rub dew from the meadow grass on their faces, to "cleanse" and masculinize them. Following this are purifications using river stones, orange forest muds, wild taro plants, cabbage palm, young pandanus-nut trees, wild ginger, brown tree parasites, white-colored forest shrubs, and blond and blue tree grasses. An extremely painful and violent stinging-nettle rite is held. Boys are dressed up and dance before the crowd in moonlight festivities on several nights. They are distinguished by having cassowary quill-bone noseplugs ceremonially placed in their noses. A day later, in secret, they are lectured on the importance of continuing to ingest semen. During those homosexual teachings, elders tell them that their cassowary quill-bone noseplugs will erotically arouse the bachelors, who will want to inseminate them in the mouth. So the quill-bone is used explicitly as a symbol of penile erection. The importance of assisting in hunting and gardening is also constantly stressed. Certain myths surrounding the origins of foods and animals are told, pandanus fruit in particular. After several more days, the boys are given a feast and allowed to sleep.

The next day boys have their final feast and are lectured again on the need to be warriors and hunters (see Photo 10). The elders implore them to ingest as much semen as possible, to grow strong. The boys have some homosexual contacts at night in the culthouse. These will increase in the coming days.

Photo 10. Shaman war leader orates in ritual teachings

Soon they are freed to return to their hamlets. For a time the danceground site is quiet again.

FIRST-STAGE INITIATION

The first initiation of Sambia boys is special in many ways. It is the longest and most elaborate initiation ceremony, and the most important in the sense of being the boys' induction into the cult. The boys' separation from their parents is dramatic, as is their virgin exposure to ritual secrets. Nor must we forget how young the boys are: what they endure, learn, and change into is remarkable for seven- to ten-year-olds. We will examine these events in detail; but still, many things must be omitted from this short account (See Table 3).

These last events started on July 27, 1975, and lasted for seven days. The new third- and second-stage initiates were crucial participants. Both Weiyu and Moondi served as initiators. This particular initiation was done at Yulami hamlet, in the lower Sambia Valley. You know already the political changes this initiation represented: two opposing phratries with a history of warfare came together for the first performance in modern times. The men were primed for staging impressive displays after the preceding weeks of higher-stage rites, each side determined to prove that its phratry was the stronger in the initiation cycle.

First Day of Initiation   We depart our village and arrive two hours later at the village nearest Yulami—Kanteilo, Weiyu, Tali, Moondi, and other men and initiates. Here several rituals will be done before moving on to the culthouse at Yulami. We are greeted well, for this is a sister-hamlet of our

TABLE 3   SAMBIA FIRST-STAGE INITIATION
SEQUENCE OF RITUALS

	Separation of initiates, guardian takes authority
Day 1	**Journey to sponsor hamlet**
	1. First ritual thrashing
	2. Shaman's ceremonial purification (black palm tree)
	3. Taro-feeding ceremony and nose-piercing
	4. **Moonlight ceremonies**
	Sugar cane rite
	Firewood ritual
	Frog-feeding ceremony
Day 2	5. **Purification at dawn**
	Ritual seclusion
	6. Moonlight ceremonies and dancing
Day 3	7. **Purification at dawn**
	8. Public ritual thrashing ceremony
	9. Possum-liver spitting ceremony
	10. Ritual nose-bleeding ceremony
	11. **Penis and flute ceremony**
	Body decoration
	Ritual parade to dance-ground
	12. Bachelor impersonation of female spirits
Day 4	13. Ceremonial songfest with hallucinogens
	14. Iwouwi'u ceremony
	15. Name-changing ceremony
Days 5–6	16. Sequence of horticultural ceremonies
	17. Bullroarer ritual
Day 7	18. Ceremony ending taboo on drinking water

phratry (the last one before crossing into Yulami territory). The first initiation events soon start. The new initiates, we learn, have been taken from their parents, who returned only yesterday from a month-long possum hunt. Three boys ran away and tried to escape into the forest. One has been found already and the others are being trailed. By nightfall they returned.

Soon, the secluded initiates are prepared for the short trip to the dance-ground. Many men and boys walk ahead of us. We wait ten minutes. The men standing around the men's house halfheartedly sing war songs. Tulutwo departs and returns: he has changed from Western-style trousers into a grass sporran and, as always, the transformation is startling. He jumps into the organization of things with such a grown-up expression on his face; how different compared to his fear at the time of Moondi's indecision!

The ritual sponsors emerge from the men's house with their wards riding on their backs, clinging to their shoulders. They cover the boys with their new bark capes so the mothers cannot see their faces. Then the pairs walk

Photo 11. Ritual sponsors cover initiates on journey to forest ceremonies

through the hamlet (see Photo 11). Women and children watch. As the novices are guided past their mothers' houses—leaving them behind forever—the women begin to wail sorrowfully. Weiyu, who is walking with me, remarks that the crying women are the boys' mothers. Off to one side I see a middle-aged woman with long tears on her cheeks. An even larger group of women stand in the brush bordering the hamlet, and three of them loudly bawl as they watch their sons leave.

As we walk up the hillside to the forest, a man shouts out over the crowd of males, but no one responds. He taunts the initiates, telling them to defecate carefully during the next thrashing ritual so their sponsors' backs will not be so messed up! The boys are scared out of their wits, he implies. Just beyond sight of the new initiates and hamlet, some men take out flutes and play them. Meanwhile, the group of initiates are halted and seated on the grass. The men, however, continue on the path around a bend where numerous men are already secretly preparing for the beating ritual. We are now about 15 minutes above the village. Foliage is cleared to camouflage pairs of men hiding on either side of the trail. Sticks are distributed to everyone for the thrashings. The men lay in wait for a signal to jump up and frighten the novices.

The boys are now lined up and their ritual sponsors hoist them on their backs. They round the corner on the path. At a signal, all the hiding men jump up and form two lines, with a passageway between them. They thrash the ground with switches, hollering and hooting, grass and debris flying everywhere. The boys look terrified. Their sponsors charge through the lines, so they and the initiates are repeatedly thrashed. Most of the boys cry. Two of them were so afraid that they involuntarily defecated.

Meanwhile, a ritual platform is completed off to one side of the men in hiding. The platform, made of roughly hewn poles, has been constructed around a young black palm tree. It is 6 feet by 8 feet in size and stands 5 feet off the ground. Two senior shamans attach the red ceremonial headband associated with shamans to the topmost palm leaves.

Now the initiates are assembled for their first purificatory ritual. The initiates climb onto the platform. Each is carefully rubbed with the topmost palm leaves and cloth (see cover photograph). The leaves are twisted into each boy's hair. Men say the black palm is like the boy's age-mate. Because the initiate's skin flakes and sweat have been rubbed on the leaves, some of his body essence enters the fast-growing tree. Like the tree he, too, will grow quickly. The shaman touches each boy's head with the red cloth and then jerks it toward the sky, making the eerie shaman's whistle (this is done in healing ceremonies too). The boys are instructed to watch the cloth, which is believed to pull down the sun's power and vitality, gliding into the boy's body via the magical headband. Here we see the sun used directly to help develop *jerungdu* in boys. Then the boy's childhood noseplug, a tiny piece of bamboo, is taken from him, another symbol of childhood lost.

These old noseplugs are collected and are placed in a branch of the palm tree. Both the leaf-rubbing and placement of the old noseplug in the tree are believed to help fortify the initiates' souls for the ordeals lying ahead. Sambia take care lest boys' souls are too frightened and "escape" their bodies, leaving them vulnerable to illness or death.

The whole group of men and initiates now return to the village. It is early afternoon, and the initiates are locked up in the village's men's house. They are guarded should any try to escape. Even when allowed periodically to go to the outhouse they are escorted. Meanwhile, my friends and I relax at the hut of a local man.

A few minutes later, Tulutwo gives us sugar cane. Kerumulyu, from a nearby hamlet, is with us. Last week his wife gave birth to her first child, and his sixth-stage initiation has made him an adult. Weiyu's younger clan brother (Tulutwo's own age-mate) sits beside Kerumulyu and jokes with him. The youth makes a pass at Kerumulyu's grass apron, jokingly attempting to grab his penis. Kerumulyu is momentarily embarrassed but they both laugh as he protests. Such homoerotic joking among males is common during idle moments of initiation. Then others begin to speak of the coming events.

The septum-piercing ceremony followed shortly thereafter. This ceremony, with its special feast foods, is said to hasten the initiates' growth. The ceremony is mainly symbolic, because most boys already have pierced noses. The ceremony draws attention to the nose and their new status, following the first purification. Food then prepares them for tonight's ordeals and moonlight dancing.

The initiates are led from the darkening seclusion of the men's house and made into a semicircle facing the men on the village plaza. Women and children are chased away so as not to see what happens. The boys wait only moments and then a line of eight colorfully decorated men (carrying long red leaves) run into view. These dancers hurriedly pass along the line of initiates and pound their chests. This is also done on older second-stage initiates, who are lined up behind novices. Then Tali proceeds to ceremonially strike each lad with a second ritual object, the *kwolyi-mutnyi*. This object is believed to have great secret power to strengthen and help boys grow, and to make the group and its gardens fertile. Another senior man produces a string bag full of mashed green leaves. This green mash was chewed by the elders, and each boy gets a pinch placed in his mouth, again to stimulate growth.

Now a new noseplug is fitted for every initiate. Two boys do not have pierced septums, which is unusual since boys and girls customarily have their septums pierced at around age four or five. (see above, pp. 109–110). The senior man performs the operation on these two matter of factly, jabbing their noses with a cassowary-bone needle. They cry. Another elder follows and spits yellow masticated root on the forehead and chest of each initiate, again to strengthen them.

Cooked taro is carried out in a raggedy bark cape. It is broken into pieces and distributed by three men, two of whom are shamans. A chunk of taro is momentarily held before a lad's face; then a spell is muttered while taro is pressed between the shaman's hands and into the lad's stomach. The spell appeals magically to the eagle and to the hard white sap of trees to strengthen the lad and dissolve his hunger: he must be strong now, as later, when he journeys on war raiding parties and food is short. (At third-stage initiation a similar ceremony is done, traditionally to anticipate real war raids.) The boys quickly wolf down the taro, their first food of the day and their last until the early morning hours. Another ritual fast now begins.

The party from our village walks the main trail to the culthouse, an hour away. It is dusk when we arrive at Yulami, the site of the great culthouse.

Yulami Hamlet   The hamlet is crowded when we arrive. I follow the initiates, who are placed in a small house near the culthouse on the danceground above the hamlet. The culthouse is off-limits to the boys until a ceremony is done a bit later. Numerous people from Nilangu and Pundei hamlets are staying in temporary grass huts on the edge of Yulami and the friendly relationship between them is obvious. A few older families camp together, sharing food and conversing. But sexual segregation is prominent. Women take up residence with their children in two large houses. Nearby, the men and older initiates stay in another house, where I also bedded. This kind of solidarity between our people and distant kinsmen from the area persisted during the initiation. On the other hand, the inhabitants of Yulami village— former enemies—did not make us overly welcome, a fact my party repeatedly complained about. Fears of sorcery were common.

A large group of men and women assemble in and near the women's house, where there emerged a lively and friendly atmosphere. Older people noisily chat, smoke, and chew pandanus nuts around campfires. Children are running everywhere.

Back in the men's quarters, our elders and senior men sit in the house, telling stories and chewing betel. Off in the distance I can see the vacant danceground. At dark, the elders begin needling the bachelors and older initiates (a common occurrence in the initiation), reminding them of their ceremonial and sexual responsibilities. The men's reprimands are at first humorous. "Why are the initiates not up at the danceground with the new initiates?" Our boys, men assert in a friendly manner, are the age-mates of the new novices. They mean, of course, that second- and first-stage initiates are all fellators, who should be concerned with "growing big." Our second-stage initiates shrug and try to ignore them. Elders say they have "worked hard" recently to elevate the younger boys to second-stage initiate status. Moondi defends our boys, saying everyone feels reticent about being here in Yulami, which is a strange and hostile place. He also criticizes the hamlet for its tiny population, a fact which is both funny and worrisome (fears of sorcery?), it seems. But Kanteilo retorts that the second-stage initiates and Moondi too (who is now a third-stage bachelor) should not be "lazy" and hang around the elders here. Bluntly, they tell the initiates to go and ingest semen. Weiyu, sitting nearby, adds: "Yes, that's true, you don't want to fall 'sick' [from lack of semen]! Go on now." So the boys reluctantly leave for the danceground.

Soon, the remaining young married men engage in their own verbal duelling, as is common between in-laws and male cross-cousins. Erunjun and Weiyu joke with men of Pundei hamlet, trying to extort pandanus nuts from them. Two of the men are their in-laws, and one of them is a cross-cousin. Weiyu chides them: "Come on! We gave you our 'sisters' quickly; they developed breasts quickly; now you should give us pandanus nut 'milk' just as quickly!" They all laughed at this; Weiyu was given more of the precious nuts.

Moonlight Rituals of the Danceground   On the first night of initiation, men perform glamorous public rituals. A great central bonfire lights the center of the danceground. Its brilliance is compared to the moon's rings. The weather is beautiful. Senior men and older and newer initiates dance, while groups of older warriors sing choruses of war songs. Women and children build small campfires just beyond the danceground, around its fence, to warm themselves through the long night. Women participate in the early dancing; later they perform their own Firewood Ritual. Here is a rare occasion in which women take a ceremonial role. What emerges in these opening rites are graphic demonstrations of the always-present antagonism between the sexes.

This mood of sexual polarity persists during the remaining days of the initiation. As "rituals of rebellion," these moonlight danceground ceremonies are inflammatory and tense. Women are not only allowed but are expected to rhetorically chastise the initiates for their laziness and unmanly conduct. In no other context of social life can women collectively launch such attacks. As the night proceeds, women extend their harangues to the men as well. Likewise, elders, in their teachings to boys, seize upon the opportunity to criticize the women. Castigating the boys for their laziness, the elders continue by condemning them for the misuse of male ritual items, such as trees and cordylines. Again, they generalize their verbal attacks by holding the mothers responsible for the boys' sacrilege of male ritual and ritual items. Indeed, at one point they even accuse women of motivating their sons to make fun of the sacred rituals in this way. Women are assailed for ignoring their subsistence tasks too. Male speeches on this opening night, then, anticipate two themes underlying later ritual acts: the rebelliousness of insubordinate, uncooperative women who challenge men's control of persons, events, and resources; and the harmful essence of the depleting and polluting women. Here we see dramatically the bitter tug-of-war between men and women over the initiates, who are, this one last time, caught between the two worlds.

There was also another theme in the rhetoric: interphratry political rivalry. The men began with the Sugar Cane Ritual.

The ritual performers carry in a structure resembling a moving fence of sugar cane. The tops of the cane leaves are intertwined to create a living wall. The initiates are first hit with the sugar cane and then surrounded by the performers. These men hold the sugar stalks between their legs, thrusting them up and down, bumping the butts into the ground as if riding them like broomsticks. As with carrying the bullroarer pole at other times, their action is blatantly phallic and aggressive. The ceremonial teaching follows. The elders first lecture the women, reprimanding them for ignoring the cultivation of sugar cane. An elder of our phratry then says to boys:

> This sugar cane is like the calves of your legs; you must put up supporting sticks when planting it. You may not eat this cane, for it is tabooed to you. This is true for the second-stage initiates too. If you eat it, you will be rubbish men. You can eat it later following third-stage initiation. This ritual is ours—not that of the Yulami people. You must plant the cane—so you can offer some to any male visitors. Do not be lazy. If your wife cuts down this cane, you should cut her with your knife as punishment! She must not think that you are afraid of her. She might want to take another man, so she will cut off the leaves of your cane. If she does so, you should take your axe and cut her, as a warning.

Here we see how ritual is used to define specific activities or foods (sugar cane) as being male. Women are told to leave cane alone. We see also that such items are sometimes used to teach about adultery. Elders' attitudes are to not "spare the rod" in dealing with such women. Such explicit socialization of sex attitudes strongly influences the boys.

Then the Cordyline Rite is begun. Another elder does the orating, but this one laments past warfare between the hamlets assembled here, long-standing rivals who had often fought before the Australians brought peace. In the late 1950s many men of the Yulami hamlet group died, and their deaths were attributed to the sorcery of men in the Seboolu group. People say the sorcery was in retaliation for a fight over eel-trapping rights in the river. (It is known that many men died in the Seboolu hamlets during the same time period, possibly from an epidemic.) Several ceremonies are performed that exemplify this past warfare.

Next is the Firewood Ritual, which temporarily overturns the men's control. Unique to all Sambia initiations, women in this event are permitted to do a ceremony face-to-face with the initiates. Perhaps this openness expresses the importance of the bond to their mothers, which ritual brings to an end.

Women begin gathering around the inner circle of men by the bonfire in preparation for the ceremony. The men make a larger circle enclosing the few women who are closer to the fire. These women carry smoke-blackened sticks of firewood, a sign of their female domestic role. They dance frantically round the fire, beating the ground with their sticks. The crowd's eyes are glued to the scene. Now the novices are brought by the men into the women's circle. The women, some of them quite aged, start hitting boys hard against their chests, stomachs, legs, and hips. The initiates bawl. The women, as serious as ever I have observed Sambia women, mercilessly castigate boys. One initiate in particular is singled out by a bitter-faced, frowning woman. She instructed a man (his father?) to hit the boy, and he did. Two women lecture the novices, "You initiates must feel sorry for us. . . . We have brought firewood for your danceground fire. . . . Later, when you are in the forest, bring firewood back for us." Somewhat later the male elders add: "You initiates must bring wood back to heat your wives' skins whenever returning from the forest. That is your manly duty, not the women's."

At last the boys are removed from the circle, crying and weary, leaving the women alone and now vulnerable around the dying bonfire. Instantly the men grimace and remark among themselves that the women went too far and said too much. Some younger men mock them: "We are no good; we are spineless for not collecting firewood, are we? That angers us." They challenge the women: "So it is only you women who collect wood! This firewood may be yours, but if we push you into the fire, it will burn you—even though you say you are its 'mother'!" But the women show no fear, and even chide the men, replying: "Are you men eels [cold and slippery] that your skins will not be burnt too [if you try to corner us]?"

The women begin a terrible thrashing of the dying bonfire. Great bursts of embers fly into the air, creating a blazing orange fountain. The circling men surround and begin pushing the women into the fire. Edged closer into the fire, the women barely maintain their dancing movements. The men joke at how the women's grass skirts may catch fire. Finally, nearly forced into the hot coals, the women exit, which triggers a triumphant war cry from all the men who have succeeded in expelling their "opponents" from the dance-ground. The men celebrate. They compete against one another by dancing, seeing who is able to bounce his grass sporran the highest. They seem un-abashedly exhibitionist as the admiring crowds of spectators look on.

This ritual sequence, like others, reveals the tense and conflictual involve-ment of women in the male cult's public activities. By assuming their com-plementary role in performing the ritual, women indirectly reinforce the male position. The cooperation of men and women in the ceremony quickly de-teriorated. Not content to criticize only the initiates, women directed their remarks to the men as a group, who responded to women as a group. The resulting exchanges, in heated words and scuffles, confirmed the opposition between the sexes.

Frog-Feeding Ceremony   The danceground quiets down in the early morning hours following the Firewood Ritual. Men and initiates continue to dance and sing, though much more subdued from weariness. The final nighttime event is the Frog-Feeding Ceremony.

This ceremony provides the initiate and his mother with their first—and last—opportunity to be reunited. For a few boys, a sort of "ritual mother" (the wives of the guardians usually) substitutes for their true mothers if they are deceased or sick. The setting is highly emotional in spite of the hour. The boys know that this is the last time to sit and eat and talk with their mothers for years to come.

The possessive way in which women remove the boys from the throng of men on the danceground is striking. Again we see the competition between men and women, here focused on the struggle for temporary control of the lads.

For over an hour women attempt to extract their sons from the crowded danceground. But the men dominate and hold back the boys. There are scuffles and even arguments. Several times men angrily curse the women, who move back only to approach again. Astonishingly, a few women actually charge into the dancing men to search for their sons. The atmosphere is tense enough for a brawl. An initiate is literally jerked from the danceground by his mother and another woman. Several moments later, however, Tulutwo raids the women's group and retrieves his initiate—for he is the boy's sponsor— loudly protesting that the women cannot "have him yet."

By 4:00 in the morning, women succeed in collecting their sons for the quiet, intimate food ceremonies. For the first time in hours the dancing stops. Each boy is led by his mother to a grassy spot outside the danceground where she sits with her other children and female kin. Women say that the boys should eat frog until their stomachs are filled, because thereafter this food is tabooed until they are married and have their own children. I see a woman place bark capes on the ground and then her own cape over them as a tablecloth. The smoked frog (stored in bamboo vessels) and some possum meat are laid out. I notice that nearly all the novices self-consciously cover their faces while eating these delicacies, continuously tugging at the head-cloak to hide their faces. This self-control is very unlike the uninitiated boys they used to be, and rather like the initiated cult members they have become. Women make quiet comments to their sons. Initiates later told me how their mothers said, "Now you must go to the men's house." Their mothers cried, saying how they would no longer be able to see them. The boys said that many of them cried too; so much so, that some boys had no appetite to eat at all.

How do we explain the difference in the boys' behavior? Earlier that day elders had instructed them to hide their faces while interacting with their mothers. The boys recall that the black palm purificatory ceremony is done on their faces, making them its age-mate. Lest they forget, elders warn boys that they will not get to be handsome if women watch them eat. It is even hinted that their mothers could somehow be harmed by watching them. Thus boys have already learned two important reasons for all later avoidance of

Photo 12. Initiates carried by sponsors in thrashing ceremony

women. It is apparent that the boys internalized this view and acted on it that night. The ritual resocialization already has shown its effects. The initiates remain with their mothers till sunrise, but they are not allowed to sleep.

The second day repeats many events of the first day.

Third Day of Initiation Another purificatory ritual is performed at dawn. The flutes are blown and the initiates are taken back to the danceground. Then the main public thrashing ceremony is held (see Photo 12).

This ceremony occurs early in the morning. Unlike the earlier thrashing, this one is public and the initiates' mother (or in her absence, the guardians' wife) plays a part in it. The ritual sponsors again carry initiates through lines of men who wield sticks with which to hit them. The boys' mothers take a complementary role to that of the guardian by attempting to shield their sons' naked buttocks. Pre-initiated boys have naked arses till first-stage initiation. This is associated with an immature state, and they are teased for it. Initiation garb includes a bark cape cover for the arse, worn the rest of the boys' lives. Men say that women lay themselves open to thrashings too by going through the lines. The women risk this because "they feel sorry for boys." Yet, men also state that the women's "interference" angers them: "If you women hide the boys' arses, you must want to be hit too!" So the boys, their sponsors, and their mothers are simultaneously thrashed. There is an ordeal for the men too: those who wish to join in the thrashing of boys must first submit to a private cassowary quill-bone thrashing inside the culthouse. Both these thrashings are very painful.

When I reach the danceground with my party early that morning, we hear men singing war songs and the flutes playing inside the culthouse. Outside there is a great throng of noisy, excited people on the danceground. Inside and near the entrance to the culthouse, warriors beat bamboo sticks against the phratry totemic bamboo posts that decorate the inner entrance.

We see the initiates lifted on the backs of their sponsors. They prepare for the scary trip between the parallel lines of men and initiates. Twenty-five of them kneel in the dusty earth on either side of a pathway that bisects the danceground. The men clamor for the thrashing to begin. Their thrashing raises so much dust that it is difficult to see to the farther side of the line. The boys' mothers are grouped at the end of the pathway, adding to the congestion of sponsors and initiates assembled there. The mothers hold green cordyline leaves in their hands. The boys are tied to their sponsors' backs with new bark capes, which are knotted. These pairs begin walking through the lines, the mother following closely behind, holding the leaves to shield the boy. Sometimes the mothers succeed in covering boys and sometimes not. The guardians move slowly through the lines, allowing the men many opportunities to swat and inflict blows on initiates. It is like a ritual whipping, and the men take delight in it. Most initiates cry. More startling is the treatment of the mothers, who are hit even harder by the men. The women are usually struck on their backs, their bark capes taking the brunt of the blows. But some are hit hard enough that they fall to the ground, and are even hit while on the ground. I observed one third-stage initiate (about 15 years old) land a cruel blow on a woman who had fallen down. He cheered and laughed to call attention to his feat. The sponsors are barely hit at all. The mothers and boys take the heaviest blows, as we can see in their faces, for even the women look afraid when walking through the lines of warriors.

Toward the end of this event there occurs a particularly striking example of an initiate's fear and resistance. A boy refuses to be hoisted on his sponsor's back (see Photo 13). He is older and bigger than his age-mates, and it takes three men to do the job. His mother approaches to take her spot, but he grabs hold of her bamboo necklace. She tries to pull away but he will not release her. Tears wash down his face as he repeatedly cries "No, no," and then "Mother, mother." The poor woman's face is a mask of sad helplessness and she is nearly in tears herself. The boy clings desperately and she struggles. At last the men direct the boy's guardian to go through the lines as the initiate holds fast to his mother. But now she is unable to cover him properly. The outcome is brutal for the boy: though the sponsor hurried through the lines, the men severely swat the boy with blow after blow, as if to punish him for his fear.

A bit later as is customary, very small pre-initiate boys, some no older than three or four, are carried through the lines and more gently swatted. They are not being initiated, but merely being tested for later. The father must decide to do this. Sometimes the mother will not agree and arguments break out. There are always a handful of men who insist upon having their tiny sons symbolically thrashed in this way. Why do they do so? They tell me it is to "strengthen and toughen" the small boys quickly. Besides this, it also communicates to tiny boys that eventually they too must be initiated. In this way,

Photo 13. Initiate holds onto mother before thrashing ceremony

such boys begin the separation process from their mothers at an earlier age than their peers—not in reality but in their hearts. I have found that these fathers are the most anxious themselves about seeming masculine to their peers. Perhaps we see here an example of how fathers' concerns about being strong are expressed in how they handle their sons' ritual treatment. Finally, this observation establishes that some boys are subjected to ritual ordeals from a very early age onward in preparation for warriorhood life. "Who will be bravest and strongest?" these fathers seem to want to know.

Possum-Liver Spitting Ceremony   Later that morning, inside the culthouse, the next ceremonial event is organized. This is the possum-liver spitting ceremony, another act of masculine performance for initiates. The ceremony captures the interest of men who show no reluctance to cheer on their hamlet's initiates and cheer against those of others. The ceremony "demonstrates" which boys will become war leaders, virile hunters, and shamans. Like the thrashing ceremony above, it is a test of manhood. Those who fail in the task are stigmatized as rubbish men. From the boys' performance in this feat, men tend to generalize about the future masculine prowess and strength of the lads in other facets of warriorhood life. Consequently, boys are placed in competition with each other, as age-mates and as up-and-coming "men." But they can only compete and succeed over peers, not their elders, who completely control the course of the events.

First a man scales the culthouse roof and makes a small hole in its grass thatching. More men enter the house as the initiates are lined up. The women outside are gone. Some minutes later, the roof "window" completed, we look up from inside to see a hole just large enough for the moon face of a shaman to peer in from on top of the outside roof. The man is a senior shaman, and once again we see how the boys must face toward the sky—they will spit toward the shaman—so the symbolism of the sun's power and the shaman's control of it come into play. The guardians lift each boy, in turn, toward the hole. A bit of raw possum liver (mixed with leaves) is placed on the tip of his tongue. The possum symbolizes masculinity and the hunt. Its liver contains the essence of possum strength, which enhances male purity. The boy's goal is to try and spit this up through the roof opening and smack the shaman's face. All of the new and second-stage initiates have a turn at it. The bachelor-third-stage initiates do not take part in the competition, for such would be inconsistent with their dominant position over the younger boys. The crowd of men loudly respond to each boy's attempt. Those who fail are dismissed instantly. The successful ones find praise, and their success is met with finger snapping, the sign of masculine bravado. Men refer to them as war leaders, as boys with *jerungdu*. Although some 50 boys took part, only a half dozen succeeded in accomplishing the goal. What matters is that here again we see but one of many ritual examples of training for warrior aggressiveness.

Of the remaining days of first-stage initiation, two key rituals stand out: the nose-bleeding and the flute ceremony. They both occur later this day, and I will now discuss these in detail. Remember that other events and smaller ceremonies occur too, though to study ritual and gender we will have to largely ignore them.

The Nose-Bleedings   The nose-bleeding (*chemboo-loruptu: chembootu*, nose; *loropina*, a verb meaning to cleanse and expand) act is considered the single most painful ritual by initiates and men alike. Their feeling is understandable. Physically, nose-bleeding is a penetrating trauma of the nasal membranes. The psychological effect of nose-bleeding is enhanced by secrecy. So when it is done forcibly by men upon boys—and by surprise at that—this bleeding is like a violent assault whose effects are probably close to producing real trauma in initiates. Boys often refer back to the nose-bleeding with expressions such as "I feared they were going to kill me." The ritual symbols and personal meaning of collective nose-bleeding are highly focused on the actual blood flow. The assembled initiators always concentrate on a generous but controlled blood flow, the sight of which is greeted triumphantly with a unified ritual/ war chant. The ritual bleeding amounts to a forcible penetration of the boy's body boundaries. For, aside from its surprise and dramatic context, the psychological impact of nose-bleeding is greater when we realize how much Sambia emphasize the nose as a part of their self-image. Only the genitals are of more importance in anatomy. Yet the nose is second to none in notions of beauty and in the image of masculine gender, as we saw in the noseplug symbols. The nose also conveys symbolism of the penis, as we saw in reference to noseplugs in general and the cassowary quill-bone plug in second-stage initiation in particular.

Nose-bleeding is hidden from all women and children, for men are some-what ashamed that they do it. Bleeding is also done in later initiations, but this information is hidden from younger initiates until they are older and experience the final initiations. Sambia recognize two different procedures for nose-bleeding that are associated with different phratries. Traditionally, the magical knowledge of these different practices was hidden from men of opposing phratries in the Sambia Valley. This is because the magic is incorporeal property: ritual customs or trademarks of the groups. (We saw in Chapter 2 how theft of ritual could lead to war.) Following the Australian peace, the opposing sides revealed some of their magic to the other side. The most common nose-bleeding technique consists simply of thrusting sharp cane grasses into the nose until blood flows. This is always used in first-stage initiation. The other technique, forcing extremely salty water down the nose, is also painful, but there is less severe penetration since no hard projectile is involved. A beastly saline solution is made from soaking water in native vegetal salt, which is then sponged into the nostrils as the face is held upwards. Blood instantly flows following this action. This technique is used mainly in fifth- and sixth-stage initiations.

The cane-grass technique was used in the first- and third-stage collective initiations by all the Sambia groups in which I observed nose-bleeding. The practice is regarded as more dangerous than the water technique, mainly because men feel there is always a chance the cane grass might break off in the nose, risking death. After third-stage initiation, the choice of which bloodletting technique to use is made by elders on the basis of the phratry of the hamlet performing the rites. Among the individual men doing private nose-bleeding on themselves when their wives have menstrual periods, personal needs, not public glory, are involved: no one else sees them do the solitary ritual. But in public the cane-grass technique is riskier and more daring, so it is seen as the more masculine form. The men's experience seems pinpointed on the need of a hard projectile actually penetrating the nostrils to achieve the painful, inward-to-outward effect of blood release. Elders see the penetrating thrust of cane grass as necessary in accomplishing the act of nose-bleeding in first-stage initiation, which in turn is crucial for boys' gender change.

There is another general reason why nose-bleeding is felt to be dangerous. Sambia believe that all blood loss from cuts or wounds is dangerous. Left unchecked, they rob one of circulatory blood and even of life itself. Large cuts are handled immediately; even with minor scrapes, men are anxious to stop blood loss. (The single greatest expense in my fieldwork medical budget was for bandages; people constantly asked for them.) Blood is vital stuff. Like ourselves, Sambia view blood loss as a critical symptom of life-risk and a key indicator for later recovery. Birthgiving and menstrual bleeding also carry medical risks, but of a different sort, because the female body is believed "naturally" to control blood flow. In other words, nose-bleeding is done even though it is painful and the blood loss is disliked: men are that desperate to remove female contaminants from the body and blood to reinforce warrior aggressiveness.

Keep in mind that the initiates have already been through three days of ordeals. They have had no sleep, little food and water, and are becoming hyperactive and afraid of the constant surprises and tricks of the elders. This very morning the initiates' mothers are told sarcastically that their sons will be killed in order to be reborn as "men." So women again begin ceremonial wailing. Later we will see how the men's play on words about "killing boys" is dramatically used against women. The boys too are threateningly warned to "watch out" because of something that lies in store. The mysterious power of the flutes—heard, yet still not seen—comes into play again, heightening the boys' growing fear of the elders' power over the spirits and themselves.

In mid-morning the boys are taken far above the culthouse into the forest. (The men are very careful about concealing nose-bleeding from women.) Since dawn the men have worked to make an elaborate ritual setting near a small creek. After waiting some time in tense anticipation, the boys are led by their guardians up to the ritual site. The boys at first confront a massive vibrating wall of thick green foliage, a fence of young saplings tightly woven together. Pieces of the shaman's red headband are tied up in branches of the green mass. Inside and unseen to the boys, a chorus of bachelors shake the foliage, while making an eerie sputtering sound associated with ritual ordeals. The effect is calculated to be bizarre: approaching from the distance, it appears as if blood were dripping from the branches. The initiates are pushed into this "bloody" chaos, tied to the backs of their ritual sponsors so they cannot escape. They enter through a small opening at its center. Many scream, some squirm and struggle to escape, but all are thrust into this green barricade and through a muddy, narrow, inner chamber that leads only one way—into an even narrower, cagelike, 20-foot-long passageway of naked saplings, tied together as a fence on both sides (see Photo 14). Here it is impossible to escape. (The passage space was barely wide enough for me to squeeze through, and I am rather thin.) Lined up on the outsides of the fence-passageway are many warriors holding wild ginger stalks, which are believed to grow quickly. As the sponsor-initiate pairs push through the fenced enclosure, they are pounded on both sides of their legs and backs. Here again the pounding is believed to help the boys grow strong. Most of the boys cry; indeed, by the time they exit into the forest clearing, many look terrified. Several boys cry out for their mothers as the all-male audience looks on.

Now the initiates are grouped round the pool of a small brook flowing down from a thicket. A huge crowd of men assemble, fencing in the boys. The nose-bleeders themselves take center stage. Several are wearing upturned pig's-tusk noseplugs (worn with the tusk points turned up only during war and these rites). The men are serious; even as their tense bodies strain forward in anticipation of bleeding the boys, some of them actually grimace (see Photo 15). A "strong" man—an aggressive war leader—steps forward and silently plunges cane grasses up his own nose: in full view of the shocked initiates, blood streams down his face. He betrays not the slightest emotion. He bends over into the water to let blood. Somewhere, still out of sight, the

Photo 14. Sponsor carries initiate through nose-bleeding passageway

flutes hauntingly serenade his feat. The crowd of men respond with a loud war cry, a signal that they want more. Only now do the boys grow truly alarmed, realizing what is to happen.

The first boy is quickly grabbed. He struggles and shouts but is held down by three men. Before we can catch our breath the initiator, Karavundun,

Photo 15. Men prepare to nose-bleed initiate

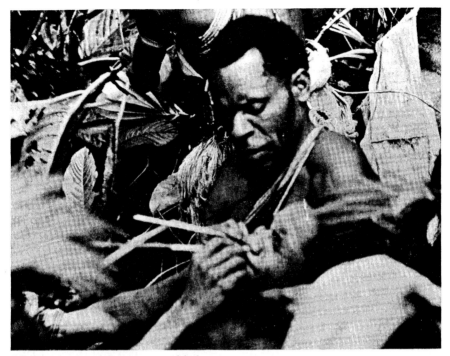

Photo 16. An initiate is nose-bled

rolls cane grasses, pushes the initiate's head back, and shoves the grasses repeatedly into the boy's nose (see Photo 16). Tears and blood flow as the boy is held and then relaxed forward over the water. Next one and then another boy is grasped and bled. One lad tries futilely to run away. Seemingly as a punishment, he is bled harder and longer than the others. The next initiate resists fiercely, so four men lift him off the ground and, there suspended, he is forcibly nose-bled. After each boy is penetrated until blood flows profusely, the men raise the ritual/war chant time and again. The smell of blood and fear sours the air. The act is almost mechanical for the initiators, who are the boys' clansmen, cross-cousins, and matrilateral kin. The guardians passively assist by holding the boys. The initiates' fathers stay removed.

Many of the previous first-stage initiates, from an initiation held several months earlier, are nose-bled again. They stood in the wings of the group. Some resisted; others did not. They were not as frightened as the new initiates. I am stunned; the emotions are so heavy, the scene nearly overwhelming.

The reactions of the boys intensify. Many struggle and are forcibly bled. The men show little pity for the lads, and those who resist are even more severely bled by prolonging the action and thereby brutalizing it. All of the initiates were bled. Afterwards, they remained standing over the stream to let the blood flow. The water ensures that women cannot discover any signs of blood, and it also allows the boys to wash themselves off. Then sponsors dab the boys' noses with ferns, wiping the face clean of any remaining traces of blood. An elder carefully collects the leaves, but we are not told why.[5]

Following the bleeding, the boys are lined up by the stream for the ritual teaching. The men's speeches describe the nose-bleeding as punishment for the boys' insubordination toward their fathers and elders. Women's pollution is also mentioned. Merumie, a respected fight leader and shaman, does the ritual teaching. He begins by telling the initiates about the norm for male hospitality:

> If a man visiting your hamlet comes and asks you for water, you must offer him some. You must not hide your water vessels. He ought to be given water; if there is none, you must go and fetch some, even if it is dark and raining.

The boys are told always to obey their elders' instructions and fetch water when asked to do so. Next Merumie reprimands the boys, saying that as children they made "bad talk" and sassed older ritual initiates. He says that if the boys defy their elders' orders to fetch water or betel nut, they will be nose-bled again as punishment. For this childish insolence, Merumie says, "We now pay you back." The boys are told they must "change their ways."

Last, Merumie lectures the boys on their mothers' harmful effects and the value of letting blood:

> You [initiates] have been with your mothers . . . they have said "bad words" to you; their talk has entered your noses and prevented you from growing big. Your skins are no good. Now you can grow and look nice.

A teaching about warrior aggressiveness was also performed until the first-stage initiation in 1973, at which time it was abandoned. Traditionally, elders stressed that nose-bleeding could help boys become more fearless during warfare. They were told to be strong and fearless on the battlefield. Having been nose-bled themselves, they must never fear the sign of their age-mates' or brothers' spilled blood on the battlefield. In fact, elders stressed, the sight of their people's blood is a challenge to seek revenge against the enemies responsible for this loss of blood on their own side. Here we see the fear of nose-bleeding converted into the opposite: a stimulus to aggressive warrior-hood.

Stinging-Nettles Ritual   The Stinging-Nettles Ritual is performed two hours later. The boys are taken to a deeper part of the forest. There is no ritual teaching here. The men say simply that this act "opens the skin" by "burning off" the fine body hair of the boy's childhood skin, making way for the growth of a new masculine skin. Fresh nettles are rubbed all over the body, including the face and genitals. This is a tremendously painful act, and it is hard for me to see this done to the boys right after the nose-bleeding. It seems so brutal, and at one point I look away. The boys must feel somewhat like they have gone through an electric shock treatment. Many scream and struggle. Afterward they look dazed. This occurs immediately before the ceremonial

---

[5] The best and most sensitive account of nose-bleedings in New Guinea is in K. E. Read's marvellous book, *The High Valley* (1965), Chapter 3.

Photo 17. An elder begins the flute teaching (Note the small and large flutes)

body decoration and the penis and flute ceremony. So the nettles' rubbing has the effect of making novices even more frightened of the men and what is to follow next. In this physical ordeal we see once more the accumulating effect of fear changing the boys' basic consciousness. The flute ceremony is the key and final activity we will examine in this regard.

THE FLUTE CEREMONY

We will now study ritual behavior focused on the secret flutes. This activity occurs in two primary contexts: the penis and flute ceremony (hereafter referred to as the flute ceremony); and the new initiates' first entrance into the culthouse, an event that leads to sexual encounters with the bachelors the very same evening. The meaning of the flutes—as ritual symbols and as gender signs—stems from their verbal and nonverbal uses. So we will see the meaning of the flutes from the naturalistic behavior of the ceremonies, as well as from what people spontaneously say about them (see Photo 17).

Sambia have several types of ritual flutes, but they lump them together under the term *namboolu aambelu* ("frog female"). Some initiates associate this name with the fact that the flute sounds like a certain kind of frog-croaking heard in the deep forest. Remember too that only women hunt frogs, that the boys were fed frog by their mothers two days ago, and that the forest edgeland is the dwelling place of the female spirits. Each flute is made from

Photo 18. Elders and men look on as jokes are made about body decoration

freshly cut bamboo left open at one end. The hollow tubes vary in length from one to three feet; they also vary according to their thickness and color. Two types of flutes are blown vertically from the mouth (like a jug pipe); another type is blown horizontal to the mouth through a blowhole. Flutes always are blown in pairs, by bachelors or adult men. The flutes are said to be hostile to women and children. They are also felt to be "married" to the initiates, as we will see.

As the flute ceremony neared, I sat with the men in my party, who casually reclined on the grass watching the ceremonial decoration. (see Photo 18). Some pranks occurred. A married man nearby pretends to copulate with an old tree trunk. He acts as if the tree is a new initiate-fellator, contorting his grinning face as if to express the breathless rapture of sexual pleasure. The men around roar with laughter at this clowning. He repeats his show three times. More laughter. Lewd jokes are cracked. We watch the guardians prepare their wards by dressing them in ceremonial decorations (see Photo 19). A man nearby jokes that the sponsors are starting to act "strange," for, as they attach the boys' new grass aprons, our men say, the sponsors' penises are erecting! A second time they suggest that the sponsors' penises are erect. This bawdy insinuation provokes huge guffaws of laughter. Some men joke about others sitting nearby on the grass: they must "smell" the new grass aprons of the boys for they are "smiling." Later they will "coax the lads into sucking them," he says, which provokes more laughter.

This lewd joking amazes me as much as the homosexual horseplay I described earlier, because Sambia never joke like this! Something is very dif-

Photo 19. A ritual sponsor prepares his ward for body decoration and the flute ceremony

ferent here. I glance over to the initiates, who look puzzled, and then scared. What is next? they must be wondering.

Then came the flute ceremony itself. The atmosphere suddenly and completely changes. It begins in military silence as the initiates are lined up, decked out in their stunning new attire. They must await the surprises in store for them.

Way off in the distance we hear flutes. They slowly move closer. Two groups, each composed of four bachelors playing flutes, arrive from the dark forest. They slowly circle the boys. There is total silence but for their music. The boys look terrified: this is the first time they have seen the flutes. The flute players are paired; one man plays a short flute, another a longer flute, their musical chords harmonizing. They play for about five minutes; otherwise there is dead silence. During this period, Karavundun (the same man who bled their noses earlier) picks up a long bamboo containing a narrower flute within it. He passes down the line of novices, attempting to insert the tip of the smaller one (contained inside the larger) into their mouths (see Photos 20 and 21). About half the boys refuse to suck the flute. Karavundun does not press them. Nor is there an angry scene such as I saw at a different initiation flute ceremony, when Moondi's bachelor-friend, Erujundei, threatened uncooperative boys with a machete. When an initiate refuses to suck, Karavundun simply smiles. He even jokes about the stubbornness of those who react with displeasure. Some men nearby openly snigger at the uncoop-

Photo 20. An older initiate shows how to suck the flute

erative and surly boys. On the other hand, those initiates who take to the act, "correctly" sucking the flute, are lauded, the surrounding spectators nodding their heads in approval.

Then—in visible anger at the defiant boys—Kokwai, a bachelor and my friend, unexpectedly enters the scene and vigorously hits the novices with a long flute. An elder shouts, "Hit them hard. It is not like you were fighting them to draw blood!"

And then the instructing elder Merumei repeatedly intimidates the boys by drawing attention to the large assembled crowd of men: "You uninitiated boys like to make jokes. . . . Go on now, make jokes for the crowd here, we want to hear them!" He commands the boys: "You boys—open your mouths for the flute! They will place it inside . . . to try it on you. All of you, look at the large group of men . . . this large group. . . . You initiates put it [the flute] inside your mouths, try it!"

The flutes are thus used for teaching the mechanics of fellatio. In their first references to it, elders use themselves as authorities to verify their words. There are two groups of well-known elders who lecture. Damei and Mugindanbu remain at one end of the long line of initiates, while Merumei is at the other end. Kanteilo is nearby.

The elders condemn the boys for their childish mimicking of the flute sounds. As they do so, the flute players again strike the boys' chests with the butts of the flutes. Some boys cry. Mugindanbu says: "When you were uninitiated, you all played a game of imitating this sound 'Um-huh, um-huh.' Now tell us, does this sound come from your mouths?"

Damei adds, "You boys think fit to imitate the flute sounds, [so] now make

Photo 21. A new initiate is tested to suck the flute

this sound, show us how you produce it. Why should we elders *show you* how to make it!" Mugindanbu butts in, and points to Damei, our great older war leader:

All of you boys look at this elder. What do you think he has done? Heard the law this moment and grown to be big? All of them [the men] "sucked" the penis . . . and grew big. All of them can inseminate you; all of you can suck penises. If you suck them, you will grow bigger quickly.

The boys are sworn to secrecy concerning the rituals and then told of the fatal consequences of breaking this taboo:

For if you do [reveal the secrets], they will kill and throw your body into the river. Sambia boys, you will be thrown away into the Sambia River. . . . Moonagu [phratry] boys, you will be killed and your bodies thrown into the lower Sambia River. The big men will not help you, they will not jail us either; they will help us hide it [the murder]. This custom belongs to the Baruya and other tribes, [to] all men everywhere. . . . The sun itself brought this custom which we hold! If you speak out, the stone axe and the stone club will kill you. . . . When you were children you saw the bodies of initiates. They are like the nice *inumdu* [shrub], green, smooth, and young. They are handsome. Those initiates suck the penises of men, and they grow big and have nice skins too. If you do not, you will not grow quickly or be handsome. You must all ingest semen.

The elder Damei praises initiates of an earlier first-stage initiation two months ago. He reveals how the elders were pleased with those boys for their acceptance of homosexual activities. He thus urges the boys to follow the example of their peers over at the Yellow River Valley:

There we performed the rites. . . . Our initiates "slept with" [sucked] the men. They drank the men's semen quickly. The bachelors were pleased with the boys. . . . They felt "sweet" [erotically satisfied]. The Yellow Valley initiation was truly good . . . ! This flute we will "try out" [penetrate the mouth] on all of you. Later the men will want to copulate with you. . . . They will do the same thing.

Damei and Kanteilo then spontaneously represent themselves as authorities, testifying and sanctifying the "truth" of the penis teaching. They relate that only by ingesting semen can the lads grow truly masculine:

Do you boys see us? We have white hair. We would not trick you. You must all sleep with the men. When you were smaller you erected the poles for banana trees and did other things. Now we have initiated you; you must work harder. When you climb trees, your bones will ache. For that reason you must drink semen. Suppose you do not drink semen, you will not be able to climb trees to hunt possum; you will not be able to scale the top of the pandanus trees to gather nuts. You must drink semen . . . it can strengthen your bones!

In the next ritual teaching, semen is likened to mother's milk. Boys are taught that they must continually consume it to grow:

Now we teach you our customary story. . . . And soon you must ingest semen in the culthouse. Now there are many men here; you must sleep with them. Soon they will return to their homes. Now they are here, and you ought to drink their semen. In your own hamlets, there are only a few men. When you do sleep with men, you should not be afraid of sucking their penises. You will soon enjoy them. . . . If you try it [semen], it is just like the milk of your mother's breast. You can swallow it all the time and grow quickly. If you do not start to drink it now, you will not ingest much of it. Only occasionally. . . . And later when you are grown you will stop. If you only drink a little semen now, you will not like the penis much. So you must start now and swallow semen. When you are bigger your own penis will become bigger, and you will not want to sleep with older men. You will then want to inseminate younger boys yourself. So you should sleep with the men now.

Another man shouts that unless the boys drink semen, they will fail to blow the flutes properly: "If you do not think of this [fellatio], you will not play the flutes well. A boy who does not sleep with men plays the flute badly, for his mouth is blocked up. . . . If you sleep with men you shall play the flute well." (Tali, our ritual expert, says this is a double entendre: first, that boys who do not suck the penis cannot properly blow the flutes; and second, that this is because without fellatio their throats stay "blocked up" with the contaminated food of their mothers, like little boys, not warriors.)

In the final sequence, the boys' old pubic aprons are dramatically cut with a machete by the elder Mugindanbu. The limp pubic coverings then become the focus of a castration threat aimed at the boys as a warning against adultery. The flutes are played again for several minutes. Merumei then lectures and shouts to the boys:

> When you are grown you cannot become sexually excited over the attractive wife of another man. You can touch your own wife, that is all right. The flute will kill you, for, if you steal a woman, her sexual moans will cry out like the flute, and her man will kill you. If you touch another man's wife you will die quickly. . . . They will kill you. We are testing you now for the time later when you might think to steal another man's wife. Then, we would not just cut your grass skirt. If your penis rises then and you want to steal a woman, we will cut it off!

The elder cuts the old pubic covering midway between the abdomen and the genitals. "No one will help you, we will cut off your penis and kill you." By this final act, therefore, not only is homosexual fellatio praised, but premarital heterosexual activities are tabooed and condemned. Now the boys know the secret of the flutes.

Following the flute ceremony, which lasts an hour, the boys are carefully lined up for a final inspection before their ceremonial parade back to the culthouse. They have been on the move and constantly frightened all day. The large group of initiates file down the hillside to the danceground, preceded by adult men who form garrisons around the area, separating the boys from the crowds of women and children who have assembled for one last view of them.

A great spectacle this is. For several minutes, led by a renowned shaman, the initiates are paraded around the decorated danceground (see Photo 22). He then conducts them inside the new culthouse for the first time. (Until now, they have slept in a shabby lean-to, next to the culthouse.) From now on the boys will sleep in the culthouse till the initiations are over. This public display is the last occasion on which women can study the boys for years to come. This is a time of honor: the boy is dressed as a novice warrior. He is proud. This is his payoff for all the pain and ordeals. Mothers try to guess which boy is their son. Yet the tranquility is short-lived.

The moment the boys are out of sight, dramatic events unfold. The bloodied fern leaves (collected from the nose-bleeding ritual) are retrieved by Moondamei from his string bag. He unveils them surprisingly before the women. The men then bark out angry accusations that the women are "bad mothers" of the boys. Moondamei holds up a handful of the leaves, silently flaunting them (see Photo 23). He says the men had to "kill" the boys to make them into men. Suddenly, without warning, two men run over to a woman seated on the edge of the danceground. She is one of the boys' mothers. They grab hold of her and violently force some of the bloodied leaves down her throat. She is cursed and castigated and pushed away. They frantically criticize the other women too for "saying bad things" to their sons, thus stunting their growth. I was astonished; the woman's treatment was ghastly and shocking. (see Photo 24). The abused mother sits downcast on the ground, looking humiliated and sad. Her women friends are furious and rise to assault her

Photo 22. Ceremonial procession of decorated initiates on dance-ground

attackers. Meanwhile, another younger man hysterically charges into a group of women. He holds more bloody leaves, and with bow and arrows in hand he curses the women and chases them. He seems to be completely beside himself. Everything is chaotic and the language so blurred that it is hard for me to follow his words. I ask Weiyu (who is also watching him) what the young man is screaming. Weiyu says: "You women say bad things to our sons. You yell at them. Now we have killed them. You can eat their 'blood' because it belongs to you, you caused it. Only you can claim this bad blood!" Weiyu added, "The big men are cursing the women so that they will not say bad things to their younger sons later." The angry women search for the two men who assaulted the mother. They want revenge. The elders try to placate them. This fails. Finally the men pick up sticks and threaten them, a show of force which works; the women recede. The rebellion fails.

This drama continued for a few minutes more; the other women are chased away as the degraded mother sits alone, speechless. This was the most remarkable and graphic example of sexual antagonism in the initiation. Why were the younger men so hysterical? It seems that the blood and the sight of women here can create violent reactions in them. Something in their gender identity is so touchy, like an unhealed wound.

During the shouting outside, another cassowary quill-bone ceremony was performed upon the initiates inside the culthouse. Their ornamentation is quickly removed. They are stung very much harder this time, and as they

Photo 23. The war leader Moondamei reveals the bloodied leaves

cry, the men raise war cries to drown out the crying and thus prevent the women from overhearing.

A while later something striking occurs. It is dusk again and the women and children are gone. The boys are led outside and fed. Then they are led back to the culthouse. As they enter the area they hear the flutes being played within. The boys are taunted. "You can't go inside the culthouse," the men say. They shout: "It's the menstrual hut of women! . . . Women are giving birth to babies. . . . The babies [the flutes] are crying!" Then another man says: "Look! An *aatmogwambu* [female hamlet spirit] is in the ritual house!" The boys are afraid. They are led into the cult sanctuary just the same, and soon something even more remarkable happens.

The boys are seated on the earthen floor of the culthouse. After going through days of initiation—especially this particularly long and trying day—they look worn out. The elders are gone, leaving the bachelors in charge. A fire has been built and a smattering of men sit idly around the hearth.

Several shrouded figures unexpectedly tramp inside, playing flutes. There are two groups of four flute players each, as there were in the earlier flute ceremony. The actors are disguised. They wear raggedy old bark capes. There is silence again except for the flutes. A man says to the boys, "An old woman spirit has come. . . . She is cold, she wants to come sit by the fire." The flute players then squat to the floor, their bodies obscured by capes and shadows.

Photo 24. Women and girls look on in horror as a mother is assaulted with bloodied leaves

They are youths impersonating female hamlet spirits. A young man says, "She is an *aatmogwambu*; she has come to cry for you. . . . Go away! Not good that she swallows her spit looking at you. [A common metaphor for erotic desire.] You must help straighten her out. [Another common metaphor, this for sucking the bachelor's penis until ejaculation, which "slackens" the penis.] If you feel sorry for her, you must help her out." The innuendos are unmistakable: boys should serve as fellators to the bachelors.

The other bachelors then joke squeamishly among themselves about this "play." The flute players hobble around behind the tense boys, playing their flutes beneath their capes. The boys are again struck on their chests with the flutes and are told not to reveal the flutes' secrets. The bachelors unmask themselves. The boys are hit one last time on the heads with the flutes, which are then thrown into the hearth fire. The lads are made to stand near the fire, warming themselves and "strengthening" their bodies from the magical heat. The formal ceremony is over, to be followed by homoerotic play.

Several of the bachelors, including those who had cloaked themselves, come alive. It is nightfall; by custom what begins are the first erotic encounters that result in private fellatio between themselves and the boys. The bachelors begin with outlandish and unprecedented erotic exhibitionism, as is also customary: they lift up their arse covers, exposing their naked buttocks to the boys, while engaging in childish games that imitate—and thereby humiliate—the uninitiated boys the initiates previously were. Yet the initiates must honor ceremonial silence, the breaking of which causes them to be soundly thrashed. The bachelors dare them to laugh. This exhibitionism and reversal of roles are telltale signs of the special ritual circumstances: that the boys are still in a liminal state of being.

What soon follows, at first initiated by a few of the more aggressive boys, is the initially awkward, soon-to-be frantic, and then steadily erotic horseplay inside the house. This leads to private homosexual intercourse outside on the darkened danceground area. Not all the initiates and bachelors join in this, but most take part. It goes on all night long. And the next night too. And before the conclusion of the initiation five days later, all but a handful of the new initiates serve as fellators, not once, but several times more.

How do we explain the sudden change in the boys' mood? There is nothing mysterious in it. They have been tied down for days. No chance to run about, laugh, have fun. Be themselves. This is the first night of release from the terrible tension and fear. They go wild with relief. And some of their wildness is channeled into homosexual activities. In this way they can also "get back" at the men for what has been done to them. Already, then, we see a blending of homosexual activity and aggressiveness.

THE REMAINING FESTIVITIES

Later that night the elders return to the culthouse. A songfest and more teaching occurs, while outside sexual play continues. The next morning the all-night songfest breaks at dawn. All the initiates are involved in this. They are then taken to the forest for the usual purification ceremonies on trees, accompanied by the flute players.

Later that morning the initiates and elders are enclosed in the culthouse. No one may leave or enter. First a shamanic healing ceremony takes place. During this, men ingest hallucinogenic leaves and tree fruit. The hallucinogens serve two ends: to alter the actors' perceptual awareness and to enhance the boys' suggestibility to being taught ritual lore and the shaman's role. Elders recognize how boys have been subjected to difficult ordeals over the past days. The shaman's healing is a response to their concern. The men believe ritual anxieties can provoke further weakness in the soul at this point, making boys vulnerable to sorcery, sickness, and soul theft by ghosts. The shaman's exorcisms allay lingering anxieties on the part of boys and their kin. Shamans also prophesy. They predict which of the novices may become shamans or fight leaders and, in a morbid vein not unlike the enigmatic role of shamans, they also predict who among the boys may prematurely die.

What ritual instruction do the boys receive? Elders concentrate on teaching food taboos and masculine rules. The men detail the extensive and onerous food taboos believed vital to a boy's growth. The trancelike state induced by sleeplessness and the hallucinogens, men say, is particularly appropriate in teaching these taboos and hunting magic. The trance state seems to tap into a deeper level of learning than ever before. Sometimes when shamans are

Photo 25. An elder warns boys against adultery in the Iwouwi'u ritual

initiated, their apprentices compete for power in these trance ceremonies. Mythology is taught pertaining to the origin of sweet potato and the bamboo knife. Again, the urgency of ingesting semen, hiding homosexuality, and avoiding women are built into the whole experience.

These activities continue until mid-afternoon. Meanwhile, other men outside prepare for the *Iwouwi'u* Ritual, while women collect food for the name-changing ceremony that follows it.

Of all the rituals performed by the Yulami people, the *Iwouwi'u* was the most striking in this initiation. The context of the performance was highly emotional and dramatic for two historical reasons. First, the ritual represented the most fearful supernatural power associated with the Yulami groups. It had been traditionally performed in secret, and men of the Upper Sambia Valley had never before observed it. Our men, for instance, said that the sorcery power of the ritual enabled the Yulami to kill them, and they truly were afraid. Second, the ritual performance conjured up a dreadful history of warfare, sorcery accusations, and death, all of which directly concerned the participants. Men say that this turmoil began generations ago. We saw in Chapter 1 how legends tell of the immigration of the Seboolu phratry into the valley. The Seboolu subsequently raided and killed the Yulami people, the original inhabitants. A combined war party of the Seboolu and Sambia phratries attacked the Yulami. They fled south, seeking shelter with the Moonagu phratry group, later settling in their present locale. In the last generation fighting broke out between a Seboolu hamlet and Yulami over wife-stealing. The adulterous Seboolu men died in the following months, their deaths attributed to sorcery by the Yulami men.

Photo 26. A Yulami village elder argues over Iwouwi'u ceremonies

An ironic outcome of this tragic history was that sons of three of the sorcery victims were new initiates at Yulami. Because this was the first initiation ever performed jointly by the former enemy groups, a Yulami elder angrily warned the Seboolu men: "If your sons steal our women, they await the same fate as their fathers" (see Photo 25). The Seboolu elder Meinji, who lectured the boyso, agreed. He related how he felt sad for the deceased men and for their brothers and age-mates who had adopted the boys and upon whom the economic burden of their support had fallen all these years (see Photo 26). Adultery, bloodshed, sorcery, and revenge are still powerful forces in Sambia society.

An hour later, women burdened with gifts of sugar cane and banana began assembling on the danceground. (see Photo 27). They are preparing for the Name-Changing Ceremony, wherein the initiates publicly lose their childhood names and receive new adult names bestowed by their parents. The boy's mother not only has a say in the selection of the new name; here she is the first person to publicly say it. Adults henceforth refer to the boys by their new names. The boys themselves are tabooed from using these names with each other, and they may not use each other's childhood names. While they live in the culthouse, they use only personal pronouns in speaking to each other. This reinforces their status as liminal people. After initiation, when boys reside in the forest rat house, with the help of the bachelors they devise age-mate nicknames for one another. Subsequently, they refer to and address age-mates by their nicknames; even when older their peers may use these nicknames. (Women never do.) They retain the age-mate names in interaction with one another until third-stage initiation. This name change recognizes the

Photo 27. Mothers bear food gifts for the name-change ceremony

personal change in boys. They must forget the past: their childhood names are tabooed because they remind boys of early memories. Their new adult names symbolize their new adult identity. After the food gifts are offered, the men worry about women's contamination. Elders carry fire over the whole danceground to purify it of women's pollution.

Over the next three days, further rituals brought the initiation to its conclusion. On the fifth day of events (July 31) there was a full day of ceremonial activities, opened by agriculturally oriented rituals. These stress the economic responsibilities of initiates. In the afternoon elaborate *Wolendiku* ceremonies take place, teaching about fire-making and hunting. This series of rites and teachings ends with the Bullroarer Ritual. Here the men teach the secret of the bullroarer, a sound-instrument also played at ceremonies, matching what boys learn of the flutes. Then the entire ritual group returns to the danceground, where the adult men engage each other in the most violent thrashing of the whole initiation. They compete with each other in a final masculine test of strength. Here the boys see the full force of adult aggression in ritual. On the sixth day there were two key rituals at night. They also stress the economic duties of initiates, convey stories, and provide lighter drama. The seventh and final day (August 2) concluded the initiation with a Water Ritual, ending the taboo on drinking water.

The initiates as an age-set are taken the next day to the forest, where they will live in the special lodge called the rat house. Here they hunt forest rats and possum. They are removed from all contacts with women for weeks. Bachelors dominate them, socially and sexually, throughout this period. They are trained to follow all orders by their seniors and are hazed, shamed, and physically punished if they disobey orders. Socialization centers on the hunt,

Photo 28. The Yulami initiate graduates pose as an age-set

avoiding women, and serving as sexual partners for the bachelors. When the boys return to their own hamlet clubhouse, they are monitored for months to ensure that ritual norms are not violated. Elders, fathers, and bachelors are their main monitors. But age-mates, too, carefully watch each other's behavior, and they shame their mates or sometimes report to bachelors if they suspect violations of taboos. Boys are once again evaluated against the abstract images of the rubbish man or war leader. Those who are active, strong, assertive, brave, and successful in hunting and other male tasks are praised, while boys who fail or cry are mocked, shamed, and stigmatized (see Photo 28).

THE WAR RAID

Until the early 1960s, the collective initiations were followed by an intertribal war raid. The new third-stage initiates were expected to participate, and, indeed, Sambia say that such raids were often launched at this time in order for the bachelors to prove themselves. We have seen that third-stage initiation is a puberty rite establishing the social and biological maturity of a youth. The ritual system expresses concerns that bachelors achieve manliness in physique and interpersonal aggressiveness. They must demonstrate, that is, their *jerungdu*, their prowess. Chief recognition of this is granted in two contexts. First, in the ritual initiatory cycle, the youth is advanced to third-stage warrior status and he then assists in the first-stage initiation that follows immediately. He is individually selected by his elders as the dominant homosexual partner for a boy initiate. Their sexual intercourse marks the bachelor's social/erotic change from being a fellator (insertee) to a fellated (insertor). Because of his insemination, the small initiate can now be ritually incorporated into the men's secret society, and the youth is thereby ritually confirmed as a biologically mature male, the inseminator. The fellatio act also changes the character of their social behavior toward each other: it confirms that the bachelor is dominant in all encounters: social, ritual, and erotic.

War raids provided a military counterpart to this process of masculinization for the bachelor. The youth went on a raid not only to acquire hard experience on intertribal raids. It had a more specific function. The raid tested his *jerungdu* in the ultimate way: by killing another human being. That act of homicide constituted a final, incorporative rite of passage, needed to confirm his warrior manliness in the real world. Cold-blooded killing was an ideal; only a few ever actually accomplished it. But the best among them did, those who were to become war leaders. The others, whatever else holds true of them, knew that they were lesser men. And it is undeniably clear that, like the Papuan tribes of the Trans-Fly river (Williams 1936), Frederick Hendrick Island (Serpenti 1965), Southwest New Guinea (Van Baal 1966), and other peoples, Sambia believed that the highest expression of masculine prowess was this war raid and its glory.

There were two other ideals concerning the war raid. If he were man enough, the new warrior could attempt to capture a woman, steal a wife from the enemy tribe. The tale recounted in Chapter 2 illustrates precisely this possibility. Furthermore, youths were taught that if they did cut down an enemy war leader, they must not kill him immediately for his body would still yield something precious. Once the warrior had fallen, his semen could be procured either by masturbating him or awaiting his body's spasmatic ejaculation. That last burst of strength was felt to contain his greatest *jerungdu*, the physical power and life-force that had made him a war leader. The ingestion of this would transfer such powers to the youth. This was, ideally, the only appropriate occasion in which bachelors could temporarily reverse roles to fellate again.

The youths returning home from these raids were real heroes in the old days. The very fact that they were manly enough to brave strange and distant places with the seasoned war leaders proved their aggressive potential. So here another psychological effect came into play. A bachelor who could kill in war was someone to respect and fear. The younger initiates would do so. And eventually the women would too for they wanted a war leader, not a rubbish man, as a husband—or so the men believed. That men had killed or were capable of killing could never be forgotten by their wives, who, like it or not, were the only soft spots in the men's lives.

FINAL INITIATIONS: MARRIAGE AND FATHERHOOD

The collective cooperation between hamlets ends with the third-stage initiation. Further male development and ritual treatment is the responsibility of the bachelor's village after that. The bachelor must undergo three additional initiations leading to fatherhood and full manhood. Achievements of the highest order they are, Sambia reckon, for even the culture-hero Numboolyu had to surmount many difficulties to attain them, myth says. Involved too in these transitions are great psychosexual changes in the young men.

Youths remain residents in the clubhouse until their late teens or early twenties, following marriage and menarche in their wives. During this period they are exclusively homosexual. Once initiated, at ages seven to 10, no heterosexual activity is permitted and initiates serve only as passive fellators who ingest semen. No other sexual activity (including masturbation or anal sex) is allowed, and research indicates that none is practiced. The only other indirect sexual outlet is wet dreams, which are common among Sambia adolescent boys. After the third stage, then, youths switch from the passive to active sexual role with boys, inseminating them. This transition is fraught with anxiety. Elders recognize this, and they counsel youths to "go easy" in their sexual contacts. Thus the situation remains until marriage.

It may be difficult to imagine the tremendous power Sambia associate with sexual arousal because our society is much less restrictive than theirs. Just looking at a prospective sexual partner is for the Sambia teenager loaded with potential for arousal, fantasy, shame, and—in the wrong circumstances—social disapproval, scandal, or even physical punishment. Their sexual behavior is extremely structured. Until adolescence, all heterosexuality is ruled out.

It is the ritual cult that applies an absolute brake on the manifest development of heterosexuality. Three mechanisms do the work: institutionalized homosexual practices, female-avoidance taboos (especially regarding menstrual pollution), and fears of semen depletion. Not all heterosexuality is eliminated, only its overt expression. Boys may have fantasies about girls but cannot express them until later. Remember that even though heterosexual contact is suppressed, boys are encouraged by their fathers and elders to acquire semen so that they, too, can achieve marriage and fatherhood. The *gender function* of the secret cult is not to destroy heterosexuality, for this would be suicidal for the society. Rather, ritual creates a fierce, powerful warrior's masculinity, which is associated with a very highly structured heterosexuality. The men desire and dislike, even fear, intercourse with women. In a word, they are as adults *ambivalent* about women. We will see in Chapter 6 how they transform their fear and ambivalence into anger and hatred of women through behavior we can call "protest masculinity." But here let us consider how the three mechanisms suppressing heterosexuality—homosexuality, female avoidance, and semen-depletion fears—change for teenagers in their transition to full heterosexuality.

Third-stage initiation or "social puberty" brings a new period of sexual freedom to Sambia youths. For the first time in years they are no longer under the thumb of the older bachelors who sexually dominated them. Now the tables are turned. The younger boys are in the subordinate fellator role. Whereas before the youths had no sexual outlet available to them, not even masturbation, now they are free as bachelors to inseminate the initiates. This proves to themselves and to their age-mates that they are strong and have *jerungdu*, because their bodies are sexually mature and have semen to "feed" to younger boys. They feel more masculine than at any previous time in their lives. So the bachelors go through a phase of intense sexual activity, a period of vigorous homoerotic activity and contacts, having one relationship after another with boys. Their sexual behavior is primarily promiscuous, for the initiates are concerned mostly with taking in semen, while the bachelors mainly desire sexual release through domination of younger boys. Occasionally a youth and a boy will pair off for a few days or even weeks. But these infatuations seldom last long, both parties fearing that others will stigmatize them as "unmanly." The norm is for intense, promiscuous activity that usually subsides to less frequent but still steady homosexual activity.

Eventually Sambia adolescent boys become more interested in females. They cannot express this interest except by whispering risque jokes or gossiping privately. This is their "locker-room" talk. It peaks in intensity at marriage. (Yet all Sambia men in later life enjoy talking and joking about women, as this provides an outlet for otherwise pent-up feelings.) Teenage boys also begin having daydreams about sexual encounters with women. This is very private talk: they share these daydreams only with their most intimate male friends as they fear being shamed or punished. These conscious thoughts are also reflected in their night dreams. At this point adolescents report that their wet dreams shift from homosexual to heterosexual images. In a sense, these are the youths' first heterosexual *experiences*, so they react with anxiety when they awaken from a wet dream, fearing a spirit woman (the flute spirit) may have stolen some of their semen. These fears pass soon enough, however, to be replaced by more powerful concerns about interacting with and marrying real women.

No interaction is permitted with women until a bachelor has his fourth-stage initiation ceremony. This also functions as the formal marriage rite. Usually several youths simultaneously undergo this ceremony, together with their brides from other villages. It is an exciting, power-filled time of new social recognition for the young men and women, for they are undergoing such profound changes in their lives, the transition from being adolescent to becoming adults. And of course they have their first sexual intimacy with the opposite sex to look forward to—remarkable and dangerous thoughts about a total stranger! Perhaps the young man's fears are eased by having such clear-cut roles to play in the ceremony itself, which dramatically represents the unequal social positions of Sambia Man and Woman, husband and wife, from the very start. The ceremony is called *nuposha*, as we have seen—a name that also means "newlywed."

Nuposha: the name refers to all the brides lying flat on their faces hugging

Photo 29. Nuposhu (4th stage) initiates fully decorated and assembled for the marriage ceremony.

the earth in the dusty soil of the hamlet plaza, completely covered by their new bark capes. They are still and lifeless, corpses arranged for public review. There, in the groom's hamlet, the marriage bargain is formally sealed for life. The elders and the grooms have returned after weeks of possum hunting. A long rope, hung between tall poles staked across the plaza in front of the clubhouse, has suspended from it a string of packages of smoked possum, earmarked in payment of each bride. Everyone knows the youths caught the meat with their bare hands, which falls into the waiting and almost greedy hands of the bride's kinswomen. The youths stand stiff and alert, in full warrior garb, overlooking their brides and the crowds, peering stonefaced into the sky as they have been directed to do (see Photo 29). This is, after all, their first public appearance before women since they were children. They must be careful not to contaminate themselves by looking directly into women's faces or to betray their inner panic (*kowuptu*) and awkwardness at this drastic and long-anticipated moment. All the pomp and ceremony disguise this feeling, which is applauded by the onlookers, for Sambia dearly love such picturesque displays. Then there follows a great feast in celebration. The newlyweds do not, however, join in; the meat is forbidden to them, and taboos still keep them apart. This is the context in which custom begins to break down the great distance dividing the newlyweds.

For bride and groom alike, the marital contract has this rigid and stony-hearted foundation. The marriage begins in a mood of festive conformity to predetermined roles. Like clay figurines, carefully molded and colorfully glazed, the newlyweds are thrown into a staged drama not of their own design. The couple begin to interact slowly and cautiously, usually in semipublic situations with their parents present. The effects of these social and erotic encounters are important for the next stage in the couple's developing relationship.

Sexuality is part of a general pattern, not isolated from everything else. Newlywed men continue homosexual activity at their discretion until they become fathers. Since they cannot have genital-to-genital sex with their pre-menarchal brides, the initiates still provide a sexual outlet. But now that they are married and nearly adult, warfare and hunting activities occupy more of their time. They also begin clearing forest land, and with their wives' help they prepare it for gardens. Newlywed men are safe from female pollution by still living in the clubhouse, which makes it easy for them to have sex with boys after everyone else is asleep.

In order for young men to begin sexual intercourse with their brides they must learn two sets of ritual techniques: purifications to eliminate the chance of menstrual pollution, and semen-replacement techniques to help them against the loss of their semen. These are the two other mechanisms beyond homo-sexual activity that regulate the development of full heterosexuality. Men-strual pollution is dealt with by nose-bleeding. Monthly nose-bleeding to eliminate this contamination begins when the youth's wife has her first period. In this way, too, we see how the final initiations and ritual changes in gender are fully complementary and interlocking for the bride and groom. Before this, however, the semen-replenishment technique must be taught, so we will look at it first.

In the fourth- and then the fifth-stage ceremony, men learn increasingly better ways to replace their semen with white tree sap. Since semen contains strength, all sexual intercourse depletes men and deprives them of *jerungdu*. Heterosexual intercourse is felt by men to be especially draining. Depletion by boys is not feared, which attests to how much more comfortable male sexual contacts are, and how much more power is contained in female sexual contacts. So men are taught to ingest tree saps called *iaamoonalyu*, "tree mother's milk," which replaces the semen lost through heterosexual inter-course. The sap is privately collected from the trees or directly drunk from the trunk. How ironic that the tree sap is symbolized as "milky mother's sap." Like the homosexual fellatio teachings in earlier initiations, men seem to model both the semen and its substitutes on mother's milk, even though semen is thought to be a vital male essence! This seems to be another expres-sion of men's envy of women. This ritual teaching paves the way for the youths to have sexual intercourse with their wives.

The customary first sexual intercourse between spouses is fellatio. This is very difficult and sensitive for the couple, and one or both newlyweds may avoid this for months. For instance, Tali has always complained how he had to chase his wife for years before he could have sex with her. He says she would avoid it because she was afraid of him and because she had not yet had formal teaching from female elders about sex with men. My female informants say that it is not until their menarche ceremony—held at the same time as the men's fifth-stage initiation—that women are instructed in sexual practices. They then learn of heterosexual fellatio and semen ingestion in the functioning of their marriages. This does not mean they agree with the men completely about the meaning of sexual intercourse, only that the rituals are performed according to custom and have their personal impact at this time.

Initial heterosexual intercourse is both hard and exciting for the men too. Heterosexual fellatio is difficult for the men to begin. After all, they have only had sex with boys for years. Not all men can overcome their fear, as I note below. What helps the young men is this: newlywed brides dress in bark capes and wear cassowary quill-bone noseplugs such that, to a remarkable degree, they resemble young boy initiates facially (especially in dim light). Their breasts are also covered. This reminds youths of their long-standing and comfortable homosexual activities. The brides' similarity to boys and the fellatio thus help to provide an erotic bridge between the homosexual and heterosexual life-styles. Thus it continues until the birth of a child. (George Devereux told me that our distant cultural ancestors, the Spartans of Greece, hit upon the very same solution—dressing new brides as boys—to get men through their former exclusive homosexual attachments.) The young men feel that this boylike appearance in their wives makes the women more attractive. Here we have a clear example of how sexual intercourse is contextualized and made specific to the images and pressures of society.

The woman's first menses changes their sexual relationship. She goes into ritual seclusion in the menstrual hut. Her husband has his fifth-stage initiation and he learns purificatory techniques that ward off his wife's terribly feared pollution. The main ritual practice is private nose-bleeding. Again, unlike previous ritual nose-bleedings, this one is taught to the young men to be done in private, after each one of their wives' regular menstrual periods. These periodic nose-bleedings seem oddly enough to be based on the *havalt-nuntu* competitive value between age-mates. It seems like the young men must bleed themselves to "keep up" with the physical activity of their wives.

What matters is that learning this practice enables a man to have genital sex with his wife for the first time. Men believe that genital intercourse can pollute their bodies with menstrual/womb blood. By inserting their penises into their wives' vaginas, blood may penetrate into their urethra. It will then accumulate and "block up" their bodies, weakening them, bringing illness and death. Nose-bleeding is their only remedy or preventive measure. Sex and menstruation thus go hand in hand for the Sambia couple.

Genital-to-genital intercourse is harder for Sambia couples to begin. They are adults, and yet they come from such different emotional backgrounds. Sex begins only in the forest, far away from public view, for Sambia are very prudish. After a few months, people (especially parents and in-laws) will begin exerting pressure on the couple to go alone to the garden or collect forest foods, to encourage them to begin genital sex. The community expects the couple to produce children, which are crucial to village survival. It is at this time that newlywed couples are vulnerable to terrible jealousy, arguments, and wife-beating. The men are very insecure of their position in the marriage, and the women are able to do only so much in allaying their husbands' fears and anxieties about menstrual pollution and semen depletion.

Usually with time, and with children, these problems subside and the couple settles down.

This is the period of bisexuality for Sambia men. The men may still desire sex with boys, who are "safer" than women, but they can have genital sex with their wives too. The men must keep knowledge of their sexual activities hidden both from women (as usual) and also from boys, for they do not want boys to know that they may be contaminated by a penis that has entered the pollution-ridden vagina of a woman. The initiates themselves express concern over this, but there is little they can do except to figure out through the grapevine which men have sex with their wives. So we may say that young men are truly behaviorally bisexual. They enjoy sexual contacts with males and females. Sambia men themselves make no great distinction between sex with boys or women, for in both contexts they are dominant, "on top."

Men play down women's sexuality. Though the women are not controllable and are adults, men try to treat them as immature children. For instance, men generally deny that women have orgasms. They say orgasm is something only men have; they cannot imagine that women experience this. Moreover, the preferred sexual technique of men is the "missionary position." Most men also say that they experience ejaculation inside their wives very quickly, within minutes. They fear their wives' bodies and therefore the shorter their contact, the less chance of pollution or depletion. Of course this must affect and limit their wives' enjoyment of the contact too. In both denying women's orgasms and by being "on top," we see the men's need to affirm control of sex through their behavioral and ritual patterns.

The men continue sexual contacts with boys until their wives have a baby. Then the norm is for them to stop. Most men feel that homosexual activity after fatherhood is immature and unimportant. Strong social pressures are exerted on them to change their behavior and so they usually conform. They are becoming authorities in their community, so to continue homosexuality is to violate norms and undermine the whole social order. Moreover, it is felt by the secret society that initiates are the "sexual property" of bachelors, not married men, who have wives as sexual outlets that the bachelors lack. This is the meaning of the ritual teaching that the flutes are "married" to the initiates. Besides, most men prefer women erotically after marriage.

Are there Sambia men who fail to achieve these sexual transitions and move onto marriage and sex with women? Research has revealed only a rare number of such men in the valley. Kalutwo, a conservative, somewhat gruff man in his late thirties, is such a person. He has been technically married four times (twice to the same woman, a widow) under pressure from the men. But he dislikes women sexually and prefers boys for his sexual outlet. In his younger years this aroused little attention. Many Sambia men have troubled marriages and fear women. Kalutwo, however, is an extreme case. Each time the elders gave him a wife he would avoid her, and especially intimacy with her. Each woman in turn left him or was taken by another man. He has told me he has had sex (oral sex) only once with a woman (his second wife) and that she initiated it. As he has aged, the men have joked about him, mocked him for his marital failures. He himself has grown sadder and more dejected. He is stigmatized as a rubbish man, as one who has failed to make the transition into full adult marriage and fatherhood. For the Sambia, a man is not truly mature or respected until he is a family man. Kalutwo's problem is not so much that he continues having sex with boys. Several other men in the valley do this, but they are married and have children, so they are respected. No, Kalutwo is stigmatized because he *prefers* boys over women, so he has not conformed to the ideal manly social role. Kalutwos are rare; I know of only two other men in the valley who have the same sexual history and homoerotic adult preference.

Sambia consider Kalutwo to be a "deviant." No other form of sexual deviance occurs, however. For instance, it is forbidden to reverse sexual roles among males; no Sambia man could suck an initiate's penis. To do so would be truly shocking for it would prematurely rob the boy of his sperm, leading him to early death. This would be a moral outrage. Only two reports of such (hearsay only) are known to me. The best known of these was by a local man who is classified as being "permanently insane" in the valley. Thus Sambia do not polarize homosexuality and heterosexuality as we do; they allow more flexibility in this area. But they do have taboos and limits and a moral sense of what must never be.

When a man's wife has her first child, this signals his final or sixth-stage initiation. His wife goes into seclusion for many days. He learns all the final ritual techniques to maintain his gender: more purifications, more nose-bleeding, and more semen replenishment from tree sap. This final initiation marks the attainment of full manhood: fatherhood. It brings to a close a whole era of his life. He moves on now to becoming a parent, a socializer of his own sons. It seems understandable that for him to do this job in an effective way he should stop having fellatio with younger boys. It is fitting and timely, then, that during this last initiation a young man has revealed to him the most secret and important of all Sambia stories: their myth of male parthenogenesis. It is a story that explains the origins of the men's secret society and of ritual homosexuality.

The hero of the myth of parthenogenesis is none other than Numboolyu, the ancestor and culture-hero. It tells how once upon a time there were only two people, Numboolyu and Chemchi (Chemchi is the secret name for menstrual blood). They were age-mates. Both were of ambiguous biological sex, having small penes and feminine breasts. They were, in short, like hermaphrodites. Numboolyu was the bigger and older of the two. He initiated fellatio with Chemchi, copulating with Chemchi's mouth, for this, the myth says, was the only available orifice. As he did so, Numboolyu's breasts slackened and his penis grew bigger. Chemchi, however, grew bigger breasts and a smaller penis. The myth then alters their sexes, so Numboolyu is fully masculinized, while Chemchi is now referred to as "she," the feminized one. She becomes pregnant and Numboolyu cuts open her genital area, creating her vagina and permitting delivery of her first baby. Now they are married and Numboolyu may copulate with her vagina. Eventually she has another boy child. (Chemchi is the mother-ancestress and is also associated with creation stories.) The story might have ended happily-ever-after here, except that their sons grow up. And when the first reaches puberty, Numboolyu was presented with a crisis.

The firstborn son comes to Numboolyu one day complaining that his own penis is erect and he has no sexual outlet. What should he do? He wants a sexual partner like his father's wife, but none is available. For a few moments the father contemplates allowing his son to have sex with Chemchi, only to reject the idea because this would make himself jealous and would lead to fighting. Therefore, Numboolyu teaches his older son to have homosexual fellatio with the boy's younger brother, who has not yet reached puberty. This solves the problem of providing the first son's sexual outlet, while masculinizing the younger boy too. Numboolyu has them hide this from their mother (though the myth is silent about why they must keep it secret). In this way, the elders tell the young fathers, male and female were created out of an amorphous male being, womanhood was established, and homosexual fellatio became institutionalized in society.

This Oedipal drama is a surprising climax to the whole initiation cycle. Why do the elders wait so long to reveal the myth? It seems that they would want to allay boys' concerns earlier than at marriage. But the myth is a tale of confrontation between father and son who would compete in a drama of attachment over the same woman. Can it be that the initiations have been concerned with incestuous feelings all along? That ritual homosexuality is a cultural mechanism to prevent incest and patricide?

In the initiations the men pound in the idea that, because the boys have been too much with their mothers, masculinity is endangered. Men also know intuitively that they must powerfully and rapidly make up for having been aloof and distant fathers. So in the initiations, the men are suddenly and overwhelmingly present. From then on boys can live only in a male world, isolated, on pain of sickness and death, from females. Cut off from their mothers, the boys are harangued, beaten, radically resocialized, and threatened with terrible physical dangers, including death. The rituals demonstrate absolutely the fathers' power to punish. Whatever incestuous yearnings the boys may have had for their mothers are completely thwarted and repressed. Yet in the same ceremonies, the boys are also enticed with the promise of growing to be one of the men, of becoming a husband, a father, a warrior, a hero, and even in time an honored ancestor.

It seems that the myth reflects some deep self-doubt Sambia males have about being fully masculine. It shows that maleness emerges out of ambiguity, even femaleness. but this cannot be revealed to boys too soon as it might frighten them, raise doubts and fears of being feminized in the homosexual fellator role. So the story is hidden until they are grown, dominant, and can identify with the happy outcome of being successful like the ancestor.

Stripped of its tremendous drama, does this scenario not also describe the culminating stage of Oedipal conflict for boys in our own, manifestly blander, world: that the child shall forgo present desire, a task made bearable by the promise that lies in identifying with adult men?

Sambia reveal both the early childhood (pre-Oedipal) and pubescent (Oedipal) aspects of the development of masculinity. For the childhood stage, there is the close attachment to their mothers. This involves the boys in their mothers' world and creates a roadblock to the expectation of social manhood. They must separate psychologically from mother. Initiation does this. Then the boy can advance to adolescent Oedipal matters: to desire to *have* a woman like his mother, rather than *being* like his mother. And, with that accomplishment, he earns the right, pictured in the myth (Oedipal conflict), of identification with a desired, feared, admired father. Homosexual activity is the royal road to this gender achievement. However, it takes a long time to make it.

The promise at the center of that identification becomes explicit in the progression of initiations made known to the boy. In time he is fit for marriage, sets up a separate household, and reaches full adult status as a father and warrior, perhaps even becoming a war leader—the highest status one can achieve. Then he becomes an initiator like his own father was. It is his right and responsibility to fill his father's shoes. This means giving up sexual contacts with boys. But what he gains in social recognition and self-esteem more than offsets this giving up of a transitional sexual pattern he has outgrown.

6/ Ritualized gender development: continuities and discontinuities

How remarkable to imagine that in just two centuries or so the refugees who entered this valley in its virgin state could homestead villages and lands and construct the ritual world of Sambia. They began unnumerous and unpowerful. Now they are settled over a wide area, which they control politically through their fierce and hard-earned reputation as warriors. They have their secret society to thank for this. Yet, ironically, where they began as unorthodox invaders, today—through their cult warriorhood—they are the defenders of traditional orthodoxy: they use cult symbols like the secret flutes to dominate other groups and to subvert the power of their own women. The combination of this warrior ethos and their cult has made them conservative and authoritarian politically, and restrictive and prudish heterosexually. Never mind that the cult's power is based on an *illusion*—that the elders control female spirits who do their bidding for them—for this is a shared cultural fantasy in the society. Nothing is true, in the symbolic reality of human culture, unless it is first imagined. As Freud said in "The Future of an Illusion" (1927), no force is more potent than a religion that promises protection if only we will swear ourselves to its moral image of the universe.

Sambia male gender development takes a special and in some ways unusual form. The strict initiations and their harsh cultural images suggest that Sambia gender identity development is fragile and needs firm ritual boundaries and social supports. We Westerners so often think of homosexuality as the negation of masculinity. This view, however, is based in our own particular model (which is also a cultural image) of gender. The traditional Western ethos saw gender as a *biological* development leading into male or female roles and into "normal heterosexuality" as an adult pattern. This was so despite Freud's (1905) belief that all humans are "polymorphous-perverse," by which he meant that they can experiment and engage in various erotic pleasures. The anthropological data from Sambia and other New Guinea groups offer a different model compared to our Western one. It seems that gender is by and large a *cultural* construction; society can affect gender identity formation in many ways. In this sense, all gender signs are learned and symbolized patterns shared by the group. Yet there are limits to this cultural influence. Gender ideas are conditioned by the specific social needs and historical challenges of the group's behavioral environment. So gender roles can change by historical period, according to such factors as warfare, marriage, kinship, religion, and aesthetic fads. Though gender is plastic, there are still bedrock requirements for survival in simple societies like that of Sambia.

More than anything else, Sambia is a warrior society. It had to be, for the world seemed to be at war with itself. It is hard for us to imagine it even after reading these pages, to summon up that ghost of past war without underdramatizing its harsh cruelty hammering into everyday existence, or without dismissing it by a few glib sentences that must stand for the Sambia reality of man-to-man stone-age combat that could cut, tear, and decapitate human bodies—men, women, children—the victims of pseudo-enemies across the river or true enemies in the next valley. The fear and horror and glory of it permeated everything, filtering into everyone's way of gardening and playing and making love, because it was always so close and so possible. Warfare more than anything else shaped Sambia gender relationships and their cultural institutions.

The traumatic nature of Sambia initiation underlines this point and the high stakes involved in making boys accountable to this Spartan cult. The ordeals also attest to the great dilemmas men face throughout later life. The stiffness that parades as conformity to ritual norms acknowledges that the initiate's gender development is dangerously disjunctive and must be controlled. Therefore, moral and sexual choices must always be situationally controlled by rituals and gender taboos. It could not be otherwise in a culture whose moral dictates are defined as much by gender negation as by affirmation. This is true even though notions of bad and good are basic to the public talk of Sambia life. Let us now examine the way in which gender rituals *responded as a cultural system* to the conflicts of war and the controversies of sexual antagonism between the two worlds of men and women.

GENDER DISCONTINUITY

Sambia culture as an overall moral order of norms and rules primarily governs social behavior in public life. But secrecy is rampant, as we have seen. The alternative secret initiations of each sex create many contrasts in the formation of cultural knowledge and emotional expression. Sexual segregation for unmarried initiates in living quarters, and the different economic routines of men and women, reinforce these gender differences. In public we do not actually see the secret elements, only their surface ripples. Private talk between intimates of the same sex seems to utilize both public and secret ideas and feelings. Both public discourse and ritual teaching are also related but distinct from each other. Adults know this only too well. Children do not, at least at first: they feel that what they see is all there is, until they are sophisticated enough to grasp that mother and father are not only different beings because of their sex, but that they also have contrary attitudes, interests, and value standards. In childhood, then, boys and girls see differences between the men's and women's worlds.

The development of core gender identity is potentially problematic. Whom do children associate with most? Who is their primary caretaker, feeder, and guardian? Mother, without doubt. Whom do they most sense themselves to be, want to be like, and want to be with, mother or father? This question is harder to answer, though it is one that Sambia would understand, because the later gender differentiation of boys and girls is so different. Boys can want to be like father, but to want to be like mother creates grave difficulties. Girls are reared by women and they take on the female role. Boys, though reared by women, cannot do so. This dilemma is inherent in all human gender development, for males, though born of females, must separate and individuate into different cultural beings: "boys" and "men." To do so means that eventually they must *dis*identify with mother and fully *identify* with father. Disidentification in our own culture is usually a gradual and early process. It hinges on the mother's self-concept, the father's role, and the quality of the parents' relationship, at least until grade school begins, which channels children into wider secondary socialization groups. Among Sambia, however, there is an intense period of maternal attachment followed by the abrupt initiation of boys.

To fully grasp early gender shaping in children, we should briefly distinguish four forces in the child's life.

(1) *Cultural norms*, especially those surrounding gender roles. Here the child confronts two clear images of normative masculine (father) and feminine (mother) routines and roles. What remains problematic for boys is the difference between their definite sex status (male) and their indefinite gender-role status (they are not yet adult men). Initiation gradually resolves this dilemma.

(2) *Economics*: Men and women have very different economic roles. In children these are blurred. Even in childhood, though, we have seen how Sambia boys are trained to hunt, climb trees, and be more independent than girls. Girls get more babysitting and gardening chores. This dichotomy nicely illustrates a finding of a cross-cultural classic study of Barry, Child, and Bacon (1959). They showed a close association between economic modes of subsistence (agriculture versus hunting) and socialization training for independence or obedience in societies. Agricultural groups train children to be obedient, because they require steady, routine garden work. Hunting groups, however, socialize for independence and self-assertion, which are valuable hunting skills. It is not surprising that Sambia boys are trained to be more independent and girls are socialized for obedience, since Sambia have a mixed economy that includes both gardening and hunting. Yet we also saw how ritual resocialization tempers the hotheadedness of boys by applying ritual obedience standards.

(3) *Temperament*: This is the patterning of the emotional expressions and moods of the child. Temperament influences the child's gender identity. Boys

are again reinforced for aggressiveness and exhibitionism. We saw how temper tantrums occur in this developmental line. Girls seem to be trained more for submission and responsiveness to others. These patterns are all eventually highlighted in initiation rites.

(4) *Parents* and parental substitutes constitute a last main force, and a very important one indeed. Parents express patterns that are openly contradictory in influencing the child's gender development. First, they are married and yet they are strangers to each other, at least initially. Marriage is a very powerful bond among Sambia, and one that children seek and emulate later in life. Second is the quality of the particular parents' marital relationship. How warm or cool are they, and how much do they enjoy each other's company? Couples vary in this respect. Here especially age is a factor, since older couples seem more content and happy than younger ones. The more aggressive and warriorlike the man, the more harshly he seems to deal with his wife. Likewise, the more a culture trains a man for "protest masculinity," such as in the machismo complex—where men are always trying to prove they are strong—the more he will be aloof from his children (see Whiting and Whiting 1975). Third, secrecy surrounds sexuality and gender, definitely shaping the child's gender development. Heterosexuality is very much affected by it. Boys know nothing of the men's secret ritual homosexuality. They grow up seeing their fathers participate only in the heterosexual role. It comes as a great shock to them years later to discover that this strong and aloof masculine figure once sucked penes. This shifts a boy's later social attitudes about adult gender roles. He unlearns what he thought he knew (father is only heterosexual) in order to learn new information (homosexuality is required). Fourth, there are expressions of unconscious communications to children from parents. Sambia is a dream culture, and dreams are regularly shared as a part of daily life. These dreams open up a channel of communication from the parents' psyche to their children's. Mothers more than fathers share dreams, however, which underlies the stronger bonds with mother. Can we imagine that such intimacy does not affect core gender identity?

A final parental factor is violence between the spouses, which obviously modifies the perceived quality of their relationship. This violence must be seen as a patterned response to warfare and men's aggressive training. Squabbling is common between parents. Newlyweds tend to fight easily and to be jealous of each other. Sex is fraught with anxiety. Physical fights are common between young couples and are no stranger to older couples either. Sambia wife-beating occurs and is an ugly strain on the tenor of village life. Even suicide must be seen in this light, because female suicides outnumber male suicides three to one, and most of these result from wife-beating and marital arguments. Not a pretty picture, especially for the children who get involved in this violence. There is no question that children almost always side and identify with their mothers, the underdogs. Boys express anger and fear toward their fathers over this abuse of their mothers. I have seen boys try to hit their fathers in defense of their mothers. The fathers may not care that much, especially if they have a second wife and family. This violence affects the child's ability to identify not only with the same-sexed parent, but also to positively value heterosexuality as an expression of the quality of the bond between his or her parents. We may say that this identification with the quality of the parents' relationship shapes children's feelings—about relating to the opposite sex, about their potential spouse as a whole and valued person, and about their general ability to form cordial and mature relations with others in life, including their own children later on. The men see this violence in relation to the ever-present conditions of war. Warfare thus influences gender relations as a common denominator of the social consciousness of families.

We must return here to ask why women generally support boys' initiation at all. Let us review the reasons. The economic causes of women's responses to their sons' initiations are clear. A boy is a potential economic helper, especially as he grows older. Boys are unmanageable, as we have seen, yet even the worst of them still babysit and run errands such as fetching water or collecting bits of firewood. They assist in gardening by weeding, as their fathers never do. Mothers rely on sons more when they are the oldest children or there are no daughters. Some of them are certainly important helpers. Once initiated, this assistance is lost. Female-avoidance taboos mean that an initiate must completely avoid interaction with his mother or other women. His domestic assistance ceases entirely, except when he helps his father hunt or clear gardens. What his mother hopes for is that his initiation will hasten his growth and bring him to manhood quickly. This ideally enables him to hunt and cultivate gardens, which will help her. But never again will she exercise authority over him as she did in his childhood. However, this mother must continue to provide her son with food. That is her motherly obligation. Thus, although she loses a domestic helper, she must continue to feed him without much reward for years. Women do this, no doubt, with several motives, including their love of and pride in their sons, as well as their own sense of self-esteem as women and mothers. The pragmatic aspect of it is that if their husbands die, their sons can support them later. Moreover, women are given no choice by their husbands' clan or the men's society as a group but to surrender their sons. Nor can we dismiss gender beliefs: no matter how cynical are women of the men's society, they still accept the need to masculinize boys through initiation.

Women's reactions to the first-stage initiation go beyond rational economics to reveal deeper emotional tensions. We saw the mothers crying for their sons at the start of initiation. We also saw how women identify boys with their fathers in the ritual context, while men identify initiates with their mothers. This tug-of-war is understandable. If a boy is in the shadow of the female sex role by virtue of his attachment and associations to his mother and her domestic chores, he is also estranged from his father's clubhouse activities. The boy is, as it were, always standing on the outside of the men's clubhouse looking in on his father's mysterious life with his cronies.

What role do mothers play in helping or hindering the boys' transition into the men's club? Aside from the immediate economic disadvantages, there is the emotional loss. This loss is sharpened because of a woman's relatively nonsatisfying relationship with her husband. We have already noted the women's lack of a choice of mate; the chauvinistic attitudes of men and the restrictive sexual rules of the culture in general; the demeaning stigma of menstrual pollution and birth pollution; the men's fear of sorcery through food and sexual pollution; and the apparent one-sidedness of marital sexual relationships. It is clear that Sambia men perceive women's gender differences in largely negative terms. There are several reasons for the men's devaluation of femininity, and one of the strongest centers on male "envy" of female birth-giving and breast-feeding powers. We will study that below. But what of women's feelings about the rigid limitation on intimacy and endearment between spouses?

One likely result of men's aloofness is that women share joy, companionship, and intimacy with their children instead of with their husbands. Women turn to their children for support and confidence, as the companions their husbands are not. Remember that women are imported from hostile villages. The mothers and sisters of her husband can be from different clans. This limits how women, who are outsiders, can support each other or be intimate companions. I think mothers are very close to their daughters. But remember here too that these daughters will eventually marry and leave the village. They will not be the same kind of economic supporters as sons. Sons are males, like their fathers, so mothers tend to respond to them as such the more they mature. Therefore, it is understandable that a woman could displace feelings about her husband onto her son, both her aggressive and her nurturant impulses. She would perhaps project her own anxieties and cares into her son's future. This emotional process starts at birth and is reinforced by the long breast-feeding and postpartum taboos that separate spouses. Women like to nurse and some seem reluctant to wean children off the breast. Why? For one thing, this means they will return to a difficult sexual relationship with their husband, which begins again after weaning. If it is true that women find affection in children as compensation for what they lack from their husbands, then we might expect them to be ambivalent or even negative about a son's growth and initiation. For all these reasons, we could hypothesize, for instance, that an only male child would experience greater problems of attachment and disidentification from mother than would a boy born into a large family of children. These are strong feelings and they are not easily changed as initiation approaches.

The main teachers of children are their parents. But because of men's aloofness, mothers are more available and, Sambia believe, the more important influence on personality. This view runs counter to male ritual dogma: men are ambivalent about their mothers' influence on them. Initiates are less so: many of them identify with their mothers. Sambia believe that the boy's soul is purely bestowed by the father and is nourished and matured through initiation. In private interviews, some initiates say they did learn things from their mothers. But most men flatly deny such an idea. Have the men forgotten what they learned in childhood? Or are they simply protesting their masculinity, denying any female influence in their personalities? Not quite. No Sambia ever denies the fact of biological heritage or subsequent maternal care, for instance. This maternal bond and the women's world it represents color the morals and personalities of all Sambia. Yet the men are loathe to acknowledge it. To be polarized against the women's world and reject it is no less a feat than the rejection of a part of one's own moral personality and gender identity.

In the Sambia world certain adult idiosyncrasies can be indulged, so long as they do not disrupt the social order. Disagreements can be settled through long talking sessions or moots. Some wrongs are supernaturally punished. Sickness and social malaise are dealt with by shamans in healing ceremonies. But make no mistake: dangerous troublemakers are eventually killed. In these contexts Sambia believe that the individual's personality has become "opposed" to customary behavior.

The social problem of how to handle uninitiated boys is of far greater magnitude for the men, however: here it is the difference between childhood personality and adult masculine expectations that motivates the initiation of boys. Boys as a cohort are viewed as socially unproductive and irresponsible. Though a part of the women's world, the women cannot control them. To make boys obedient to elders and to ritual customs, they require initiation to bring their personalities into line with ritual directives. So they are drafted into the secret society. Nevertheless, the outcome is a problematic discontinuity between the personality and domestic world they experienced as children, and the ritual roles that make them opposed to the men's negative images of mother and childhood.

The two broad contexts of socialization, childhood and initiation, are associated with the very different value standards of the two worlds. Boys and girls are both exposed to the women's domain, but trained somewhat differently in childhood. The differences increase as they age and mature in relation to context-specific factors.

1. Values underlying male/female sex-role socialization are explicitly different: assertiveness and independence are stressed for boys, while compliance and dependence are reinforced for girls.

2. The authority and control over socialization change. Infants and children are primarily trained and disciplined by mothers. They are controlled by women and are thus responsible to the norms of women. Once initiated, however, boys are removed from women's authority and kept under strict control by older males. Girls are fully involved and under the authority of older women until marriage.

3. Because of the great disparity in the ages of males and females at initiation, each sex differs in its susceptibility to ritual socialization. Being only seven to 10 years old, boys are highly susceptible to coercion in their ritual gender changes. (We will review this idea in the next section.) Girls are in their late teens at the menarche initiation, and they seem less susceptible. Early initiation creates great transformations in boys' social and sex roles years before those of women. Female socialization is thus steadier and more continuous than that of males.

4. Boys are therefore socially pressured to conform to adult roles earlier than girls, and they are exposed to more behavioral dangers in warfare than girls. The early age of Sambia ritual resocialization, which opposes early training by mothers, is a function of the dramatic changes expected in males' adult behavior. In general, the greater the pressure to dramatically change male social behaviors in New Guinea societies, the earlier initiation will occur.

5. This pressure includes coercion to "unlearn" behaviors learned in the female world, and to learn to perform skills and attitudes expected of the adult men's society.

6. Socialization for sexual behavior also differs between the sexes. Boys experience sexual behavior years before girls do. They engage for at least a decade in promiscuous homosexual activities, then they marry and experience heterosexual behavior the remainder of their lives. Girls, as far as is known, do not engage in homosexual activities. They are trained only in heterosexuality. Discontinuity is marked by secret versus public sexual role-behavior models, since boys have only the father's heterosexual role to model themselves after in childhood, whereas they are expected to have only homosexual behavior after initiation. After fatherhood, they can have sex only with women.

7. Socialization after initiation is done by the same sex. Boys are trained exclusively by their fathers and other initiated males. Girls are trained by their mothers and other females. These same patterns are perpetuated in adulthood because parents rear children the same way they were reared. Thus the two worlds remain antagonistic.

RITUAL BRAINWASHING

The ritual resocialization of first-stage initiation leads to a new gender identity in a boy. The processes of identity change are very clear, and their final success is determined by visible outcomes (body physique, masculine personality traits such as prowess, and masculine achievements in war and hunting) the men's society wants and needs. The changes are defined by men as "purely masculine, not feminine." Let us focus now on how these collective rituals act as a process of internal "thought change" in boys. Or, to put it more crudely, how they "brainwash" the boys' childhood identity. Whiting et al. (1958) introduced the brainwashing analogy. As an analogy the idea is fine, but it should not be taken too literally compared to modern political torture.

Various manifestations of extreme and often traumatic ritual actions occur in initiations. We saw how elders use nose-bleeding rites to force obedience to their authority. These traumas force boys to accept their lowly positions in the men's cult. But this does not explain why and how boys *internalize* the concepts and explanations of the men's rituals. Boys' experiences differ so radically from those of the secret ritual world. What is the mental process by which these identity changes occur? Remember that the boy has been forcibly separated from his parents and that his separation anxiety is the foundation of the rituals. The boy feels he has lost his mother. Then he experiences intense fear, excitement, uncertainty, and exhaustion in the ritual ordeals. Let us review these events at the Yulami initiation:

1. The boy has no sleep for the first two nights. When he dozes, he is awakened, sometimes forcefully, to frighten him. He becomes worn out.

2. He is led in continuous dancing for approximately 10 hours on the first night of moonlight ritual. There is singing, excitement, heated rhetoric, and physical pain, inflicted both by men and women. Then in the wee hours his mother gives him rich food in a highly emotional setting. He and his mother cry and then part. More dancing occurs on later nights.

3. He experiences many terrifying ordeals. By the third day, when he experiences the flute ceremony, the boy has had two beatings, two thrashings with cassowary quill-bones, numerous "ceremonial" (often painful) blows, been forcibly nose-bled, and rubbed with painful stinging nettles. Quite a change from his boyhood freedom and lack of discipline!

4. He has had no water and little food.

5. He is subjected to mental confusion by being persistently bombarded with surprising and frightening assaults, such as the thrashing rites and Nettle Ritual. He is repeatedly tricked into expecting one thing, only to have something else occur. Since he is not informed honestly but is exhorted with deceit, he becomes mistrustful and uncertain.

6. He is ritually secluded and hardly sees his father. The boys say they feel sorrow, longing, and also anger toward their parents during this liminal period. They feel betrayed and abandoned.

7. He is verbally assaulted, often with vicious language, by his own elders, who are loved authority figures. This is extremely unusual behavior. Men do not curse children or initiates, as we saw. But in ritual they have the license to do so, and the harsh language itself is enough to make the bewildered initiates cry.

8. The initiate is continuously threatened. He is threatened with death when the secrets of the flutes and homosexuality are revealed to him. He is threatened with castration if he commits adultery. His parents, and especially his mother, are also threatened by implication if he betrays cult secrecy.

9. He is bombarded with shocking information and sensations. Some of this information is secret and must remain so upon pain of death. He has many new beliefs and notions suggested to him. For instance, he is told that the flute *is* penis; that semen *is* mother's milk; that his eliminated blood (from the nose-bleeding) *is* polluted; that all women *are* polluting; and that semen *is* the only means of attaining strength.

10. The boy must submit to various acts which make him feel dominated, even ashamed. A powerful one of these is his fellatio performed on a bachelor marked for him by the elders. His sponsor and older initiates (and perhaps his father) act as authorities in persuading him that this act is vital to his masculine growth. The spirits back up their power.

11. Finally, he loses his childhood name and attire, and is given a new name with new social rights and obligations to others.

Similar ritual techniques have been widely reported in Sargent's (1957) well-known study of the psychology of religious conversion and political "thought reform." Sargent was impressed by the remarkable parallels in the methods religious and political cults used to achieve the same brainwashing results. His approach questioned the physiological mechanisms underlying "how beliefs can be forcibly planted in the brain" (Sargent 1957: xxiv). His examples came from historic English Protestant reformist groups, brainwashing techniques used in modern warfare, as well as initiation rituals in New Guinea and Australia. He showed how brainwashing used isolation, fatigue, tension and sustained uncertainty, fasting, and vicious language to initiate change.

Sargent explained how the brainwashing works in this way. First, anxiety arouses attention, which increases the person's suggestibility and receptivity to new beliefs. Second, tension and excitement induce mental conflict, which impairs normal judgment. Third, so much excitement and anxiety not only heighten suggestibility, but create mental confusion, enabling radical thought reform in a person. Once the stress is removed, the suggested information remains in the mind, as occurs in hypnosis. Finally, Sargent argued that ritual experience in New Guinea uses the rhythms of dancing and percussion instruments like the flutes to "disorganize and exhaust the brain." The rituals suppress old behavior patterns through pain and fear that carry boys to the point of "emotional collapse and increased suggestibility," making them embrace the "salvation of a cult life" (Sargent 1957: 88-97). This causes boys to surrender their "childhood habits" (Sargent 1957: 94-95). Here we see, then, a psychological model that explains the power of Sambia initiations to fundamentally alter boys' deepest core identity.

Research in other areas of the world supports this same viewpoint. The susceptibility of humans to stress and coercion was documented in controversial experiments at Yale by Milgram (1974). He found that people would take orders from authorities to the extent of giving lethal shocks to experimental subjects. Why are humans prone to accept authority? The Spindlers (1982) have shown that in many areas of the world initiation and other cultural institutions reinforce basic cultural emphases that are unacceptable or unknown elsewhere. They are relative and become meaningful in their cultural context.

Brainwashing is a "stripping process" in which boys have elements removed or stripped away from themselves. The physical part of the process emphasizes the removal of female residues or essences, like skin flakes and blood. The mental counterpart is the negation of "feminine feelings" or behavioral traits, such as crying, shyness, and gardening or babysitting habits. The negation is involuntary. The coercive initiations leave boys no exits of escape from the identity changes. Later we will see, through boys' own words, how they internalize the coercive teachings. This brainwashing resocialization stresses only the negative side of rituals. Now let us see the positive side of their new identity formation.

THE LIMINALITY OF AGE-MATES

Earlier I noted that ritual has been called a *liminal* period: the social and psychological arrangements of initiation place boys outside the realm of "normal society," on the margins of everyday life. Liminal people such as initiates live in culthouses where there is a sense of timelessness, because what they are doing is special and they have never done it before. Time passes slowly when we discover new things. It is an amoral period too, when regular moral rules are suspended. We saw this at the culthouse, where blatant homoerotic horseplay goes against the ordinary rule prohibiting sexual exhibitionism. The grotesque and bizarre are highlighted, both from the elements of culture (the nose-bleeding ceremony) and from the unconscious (boys' dreams). Myths told at this time stress fantastic events that explain why the rituals are performed. The myths too turn normal morals on their heads. The parthenogenesis myth speaks of incest desires otherwise unheard of and unthinkable to Sambia. The initiates reflect on their new personalities and social positions during the long quiet hours of painful seclusion following ordeals. As true liminal beings, they wonder who they are becoming and contemplate the basic identity question, "Who am I now?"

But the fact that boys undergo this transition experience as a group is another important part of the identity process. May we say that they see in each other another self like themselves? Yes, for they know that they are not alone. Though the group treatment denies their individuality, it has the positive function of permitting them to form deep new bonds of male friendship and masculine comradeship with other boys. In this sense boys withdraw a large part of their feeling of themselves—their mental energy—from their parents and reinvest it in their age-mate group.

Age-mate bonds are thereby created in this liminal period of initiation. The bonds have wide ramifications for society. The age-mates become comrades-in-arms. Some become devoted to each other as lifelong intimates. The initiates, parents, and others involved also experience changes in their normal routines and social relationships. For example, the food and sexual taboos of the boys' fathers alter relations between parents and the sexes in general. The men's hunting and rituals temporarily restructure residence and cohabitation. Yet, it is the initiate who is the real object of these changes. We have seen him taken through the gamut of ritual transitions: first separated from parents and siblings, then isolated and enclosed (at the culthouse and then in the rat house), and finally, he is re-incorporated with a new identity and role into the men's clubhouse.

Ritual treatment of boys as members of a unit constitutes an alternative type of learning to that of the Western classroom setting. We may call this learning by group identification. Boys are identified as a cohort by the men. This is why they are fixed the rest of their lives as an age-set. They are treated as a batch. Indeed, sociologist Erving Goffman (1961) has referred to a similar process among psychiatric patients as "batch living." The total needs and living arrangements of the initiates are handled as a batch by the institution of the secret society. Boys are treated not as individuals but as members of a team unit, the warriorhood. Their identification as age-mates, and their feeling of camaraderie with each other, are waited for as sure signs of their transition from unruly childhood.

What is the emotional impact of sharing these experiences with other initiates? They support one another during ordeals. Silently they sit and eat together, or stand together and hear ritual harangues. Their common suffering in painful rites makes the boys fond of saying of age-mates, "We cried together." They are exposed to the same taboos and social obligations. All these experiences boys see as ordeals. Years later when comparing their initiation experiences among themselves, they appeal to each other's understanding and make light of as much as possible by recalling the funny moments. They do not like to remember the pain. In these ways age-mates experience rituals that mold close associations.

The implicit competitiveness between age-mates becomes more important as they mature. Even in the rituals there is competition. We saw a good example of this among the novices during the possum-liver spitting ceremony at Yulami. This is a test of strength. Initiates are awkward and tired, but they still met the task. Elder brothers and clansmen were keen to see their boys succeed and be called "strong." Their relative achievements quickly labelled the boys as rubbish man or war leader. In this simple ceremonial act, the lads are brought into competition with each other.

We can see here the politics of the secret society already invading the boys' lives. The initiates perform for a special audience, their seniors. These men belong to opposing hamlets and phratries. The importance of this political audience increases as the boys mature and are advanced in rank through subsequent initiations. By then the fathers are elders, spectators for the youths who are older and aggressive. In the first initiation, ceremonies such as the possum-liver spitting are an expression of ideal values. Boys should ideally be strong, in this ceremony as elsewhere, for it is an indication of their budding masculinity. If one of them excels, the others should match his achievement. This is the result of the value on equivalence. Equivalence implies a sameness of size and ability, which is embodied in the image of the age-mate bond. So if a boy fails at performing, the competition is plainly exposed, the age-mates' cohesion is jeopardized. The village gains by the reputation of its strong new warrior. Such tests lead to the bravado of bow fights, which lead to intervillage wars. So we can see why boys' performances in these first competitive matches are evaluated by elders in the language of warfare: rubbish men versus war leaders. Another example of this process was when boys were praised for being brave during ritual ordeals or were criticized for showing their fear. Men also compared the decorations and appearance of the lads during ritual processions. Boys are even compared on the basis of who are the most willing fellators. These competitions become more direct and aggressive as they mature.

The initiation shows that age-mates have divided loyalties from the start. They are reared in a hamlet and their primary allegiance belongs to its kinsmen. Their kinship and residential ties are thus in potential conflict with their obligations as age-mates. The political dilemma in the relationship between age-mates is simplified if we compare their bonds inside versus outside of the hamlet. Yes, ritual does create emotional camaraderie between initiates, but boys of the same hamlet are more closely identified with each other than with their mates in other villages. Boys of a hamlet are, after all, reared together as "brothers." They have been constant companions from childhood. Their guardians treat them as natural age-mates, which is the normal development cycle in all Eastern Highlands tribes such as Sambia. Mates reside in the clubhouse of their own hamlet, and this is where they spend most of their time. They may be friendly to age-mates in other hamlets, but their loyalties always belong to their clansmen. When push comes to shove and a fight breaks out in the valley, age-mates do not hesitate to battle each other. They do so not to kill each other, but to put them in their place and remind them that they will take no guff. If the valley were attacked from outside, however, these conflicts would be put aside. The mates of the confederacy unite to repel the invaders. What matters, then, is that age-mates could fight each other but would form a coherent group in dealing with foreigners.

RITUAL SYMBOLISM

Ritual socialization and gender identity change do not occur only through the process of group identification between age-mates. The collective cultural symbols of initiation ceremonies are another means of learning. This type of socialization is symbolic learning. It occurs at both conscious and unconscious levels of experience. We may identify three types* of symbolic learning in ritual: (1) verbal meaning, which stresses the conscious meanings through what people say about the symbols; (2) operational meaning, which is more conscious and is based on how symbols are used in a single ceremony; and (3) positional meaning, the experience of a symbol that emerges from being exposed to it in a whole range of ceremonies. This latter type is mainly unconscious. All three types of meaning are interrelated and reinforce each other. It is best to study symbolic learning through an actual analysis of rituals: We will look at nose-bleeding and then the flute ceremony. Nose-bleeding involves more of the operational and positional meanings, whereas the flute ceremony uses all three types but emphasizes the verbal teachings and learning of the boys. Review of symbolic learning in these ceremonies will serve another aim. We will see how these rites structure sexual behavior development as suggested in Chapter 5: through female avoidance, homosexuality, and beliefs that make males fear pollution and depletion.

* Adapted from V. W. Turner (1967).

NOSE-BLEEDING RITES

Forcible nose-bleeding is one of many social control mechanisms used to create and maintain the social dominance of the ritual cult. The hamlet warriorhood, into which boys are conscripted, backs up this cult hierarchy. Elders are at the top of the ritual dominance ladder. Fully initiated married men dominate over bachelors, who themselves dominate initiates. Though women and children are excluded from the cult, it nonetheless politically controls them. Men, including the boys' fathers, use initiation to separate boys from their mothers and masculinize them in conformity to the adult male role.

Initiation begins with boys being taken from their mothers in such a way that it ensures they will be afraid. The initiates know they can never go home to their mothers' world. First-stage rituals make use of this traumatic separation to resocialize boys. Both parents are removed from the scene, a ritual sponsor is introduced, and for days boys undergo the ordeals described above, including the great revelations of the flutes and ritual homosexuality. After separation from mother, an insecure feeling develops. The boys do not know who to turn to for security and affection. This is called "insecure attachment"; it comes from the boys' fear and the unpredictability of rituals, while being denied access to the key protective attachment figure, mother. Nose-bleeding is most terrifying of all. It leaves the boys numb and creates what psychologists call *detachment*: despair, crying, searching behavior, depression or its suppressed counterpart, anger. Sambia rituals generate such feelings by making familiar persons or surroundings seem alien, bizarre, even terrifying.

But what about later nose-bleedings, such as in third-stage initiations? Why is it necessary to keep violently nose-bleeding the older bachelors years after they have been detached from their mothers, have avoided women, and have adapted to warriorhood life in the clubhouse? Why, in other words, do males require this repeated symbolic learning?

To understand why, we must summarize the political context of ritual domination. The presence of a warriorhood in every hamlet is a function of meeting certain social needs that concern the elders. First is the perpetuation of social and economic stability in the community, which requires control and use of the products of women's bodies and their labor, including sexual services, babies, breast-milk, garden food, and domestic services like cooking and babysitting. Then there is the need for authority over boys, whose allegiance as supporters and young warriors is vital to the elders' authority and hamlet defense. Last is social control over female children—daughters, sisters, nieces, cousins, granddaughters—who are needed to obtain future wives for the bachelors. The elders control the bachelors, in turn, by keeping all responsibility for exchanging these females and arranging marriages. But the success of all these political ploys depends on first separating boys from the women's realm. Only then will they become fierce warriors obedient to the secret society, as symbolized by the elders.

The positional meanings of nose-bleeding reveal that elders are faced with a dilemma that initiation resolves. As uninitiated boys, males are controlled by their mothers, who are their caretakers. Initiation transfers this control to elders and bachelors. Initiates are removed from direct interaction with females. Age-mates become comrades and competitors, matching their achievements in hunting and fishing. By puberty, then, bachelors dominate initiates but are controlled by elders. Women are tantalizingly nearby, but they are roped off and kept out of reach. And here is where the ritual violence of nose-bleeding is reintroduced to keep bachelors under control.

Nose-bleeding, periodically performed as a surprise in later initiations, is the most powerful symbolic learning that reinforces boys' obedience to authority. Next to threats of death, nose-bleeding is the clearest act of "raw aggression" (Tuzin 1980: 74) over youths. The aggression against boys comes first in late childhood, when they might try sexual experimentation with girls. That is ruled out. The next bleeding comes at puberty, when a powerful control is again needed to ensure the repression of heterosexual impulses in bachelors. Nose-bleeding is therefore like a kind of "symbolic castration," or perhaps even "phallic aggression" (Vanggaard 1972: 101-12). It is a traumatic but very effective means of channelling bachelors' sexual impulses away from women and toward younger initiates. Here is where ritual beliefs about the deadly pollution of women's bodies rationalize bachelors' fears and avoidance of women. Then a war raid follows bachelor initiation. The bachelors' frustrations and anger are thereby conveniently directed outside of the village, away from the elders, and toward external enemies. No wonder nose-bleeding is so violent: the problems it controls are very great.

Forcibly inserted into the secret male rites, nose-bleeding is a most powerful way to penetrate a boy's body—and identity. Although mother is removed, blood is used as a symbol of her. Therefore, cutting the nose releases *mother's* blood. Boys symbolically learn in ritual that this blood is the contaminated femaleness of boys—which represents the womb, nurturance, softness, and curses, an essence of femaleness that cannot become an essence of maleness. It is not just that the body changes. In New Guinea societies we see the body and skin surface treated as what we Westerners call the "self" (M. Strathern 1979). Nose-bleeding violates one's body boundaries in order for the whole self to be reclaimed as exclusively male by the ritual cult.

Only after the completion of nose-bleeding can appropriate homosexual fellatio occur. This "fills up" boys' insides with semen—"biological maleness"—displacing the female essences. The critical symbolic learning is this: the boy can now nose-bleed himself to eliminate femaleness from his body, a ritual that separates the boy's identity from his mother and all femaleness. This act in time becomes a sign to himself that his identity is purely male.

THE SECRET OF THE FLUTES

The ritual flutes are the dominant symbol of the men's secret society. Hidden in the flutes' symbolic meanings are many great questions and answers about Sambia gender.

The flutes are *naturalized*, that is, they are treated not as manmade but as supernatural forces, beyond human control. The flutes are odd in two ways for the men. Myth tells how originally women, not men, made the flutes. This is a common theme throughout New Guinea. Second, the spirit of the flute is not male but female. Like the phantom cassowary, though, this female is not passive and obedient like real women, but is aggressive and dangerous. Men control the flute spirit power, but they know that they use deception to do so. Why should a warrior cult that prizes masculinity and disparages women have selected a symbol that in its origins and present form is female? This puzzle we will solve. Remember that the answer does not have to come only from the conscious, rational mind, for symbols like the flutes appear in dreams and seem also to have unconscious significance. This explains why what seems to us a contradiction—femaleness at the heart of the male cult—is never questioned by Sambia themselves. They are not aware of its full meaning.

During performances of the Flute Ceremony in two different initiations, one thing was striking to me: the men were mainly revealing to boys erotic information about the mouth and penis—penile erection, sexual impulses, semen, homosexual activities in particular, and genital eroticism more broadly. These revelations come when boys are being taught about homosexuality and ritual secrets. They are threatened with death if they tell the women what they learn.

Boys' Initiation Experiences   How do boys experience the Flute Ceremony? Let us refer to their own words to understand. What follows are examples of what they told me in interviews later. In boys' remarks we learn that they perceive different values associated with the flutes and homosexuality. Their values are in conflict because they still are in transition between the female and male world views. Boys begin with responses to the penis teaching. They feel shame about it. They refer back to their earlier socialization. Kambo (a 12-year-old) says: "I thought—not good that they [elders] are lying or just playing a trick. The penis is not for handling; if you hold it you'll become lazy [our parents told us]. And because of it [in the culthouse] I felt—it's [penis] not for sucking." Childhood experience is the cause of this shame about fellatio: children are taught to not play with their own genitals. They must forget this and learn something new. Kambo's remark pertains as well to the sexual naiveté of children and to the boys' prior lack of knowledge about their fathers' homosexual activities.

Another new learning concerns the perceived nutritive value of semen. The boys are told that semen will make them grow strong. The source of this idea is the men's ritual teaching that semen is mother's breast milk. Do the boys understand and accept this belief? They seem to adopt it quickly in their own subjective orientations toward fellatio, as we can infer from things they say. Moondi talked to me about the matter. Here is a typical example of his semen beliefs resulting from the Flute Ceremony:

The juice of the pandanus nuts. . . . It's the same as the water of a man, the same as a man's juice [semen]. And I like to consume a lot of it [because] it can give *me* more water. . . . For the milk of women is also the same as the milk of men. Hers [breast milk] is for when she has a baby—it's for the baby who drinks it.

The association between semen and breast milk is widely recognized. Here is Gaimbako, Moondi's age-mate: "Semen is the same kind as that [breast milk] of women. . . . It's the *very same* kind as theirs. . . . The same as pandanus nuts too. . . . But when milk [semen] falls into my mouth [during fellatio], I think it's like the milk of women." Thus boys' semen beliefs motivate their homosexual activity.

There is another shame-laden side to the teaching too. This is a powerful reactive attitude: boys feel they are "sucking a penis" like their own. Kambo felt this way immediately on hearing the penis teaching of the flute: "I was afraid of [their] penis! It's the same as mine—why should I suck it? It's the same kind, [our penes are] only one kind. We're men, not *different* kinds!" What is Kambo saying? He is first shocked by the idea of fellatio, it is so new. But he is also complaining that fellatio is not right since it is sexual activity between the same sex. He suggests, then, that males are of one kind, as distinct from females. This reveals his childhood view that only men and women should have sex together. He senses the power play in the homosexual dyad; remember the coercive nature of the Flute Ceremony. The men's hostile jokes made during the preceding body decoration convey clearly to boys that they are to be the men's sexual outlets. Initiates are sexually subordinate, a fact expressed by the saying that the boys are "married" to the flutes, which symbolize the bachelors' penes. Boys suck the small flute, which represents the mature glans penis, further symbolizing their passive role. Reference to flute marriage makes boys sense that they are being compared to women and to wives. As age-mates they are equivalent only to other immature initiates. Sucking a man's penis directly expresses their inferior position. Eventually, then, they aspire to get semen to be strong like bachelors so they will be independent agents.

Nearly all initiates perform their first act of fellatio during the initiation. Their experiences are very important for subsequent masculine development. Moondi has said:

> I was wondering what they [elders] were going to do to us. And . . . I felt afraid. What will they do? But they inserted the bamboo in and out of the mouth; and I thought, what are they doing? Then, after they tried out our mouths, I began to understand . . . that they were talking about the penis. Oh, that little bamboo is the penis of the men! My whole body was afraid, completely afraid. . . . And I felt heavy, I wanted to cry.
>
> Then my thoughts went back to how I used to think it was the *aatm-wogwambu* [flute spirit], and then I knew that the men did it [made the sounds]. And . . . I felt a little better, because before [I feared that] the *aatmwogwambu* would get me. But now I saw that they [the men] did it.
>
> They told us the penis story. . . . Then I thought a lot, very quickly. I was afraid—not good that the men shoot me [penetrate my mouth] and break my neck. Ay! Why should they put that [penis] inside our mouths! It's not a good thing. They all hide it [the penis] inside their sporrans, and it's got lots of hair too.

"You must listen well," they said. "You all won't grow up by yourselves; if you sleep with the men you'll become a strong man." They said that; I was afraid. . . . And then they told us clearly: semen is inside—and when you hold a man's penis, you must put it inside your mouth—he can give you semen. . . . It's the same as your mother's breast milk.

"This is no lie," the men said. "You can't go tell the children, your sisters." . . . And then [later] I tried it [fellatio], and I thought: "Oh, they told us about breast milk [Moondi means semen]—it [semen] is in there."

What becomes of these feelings in later months and years? Many things could be added. For instance, despite great social pressures, some boys show low interest and seldom participate in fellatio, while others feverishly join in. But those are the extremes: the great majority of Sambia boys regularly engage in fellatio for years as regulated by taboo. I mentioned earlier that males cannot have sex with any kinsmen. This taboo is the ideal. In fact, however, male cross-cousins and distant kin do have fellatio sometimes, though it is kept quiet. Boys who are considered especially attractive are pursued in this way, even though they are kin. This suggests that sexual excitement is a factor in men's homosexuality too, not just the ideal belief that it "makes boys grow." Homosexual practices are a touchy subject among males for many reasons. They begin in a ceremony, it is true, but their occurrence and meaning fan out to embrace a totally secret way of life. What matters is that boys too become just as involved in this hidden tradition. We should expect them to acquire intense feelings about bachelors, fellatio, and semen, as indeed they do.

Here is an eloquent example. One day, while I was talking idly with Kambo, he mentioned singing to himself as he walked in the forest. I asked him what he sang about. From this simple question he surprised me by saying:

When I think of men's name-songs then I sing them: that of a bachelor who is sweet on me; a man of another line or my own. When I sing the song of a creek in the forest I am happy about that place. . . . Or some man who sleeps with me—when he goes elsewhere, I sing his song. I think of that man who gave me a lot of semen; later, I must sleep with him. I feel like this: he gave me a lot of water [semen]. . . . Later, I will have a lot of water like him.

Not only do we see pinpointed here the male belief that semen accumulates and makes you strong. Even a simple activity like singing can trigger a mood of reflecting on past male associations and prolonged homosexual contacts. Kambo shows us his wish: that he too will acquire abundant manliness, like the admired friend of whom he sings.

The men's flutes come to symbolize a whole lifetime of experiences like these. Initiation thus creates a line of development that has definite effects on a boy's sense of himself and his maleness, his gender identity.

This leads us to the bachelors' impersonation of the female hamlet spirits. What does this symbolic learning mean? What about the bachelors' motives? Why do only certain bachelors volunteer for this impersonation? Gaimbako recalled that the bachelors presented themselves as "wailing old women spirits." He noted that the men told "stories" about the "milk" of the flutes.

"This flute isn't crying out for just anything—it wants the milk [semen] of men. You must all drink the milk of men." The significance of the flutes is clearly complex.

The flutes are of male and female types, the shorter ones contained in longer bamboo tubes. They are likened to mother's breasts and nipples, and are compared to the penis and glans penis. The fluid exuded by the penis is semen, but it is said to be equivalent to mother's milk. The bachelors dress as hamlet spirits to entice the new initiates into homosexual fellatio.

What is going on here is a symbolic transformation of female things into male things (Lidz and Lidz 1977). The bachelors get to blow the flutes and inseminate boys for the first time. They proudly boast of their *jerungdu*. The initiates are often scared, worn out, and unhappy. They have lost forever their primary caretaker, mother. They are offered substitutes for her instead. Boys are "going it alone for the first time." They are now on their hero's journey to becoming men. But it is not so easy to leave the security and innocence of childhood behind. Not for Sambia, nor for any of us. So the boys are provided with what we can call transitional symbolic objects to help them through the process.

Transitional objects are things that a person symbolically treats as halfway between himself and another person. Dolls treasured by children and used as comforters, but which do not have the full value of a person, are transitional objects. Such objects help children make the transition from infancy and dependence to self-reliance. They are the next best thing to the parent when a child is lost or frightened. Eventually, children outgrow them and become independent without the object. As adults, they may even repress memories of the object.

The Sambia flutes are such a transitional object for the boys in initiation. They provide a means of linking boys with substitutes for their mother, a penis for a breast, semen for milk. The flute spirit is a transparently disguised symbol for mother herself. The wailing old hamlet spirit does what mother did when the boy was taken for initiation: cry for him. Only the spirit is *powerful*, will protect and nourish the boy, whereas mother was powerless to help him. So the spirit offers a new kind of powerful protection to be desired. There are actually three transitional objects in initiation:

1. The boy's ritual guardian, who removes him from and replaces his mother, protecting and comforting him during initiation;
2. The flute spirit, which is a symbolic female but imparts male essence; and
3. The bachelors, who are first disguised as the spirit, and who later act as inseminators to provide the breast milk substitute.

These are elements of what we could call the shared *fantasy system* of the men's cult.

This fantasy system has several functions. It motivates boys to engage in homosexual activity: the image of mother and her milk rationalizes fellatio.

After ritual brainwashing, they change their beliefs about the flutes. The flutes as transitional objects help motivate them to internalize the men's secret beliefs. The fantasy system creates a double identification: the boy identifies with the guardian as a nurturant man, and with the spirit figure as a powerful, fictional female creature—a phallic female, we could say, having attributes of both males and females. This final symbolic learning suggests that boys' core identity contains both feminine and masculine elements that are difficult for them to consciously accept or act out. The fantasy of the flutes provides a symbol that can unconsciously express this core need for the males as a group.

In their identity formation, boys reach for a compromise solution. They reconcile their own promiscuous and passive homosexual activity with their independence and growing sense of masculine power. Interestingly enough, they often relate their feelings of having lost mother to their secret homosexual life-style. Note this vivid line of thought in a final comment by Moondi regarding the changes in him following initiation:

> I felt sorry. I thought, why should I lose my mother? I thought a lot about Momma and Papa. . . . I was sorry for [them]. . . . I was sorry when I was still a first-stage initiate. I wanted to remain an uninitiated boy with her [mother]. Later, later, I was a second-stage initiate. I slept around—I didn't worry much. I thought, "Oh, it's nothing." After I was initiated I stopped worrying about Momma and Papa. When I was still an initiate I thought: What will I do if my parents die? Who'll give me food and things? Now that I'm a second-stage initiate I sleep with all of the men, I don't worry. It's nothing: I've lost my Momma and Papa now.

Moondi obviously is rationalizing his detachment from his mother and father. He seems to have reached a compromise with himself. He longed for his mother and resented initiation, but he soon recognized that he was powerless to prevent it. Initiation brought homosexual relationships, and these somehow lessened his need and worrying about his parents. This has changed Moondi's concerns about homosexuality. He says that fellatio is "nothing"—neither unusual nor scary—a feeling that expresses his recognition and acceptance of having forever lost the world of childhood.

The secret of the flute is that in its core it is female and that it symbolizes, for the men, a set of transitional fantasy objects kept secret from the women because they create in men their masculinity. Women are naturally fertile and reproductive. Men are not. Yet the men are ashamed of this idea. It is a fantasy, not a fact, for it is a gender belief of the men's world. Men dread that women will learn that they were once passive insertees of older men. They fear this because they feel women would mock them if they knew the secret. Women would want to be "on top" sometimes too. They cannot allow that to happen. This is why the men keep their rituals hidden: they shield a secret identity. For they seem to feel—as their fantasy system expresses unconsciously—that women really are more powerful than they. The men do not see that what they fear in the secret part of themselves is their feminine side.

PROTEST MASCULINITY

How does this secret identity affect men in later life? Their self-doubts cause conflicts in them. They are in conflict about how often to have sex with their wives; they are torn about how close they should be to their children. But their rituals and the warriorhood clubhouse provide ready-made responses to these situations. The men protest often that they are in fact masculine and strong. Yet they are adult men—long removed from their first initiations. How do the boys we saw in the initiation rites achieve this final identity state?

Take note that the initiation first uses principles of *negation*. Before boys can be masculine, they must separate from women and be rid of female essence. Only then can the development of masculinity occur. Their ritual advancements require brainwashing of childhood attachments, activities, and desires. They negate their boy-child identity. Then they incorporate: ingest male essence in one's body to become a strong warrior and provider. The rituals provide a new way of saying: "I am being masculine [in such and such a way]." In this way the initiate's formal role shows others he is "contra-suggestable to the female ethos" (Bateson 1958). Yet, the negations precede the positive ritual status changes for years later too. Third-stage initiates as well are nose-bled before they ingest ritual foods and leaves. I believe that this negative-to-positive developmental line in initiation lays down a behavioral pattern for all later social behavior. To do masculine activities even in adulthood, men must first negate the feminine influence on them. Thus, warfare, hunting, ritual, and sex—the key contexts for performing adult masculinity—are always preceded by purificatory ceremonies that remove feminine elements. This is why even "brainwashing" is too simple an analogy. Why does one need in adulthood to keep removing what has already been removed? The answer must be that these negations or removals are never completely effective, they are never finished. Men need to keep proving that they are strong. When the men react to their own fears that they are not masculine, they compensate by acting all the more aggressive. We can call this *protest masculinity*. It has consequences not only for gender but for morality too.

Every society makes use of ritual manipulations of gender development to teach crucial standards and goals for the individual. Boy scouts and girl scouts, sororities and fraternities, even the military, do this in our society. The timelessness one glimpses in the ordeals of Sambia initiation provides such a stage of reflection necessary for boys' learning and unlearning. Nevertheless, the Sambia negations described above provide a most extreme case. The initiations point toward critical changes in the boys' moral norms, which oppose them to their earlier childhood notions of good and bad.

What is the nature of these moral splits? The most fundamental one is the negation of the women's world. Sambia boys are reared to be good people by adults (mother and father) whom they see as good people. What makes mother good is the love she gave for years and the fact that her mothering

is defined in public, especially by women themselves, as good, not bad. Whatever badness the uninitiated boy feels about his mother (whether it stems
from his own feelings or those of peers and elders) takes backseat to his love
for her. The bedrock of these public feelings of what is good persists. Initiates,
like all other Sambia, should not be lazy, steal, rape, or assault their fellow
villagers. What the men's society does is to substitute negative images of
women. We saw many examples of this at Yulami. When elders said that
women (that is, mother) have bad stuff in them which they transmit to boys
and which must be purged from their bodies at all costs, they were negating
the boys' childhood images of mother. Thus the men rationalize the harsh
ordeals by making women responsible for boys' pain. We saw how men raged
against women over the cursing associated with nose-bleeding. Being wounded
does not make one forget. Is it possible to forget the happy, innocent world
of childhood and mother? I doubt it: mother remains a memory forever,
which can cause conflict in being so negative to women.

We have seen that secret rituals help control and hide the conflicts in core
identity, and this too has a moral side. Homosexual practices and nose-
bleeding, the most secret of ritual activities, speak to this issue. They draw
their excitement, in part, from qualities such as mystery, envy, and sexual
power—which polarize maleness and femaleness in the world and in one's
self. Men project the polarization into nature and carry it over into their
families. The secret expression of these forbidden ("feminine") parts of self—
the negations never successfully eliminated—create double standards. Damn
women for menstruating, but secretly nose-bleed yourself. We see also a
dramatic split in the moral norms of sexual behavior: on the one hand, boys
are applauded for being promiscuous parties in homosexual practices for
years; while on the other hand all heterosexual activity for them is condemned,
and Sambia men are, by and large, prudish and suspicious regarding adultery
and their erotic enjoyment of women. Such double standards create guilt that
is turned into anger instead: protest masculinity.

Seen this way, the initiations are a *system of gender identity contexts* that
layer upon one another in the male life cycle. Each successive initiation
introduces changes in gender that unfold and structure the boys' gender experience. To overturn childhood and maternal love through the warrior role
is what the men's secret talk of private nose-bleeding is all about. This is a
true dilemma: that a man live and be sexually intimate with a woman while
staying aloof from her; that he must be secretive, fierce, and manipulative
by initiating sons and trading off daughters in marriage. The adult man's
private self-bleeding maintains this touchy holding pattern. The ritual cult re-
inserts itself, with each successive nose-bleeding, into gender identity and the
man's marital relationship. And this is how it must be: enjoying women and
sexual release in coitus is a dire necessity to manhood. Bloodletting becomes
a habitualized style for checking one's affections and lust, one's self-doubts
about being alone with, and inside of, a woman again. It is humanly impossible
for men, without coitus, to create children and reap the rewards of hard-won
sexual access and manhood, but they take their lives into their own hands

each time they do so. This complex meaning is contained in the masculine protest "I *am* masculine!"

WOMEN'S REAL POWER

Two rituals have been analyzed to reveal that at rock bottom men regard femaleness as more powerful than maleness. This idea consciously contradicts their own public ideology and rituals. In the nose-bleedings we saw the elimination of blood. Men themselves compare this act to women's menstruation. Sambia do not say that this is the *same* as the menses (which other New Guinea peoples say), but their comparison hints that the *power* involved is the same. The fact that the ceremony must be hidden is especially important. We may say that in this special ritual situation the men openly express their envy of the women. The envy, apparently, is of women's natural powers. Perhaps it is also an earlier childhood envy of a power that their mothers had over them that they now seize symbolically and master through the secret nose-bleeding act. In the Yulami initiation, the young men who acted hysterical and charged at the women with the bloodied leaves may have been males who never resolved their envy and rage toward women. But this is an individual instance. On the group level, the flute ceremony reveals envy through symbolization of the female functions of breast-feeding with natural milk. In both these rites we can see what Sambia women cannot: the secret identity of their men.

This secret identity reveals the deepest part of men's gender conflict and sex envy of women. It must be hidden to keep women politically inferior, and it must be carefully controlled in oneself to keep being fierce. Ritual provides the boundaries for this part of the self. The rites set up strong taboos that regulate when and where these needs, this deeper part of oneself, *can* be expressed. Only with men, and only in private, can the secret identity be revealed. The secret rites of nose-bleeding and fellatio express a man's power, his *jerungdu*, yet men fear women would laugh at them as rubbish men if the secret became public. The rites express sex envy. There are many sources of this envy: psychological, economic, political. It is overdetermined by the nature of the whole Sambia ritual system. After initiation boys are allowed to express in secret their unconscious envy of women in this controlled and masculine way. Yet in public life they protest all too much that they are phallic and condemn women the more severely for their female weakness. Why is this so?

The myths and rites of Sambia suggest that humankind in its origins is not distinctly male or female, which contradicts the men's own belief that they are purely masculine. That mythical women invented the flutes and other male symbols tells clearly that men envy their powers to create. The men imitate this *natural* creativity through their *cultural* creations—the great rituals, which imitate women's fertility—for they hold life's true power: creation. Male mythology thus hints that women have more real power in everyday

194

Photo 30. Women shamans

life than the men say. Perhaps there is a more tenuous political struggle
between the sexes going on than we had thought. It seemed earlier that the
women's power was restricted to the domestic households of the hamlet. Yet
the men's ritual envy of women contradicts this idea. So do certain symbolic
images in male culture. The aggressive female cassowary is one: myth tells
how the cassowary was originally a woman who changed into the animal. This
myth, like many others so common in New Guinea, tells that women are
close to nature and its fertile powers, which are, like the cassowaries, slippery
but real.

But another social figure is more fascinating and even puzzling: women
shamans (see Photo 30). How very curious that a male-dominated society
with a phallic cult should have in its midst women shamans. This is especially
peculiar when we recall the great popularity of the shamans and the heroic
hope they provide.

Sambia recognize different sex-linked cultural patterns that characterize a
shaman's calling. For men shamans, on the one hand, childhood experiences
such as visions and dreams of spirits are later channeled into the ritual cult
ceremonies. In the ceremonies, the signs of a calling are publicly reinforced
and accepted. We have seen that women, however, are not abruptly separated
from their mothers or childhood routines. So the dreams and childhood experiences of women shamans, foretelling their calling, are recognized in mystical situations that lead to possession and trance. In both cases, the young
shamans are then apprenticed to older ones, men for boys, women for girls,

who teach them how to heal. This leads to important sex-linked differences in Sambia shamanism. First, male shamans used to outnumber female shamans by a four-to-one margin (which has now evened up due to culture change). Second, the traditional cultural emphasis on the shaman's role highlights the *masculine* functions. Men shamans did magic ceremonies before and after warfare in past times. More social pressures are thus exerted on male shamans. The discontinuity and emotional upheaval of male cult initiations, with intense stresses resulting from psychosexual and aggressive demands, are hard on boys. After childhood there is no structural outlet for them to satisfy underlying needs, such as nurturance, in everyday life. These observations tend to confirm that there is no role except that of the shaman for the sensitive boy. And indeed, men shamans tend to be the most nurturant and sensitive of Sambia men. Women shamans are sensitive too, but they tend to be the most aggressive and flamboyant of women. For them, the shaman's role also provides an alternative outlet, only the reverse to that of the men—they can be more assertive.

There is a well-known story among Sambia that portrays the strong and heroic qualities of the woman shaman. The infant son of a war leader was found missing one afternoon. A search party could not locate the child and the parents blamed themselves for having selfishly left him in the care of his elder brother (implying, that is, a wish for the solitude of their garden to have sexual intercourse). As darkness fell the parents became distraught and began wailing for the child. They feared he had been abducted by ghosts. Kaiyunango, the woman shaman, was overcome with sorrow at the sight of the war leader and his wife shamelessly bawling and muddying themselves, starting the pitiful bereavement of Sambia funerals. A storm broke, yet Kaiyunango persuaded some girls to accompany her beyond the hamlet to search again for the child. Soon afterward, however, the girls became frightened at a noise near a gravesite and they fled to the hamlet. They thought the noise was a ghost, but Kaiyunango was not scared. Alone but undaunted, she searched for the child for she had seen in a trance that he had been stolen by ghosts who intended to eat him. She called the child's name into the rain and gloomy fog, finally discovering him crying and soiled and bewildered. There, she claims, a great black ghost suddenly appeared before her. The ghost struck and pursued her, finally ripping off her bark cape. She escaped, nearly naked, and returned to the hamlet with the child, where she was greeted in triumph for her courage. This tale was told to me years after the events by the war leader himself and other villagers. It offers an important moral: though female, Kaiyunango's powers as a shaman gave her extraordinary strength to brave ghosts in a dreadful storm and accomplish a heroic deed at which even a war leader had failed.

The hermaphroditic shaman Sakulambei provides another side of shamanism. Saku has proven many times over that he has the power to cure and the will and kindness to pull others through sickness. Some years ago I sat one evening in a healing ceremony, watching Saku and Kaiyunango work together, trying to save a gravely ill child. They used all their powers. For hours Saku sweated profusely, laboring over his patient. Afterward he leaned forward, exhausted and speechless. There was no question in my mind that he truly had spent himself; that in the service of the child he had used everything he knew. He impressed me with his compassion. This went well beyond the call of duty—it was more like a parent's effort to save the child. I commented as much to my friend Weiyu. Since Saku is his clan brother and close friend, I thought Weiyu could help me understand this sacrifice. Weiyu said:

> That's just his way. He helps people. He's a good man. Years ago, the year before you arrived [1973], I was dying. I had a terrible illness [malaria]. He sat with me, day after day. He nursed me, fed me. He was like my mother. How many times did he do healing ceremonies over this body of mine? Many!!! I couldn't count them; I was delirious. He didn't abandon me even though everyone else felt I'd die. He saved my life. That's why I will never turn my back on him.

Saku's powers are all the more remarkable because he is a hermaphrodite. He has had to overcome trauma and humiliation, rejection by his father, and who knows what else. And yet he is not bitter. He did not abandon humanity or take up the dark side of his shamanic power (sorcery) out of rage and vengeance. His compassion for others has prevailed. His care expresses a deep nurturing side of his personality, a soft side—kindness—many Sambia men lack. His religious role allows him to be more nurturant, like women. In short, through Saku we see again the need to draw both on masculinity and femininity in the shaman's role.

These two remarkable shamans are important in understanding that there is another dimension to Sambia society. It provides a stage for demonstrating *human* powers and goodness, for the heroic acts of a woman and a hermaphroditic man go beyond the normal rigid stereotypes. It seems that in the shamanic figure, Sambia are asking "what can men or women be, and do, beyond their cultural positions?" Is it for this reason that the male shamans can nurse people to health, detached and defiant of masculine stereotypes? The men and women shamans can even appropriately touch those of the opposite sex during the healing ceremony, which is unheard of otherwise. Saku, with his androgynous face and temperament, has become a powerful shaman in spite of his flawed body; Kaiyunango has journeyed into night with aggressive aplomb to recover the child and return with a hero's welcome. In such cases the shaman stretches the rigid "natural" notions of Sambia femininity and masculinity in new directions.

Sambia have, therefore, invested in the shaman a humaneness and plasticity transcending the terrible gap between their own models of manhood and womanhood. That women are shamans is interesting; that they can be prestigious and powerful in a masculine society seems remarkable.

Only grudgingly or in despair do men privately allow their dependence upon women's contributions. My friend Weiyu once gave voice to men's silent appreciation of the burden of women. At the back of my house one afternoon we stood talking, looking out into a bitterly cold and rainy last light of dusk. Women appeared from a garden, and we watched them as they filed past.

They were returning from their daily chores, rain-soaked, burdened with food, firewood, and babies. They looked so wretched. Weiyu shook his head and then added spontaneously: "Sorry. Women . . . women are just like our mothers." I asked him how that could be and he said, "If only we did not copulate with them, they would truly be like our mothers. They provide us with our food, everything . . ." His voice trailed off, his sentence incomplete. This moody comment, triggered by the hard sight of the women and conveyed to me in tones of quiet sadness, unveils a sense of longing and guilt normally disguised by men's bravado.

7/The relativity of gender

What can we conclude about the structuring of sex and gender in humans? Our anatomical sex is fixed at birth. The fluids and reproductive potentials of males and females are therefore present and awaiting maturity. Some level of sexual drive seems also to be biologically determined. Yet these facts do not fully define the content of gender in cultures. Societies assign meanings to the biological givens. Their values and symbols influence male and female development after birth. They condition sex drive and the forms of sexual behavior preferred or accepted in a society. In other words, the gender code of a culture establishes broad limits for being male and female, and for expressing such being through sexual and nonsexual relationships.

But how much do these social limitations affect the biological facts of sex? The sexual freedom opened up in the 1960s has raised this question in a new way. Contraceptives have created choice in the matter of whether to have children. The controversy over the morality and personal choice of having an abortion still rages in the United States as elsewhere. The Women's Movement has strongly advocated the need for women to make choices in these matters according to their own conscience. Opponents see abortion as the taking of a human life no matter what the circumstances: whether the birth is wanted or not, the result of rape, or the source of medical or mental risk to the mother.

Feminism has challenged basic gender role definitions. The increasing numbers of working mothers testify to women's desires to have careers and identities apart from the question of whether to be married or have children. Working women suggest that the economic needs of society are changing too. No longer is everyone expected to be a mother or father. The population boom underlies this change. And the development of the Gay Movement since the late 1960s dramatically emphasizes the desire of homosexuals and bisexuals to live openly according to their sexual preference. These social changes in gender are expanding previously held views about the biological limits of sexuality.

It is fitting that anthropology has joined this debate again. Anthropology and other social sciences confronted these same issues in the 1920s with strong concerns. At that time both sex and gender were seen as biologically structured. Blatant racism and bigotry were part of society. Margaret Mead's (1928)

199

study of Samoan teenagers had a large impact on the debates. She suggested that Samoan adolescents do not experience the social and mental conflict associated with puberty and the transition into adulthood that is so well known in Western culture. If biology is not the reason for teenage stress then culture must be, she argued. Her work widely influenced psychologists, teachers, social planners, and others in American society. Derek Freeman's (1983) recent book has challenged Mead's work. He shows that certain of Mead's interpretations and facts were either incomplete or incorrect. Freeman's work focuses attention again on the biological influences on gender and other human behaviors. Moreover, this controversy points out the critical "human element" in studying gender. It is not always easy to be sure that we are being objective. Anthropologists are humans, not machines. Yet, at the same time, Freeman and others suggest that we need to more fully consider the overall effects of the *interaction* between culture and biology in studying the human condition (Herdt 1981: Chap. 9; Levy 1984; Lidz 1976; Luria 1979; Mead 1949, 1961; Rosaldo 1974; Spindler and Spindler 1982; Spiro 1979, 1982; Stoller and Herdt 1982).

It is premature to suggest which side of the equation—culture or biology—is the stronger influence. Part of the reason for the uncertainty is that each topic posed for research involves complex factors contributing to the behavior or experience in question. To ask, for instance, why men are aggressive and dominating requires us knowing the particular social situations, resources, and people over which they dominate. Then we need to establish a reliable and systematic method for studying the aggressive behavior. And *then* we still have to interpret the findings of the study. Interpretation requires knowing the actor's views and recognizing our own cultural point of view or biases. This is not easily settled at one point in time. Meanwhile, the society and people studied are changing. So restudies—replications of the original research—must be done to take account of the social changes that have occurred. This is why it is difficult to argue in black-or-white terms that either culture or biology determines gender.

In a recent review of "Human Sexuality in Biological Perspective," Thomas Ford Hoult (1984) has written:

> How convincing is the biological evidence that the details of human sexuality are directly due to innate traits and processes? The answer is that the evidence is far from persuasive. We may conclude that the biological perspective on human sexuality has not yet made a substantial contribution to the "balanced biosocial synthesis" some have recommended.
>
> This conclusion is not intended to imply that biology has nothing to do with human sexuality (since the two are, of course, inextricably intertwined). It means simply this: The claim that biological factors have an immediate, direct influence on such things as sexual identity, behavior or orientation remains unproven. When biology seems to be critical in such matters, an intervening cultural factor is often more immediate. For example, physiological feminization or ambiguous genitalia in males can affect sexual identity if the culture stresses the value that "real" maleness requires stereotypical male appearance and aggressive action. Such cultural influences do not, of course, play any part in the formation of genitalia and

basic sexual drive. For these, all animals are "indebted" to biology alone. What humans do with such biological resources, however, and how they are regarded, appear to be heavily dependent on what is learned in social interaction. (150–51)

For the same reasons, it is hard to argue definitively whether homosexuality and heterosexuality are biologically determined. The data we have are still incomplete. Yet there is reason to believe that homosexuality in one form or another occurs in many societies (Carrier 1980; Ford and Beach 1951; Greenberg and Bystryn 1982; Minturn et al. 1969). Certain societies have negative attitudes about the expression of homosexuality. Others, such as the Sambia, institutionalize it. Here again there are complexities. The Sambia make homosexuality obligatory, but only for the years leading up to marriage. So their flexibility is tempered by the fact that they require men to marry, have children, and give up homosexual relations with boys. This is a pattern found in certain societies. There are limits on how far obligatory homosexuality can extend. Perhaps a society's sexual flexibility or bisexuality is a key here. Their socialization practices are effective in implementing and then stopping exclusive homosexuality among males. This flexibility may be what is most crucial for us to understand. As D. S. Ford and F. A. Beach (1951) concluded after studying the anthropological data on homosexuality throughout the world:

Human homosexuality is not basically a product of hormonal imbalance or "perverted" heredity. It is the product of the fundamental mammalian heritage of general sexual responsiveness as modified under the impact of experience. (259)

Culture is what structures this experience and learning. What is this experience of homosexuality like in other societies?[1]

The Sambia type of ritualized homosexuality occurs widely in the southern coastal and southwestern areas of New Guinea (Herdt 1984). At least 30 different societies practice this, which is associated with the same basic cultural patterns described above for the Sambia. Warfare, sexual antagonism, men's fear of women's powers, thin population, and marriage exchange are the key traits shared by these groups. Here too secrecy facilitates the domination of women and children. Ritual flutes and bullroarers are cult symbols. The same complex of ritual homosexuality is found in similar areas of the New Hebrides, New Caledonia, New Britain, and in certain northern tribes of Aboriginal Australia (Dundes 1976; Herdt 1984).

Ritualized homosexuality among women (lesbianism) in this region is very rare. It is reported only among the Big Nambas tribe of the New Hebrides near New Guinea (Deacon 1934). The Big Nambas practiced ritual homosexuality among males on a widespread basis. Yet Tom Harrison (1937:395) mentions only that "the women have developed a parallel pleasure system of their own, less elaborate than the male." However, in Central Australia, where ritual homosexuality occurs among males, sexual relations among women

---

[1] I am indebted to B. Adam for selected examples drawn from his recent and excellent review of this subject.

are common and widespread (Roheim 1932; Strehlow 1913: 98). Roheim (1950: 174) writes: "Two women of Tauru (Fergusson Island), cross-cousins, ran away into the inland and lived there doing cunnilingus to each other." In these groups we may see a greater acceptance of sexual flexibility for women too. The question still arises why institutionalized lesbianism is so rare compared to the male practices. Male dominance is certainly a factor in the reported rareness of lesbianism. To my knowledge, Sambia women do not practice sexual relations with other women. My women informants denied such, but I cannot be absolutely certain, having not seen their ceremonies. Doubts must remain because many of these same societies have been studied by male anthropologists, some of whom even ignored the male homosexual practices. So we must be cautious in concluding that women have no similar practices.

Beyond New Guinea, ritual homosexuality has been reported by anthropologists in scattered areas around the world. The Amazon basin in South America contains groups whose male homosexuality, warfare, and sexual antagonism are strikingly similar to that of the Sambia (see Murphy and Murphy 1974). Even ritual instruments such as flutes have similar meanings there. In Africa, the British anthropologist Evans-Pritchard reported the same pattern among the Azande tribe. Like the New Guinea examples, homosexuality was age-structured between older Azande warriors and younger boys. The king's household included hundreds of wives and some boys, all of whom were "married" to him. The Azande were fierce warriors; theirs was a kind of "military homosexuality" too:

> Many of the young warriors married boys and a commander might have more than one boy wife. When a warrior married a boy, he paid spears, though only a few, to the boy's parents as he would have done had he married their daughter. (1971: 199)

> He gave the boy pretty ornaments; and he and the boy addressed one another as *badiare*, "my love" and "my lover." The boy fetched water for his husband, collected firewood and kindled his fire, bore his shield when travelling. . . . (1970: 1430)

After these boys grew up, they were given bridewealth by their former lovers in order to marry. They could then take boy lovers of their own.

Perhaps the best-known case of age-structured homosexuality is that practiced by the Ancient Greeks. Virtually all of the famous figures in Greek philosophy—the teachers such as Socrates and his students Plato and Xenophon—engaged in homosexual intercourse. It was part of the educational process. The teacher transmitted knowledge, morality, and the concept of masculine honor to his pupils, which were believed to be facilitated by experiencing love and sex with them. "As the philosopher Jeremy Bentham pointed out to the dismay of Victorian scholars who refused to believe that their Greek heroes were eager homosexuals: 'Everybody practiced it; nobody was ashamed of it' " (Harris 1981: 104). Greek homosexuality probably had its origins in warriorhood life. The Thebans and Spartans were said to have taken their male lovers with them as comrades and sex partners. The youths, likewise, learned warrior values and the military arts. Many classic texts tell stories of how male lovers destroyed tyrants and defeated invaders side-by-side. The early anthropologist Westermarck (1917) quotes Hieronymus, Plutarch, and Plato on the subject:

> For, "in the presence of his favourite, a man would choose to do anything rather than to get the character of a coward." It was pointed out that the greatest heroes and the most warlike nations were those who were most addicted to the love of youths; and it was said that an army consisting of lovers and their beloved ones, fighting at each other's side, although a mere handful, would overcome the whole world. (479)

Here again we see the pervasive link between ritual homosexuality and the warrior ethos, this time at the roots of Western culture.

A similar form of marital homosexuality existed in several parts of Ancient Asia. The Japanese were one such group. In the seventeenth-century novel by Saikaku Ihara, *Comrade Loves of the Samurai* (1972), we find romantic tales of how the sons of samurai families were urged to form homosexual alliances with warriors, which often matured into lifelong companionships. Masculine training, warrior life, and love were all present here too.

The structuring of homosexuality by culture requires that we try to understand its occurrence and meaning in each social context. The factors that influence its meaning are many. The great expert on the Ancient Greeks, Professor K. J. Dover (1978), has put the matter this way:

> Homosexual relationships are not exhaustively divisible, in Greek society or in any other, into those which perform an educational function and those which provoke and relieve genital tension. Most relationships of any kind are complex, and the need for bodily contact and orgasm was one ingredient of the complex needs met by homosexual eros. (203)

We should not think that every society past or present supported homosexuality. Not all cultures permit the expression of homosexual or bisexual desires. But the fact that we find these similar forms of warrior homosexuality in such diverse places as New Guinea, the Amazon, Ancient Greece, and historical Japan testifies to some universal capacity to engage in transitional homosexuality as a part of normal masculine development. Nevertheless, institutionalized homosexuality is today an unusual phenomenon.

Warrior societies go to great lengths to emphasize the differences between males and females. They do this even though they institutionalize homosexuality, which seems to blur the difference between masculinity and femininity, in our Western sense. But their form of homosexuality, as among the Sambia, is not expressed among equals. Nor are they exclusively homosexual all their lives, and they seem to experience no great difficulty in being bisexual in this way. We, on the other hand, play down the differences between the sexes, expressing a belief in their general equality. But we find it hard to understand how homosexuality and heterosexuality can be combined in the same person. The Gay Movement in the United States provides a different cultural pattern.

Many gays are exclusively homosexual their whole lives. Few marry or have children. And many gays seek partners who are their equals (though others do not: Bell and Weinberg 1978). In this sense the Gay Movement is a totally new social phenomenon. One might even ask: Is not the Gay Movement a response to the extreme polarization of heterosexuality and homosexuality in our own society?

This question raises the general problem of why certain societies completely taboo homosexuality. Their negative attitudes require an explanation as much as does the complete acceptance of homosexuality. Anthropology has shown that few cultures completely forbid *all* expressions of homosexual behavior. Ours was traditionally one of these restrictive cultures. I am told, for instance, that in World War II the United States was the only Allied country not to allow homosexuals in its armed forces. The Gay Movement is changing this negative attitude, though it is still widely held.

What seems to be at issue in our society is a very specific kind of polarization. Tribal societies such as the Sambia polarize male and female, masculinity and femininity, as we have seen. On the other hand, we polarize homosexuality and heterosexuality. In New Guinea ritualized homosexuality seems to incorporate males into a socialization pattern leading to heterosexuality. That this surprises us should lead us to wonder why we play down the difference between masculinity and femininity, but underline the polarity between homosexuality and heterosexuality. Yet our categorization is special and, to repeat, unique to Western culture. For the "gay role" presents a new cultural category different from that of other societies. Gay people can be identified with a lifelong, habitualized, and exclusive preference for same-sex contacts. Rarely has such a life-style been accepted as such elsewhere in human history. This social change has been made possible by the way we have urbanized and decontextualized sexuality as separate from the total social environment and other roles of a person. "Sex" is treated as a noun category unrelated to anything else in American culture. This does not occur in traditional New Guinea societies. So what is set in motion in our culture is a process in which someone who engages in homosexual behavior is then categorized permanently in the gay role. When they internalize this categorization in their selfhood and sexual identity, they are a gay-identified individual. In this way, we overlook the possibility of bisexuality as an intermediate state between homosexuality and heterosexuality. Paul (1985) has shown that bisexually oriented people experience pressures from both sides. Their heterosexual friends and relatives want them to declare themselves completely heterosexual. Their gay friends feel they are simply afraid to declare themselves homosexual. It seems, in this sense, that American society still pressures people to conform to the exclusive dichotomy of being either "gay" or "straight."

Various explanations are being offered to account for this negative attitude toward homosexuality in Western culture. Some see Christianity as the source of the taboo (Boswell 1980). Hoffman (1984) suggests that the change from polytheism to monotheism is associated with the development of negative attitudes toward homosexuality. Others see our capitalist economy, which promotes family reproduction and is threatened by sexual variations, as the cause (Harris 1981). There are no complete explanations yet, though historians and other scholars are intensely at work on the problem.

Whatever the final answer, the case study of the Sambia and examples from these other cultures indicate that there is greater flexibility and potential in gender than our own Western views have led us to believe.

Both the Gay Movement and the Women's Movement emphasize historic changes in society. They are testing the limits of what is possible and permissible. They have opened up important debates on what is cultural and what is biological in sex and gender. The capacity for flexibility, for equality, and the relative acceptance of alternative life-styles are all being examined. Ford and Beach (1951) found that homosexual behavior was considered normal and socially acceptable for certain people in 64 percent of the 76 societies on which information is available. They concluded:

> When it is realized that 100 percent of the males in certain societies engage in homosexual as well as heterosexual alliances, and when it is understood that many men and women in our society are equally capable of relations with partners of the same or opposite sex, and finally, when it is recognized that this same situation obtains in many species of subhuman primates, then it should be clear that one cannot classify homosexual tendencies and heterosexual tendencies as being mutually exclusive or even opposed to each other. (236)

Today women expect and deserve equal treatment and opportunities in education, work, and the arts. Today the Gay Movement asks society to set aside the old stigma and hatred of homosexuality, and provide fair and equal treatment for gays relative to their contributions to society. These changes are forcing us to revise our views of male and female. Like the Sambia and their ritual flutes, we are thus confronted with symbols that have an old, unconscious significance now being brought out into the light of day.

Here is Dover (1978) on the Greeks again:

> The modern sentiment which I have heard expressed, more than once, in the words "It's impossible to understand how the Greeks could have tolerated homosexuality" is the sentiment of a culture which has inherited a religious prohibition of homosexuality and, by reason of the inheritance, has shown (until recently) no salutary curiosity about the variety of sexual stimuli which can arouse the same person or about the difference between fundamental orientation of the personality and episodic behavior at a superficial level. The Greeks neither inherited nor developed a belief that a divine power had revealed to mankind a code of laws for the regulation of sexual behaviour; they had no religious institution possessed of the authority to enforce sexual prohibitions. Confronted by cultures older and richer and more elaborate than theirs, cultures which nonetheless differed greatly from each other, the Greeks felt free to select, adapt, develop and—above all—innovate. (203)

The modern Western world has a far richer and more diverse cultural history than did even the Greeks. Our conceptions of gender are being stretched, revised, expanded. A new frontier—the reaches of outer space—is opening up. A woman astronaut has journeyed there. Will we be able to meet the new challenges? Will we have the wisdom and common sense to draw upon all members of society to do so? What we teach and permit regarding all types of people reflects the benevolence and consciousness of our own age and time. Opening up gender to searching inquiry in anthropology and the social sciences suggests that we are awakening to the new challenges, that we are healthy enough to now look publicly at the secret side of our own identities.

Afterword:
whither the Sambia?

Several bitter wars in the 1950s left scars and old scores to settle in the Sambia Valley, and these were still smoldering at the time of first contact with Westerners in the late 1950s. We saw the last great battle and its casualties in Chapter 2. The government forcibly intervened then to stop all warfare. But we have not seen all the effects of this momentous intervention. Here is a native's account, taken from one of the warriors who was there and translated by me from his own words.

Another battle flared up, this time between Nilangu and Moonunkwambi [a now extinct neighbor hamlet]. Shortly before, the initiations were held again. Weiyu's age-set was made a part of the cult. No sooner was it done than another battle started, this time with Nilangu torn apart because the men took different sides in an argument over game stolen from a river trap. [This was in 1962.] That argument led to the last great battle. Many men were wounded. It seemed as though it would turn into a big war when the red skins—the government patrol officers—appeared. They seemed to ignore the fighting and went away. But in a few days they returned with a great line of black-skinned police. They built a hut [government rest house] over near Kwoli hamlet and made a speech. A distant Kaimeru man—a Sambia who'd gotten to be a government interpreter—was his translator. They said they wanted to put the men's names in a book, so we were all to assemble the next day. But we were tricked: the police circled all of us, took our weapons, and put us in handcuffs. It was terribly humiliating.

Forty men were chained, endured a two-days' walk to Mountain Patrol Station, and were jailed. They were treated as—what is the right metaphor?—savages? animals? When one man wanted to defecate, the whole line had to stop and wait for him. This was so shameful for the Sambia, who are terribly shy about toilet training. They had no food. They were kicked and sometimes beaten. In jail they were treated little better. In a few weeks they were released and warned never to fight again. That was in 1964. War was done with.

Several years later some missionaries arrived. They were strange, they wanted to learn the language. They lived down by the river and made a settlement of their own (KwatSambia) in time. People distrusted them at first, but soon came to like them: they never hurt anyone. Around 1971 Moonunkwambi was abandoned and its people moved into Nilangu, the former pseudo-enemies now living together peacefully. Two years later Mountain Patrol Station was built. Some Sambia helped build the airstrip.

Six years later I arrived. Nilangu seemed idyllic. People were friendly and war was a living memory. People were glad it was gone. Three initiation cycles have been held since that time. Moondi's was the first in 1968. The next year, 1975, the full initiations you have read about were performed. It lasted weeks and wore me out. New Guinea was decolonized that year, and it became Papua New Guinea, an independent state. In 1979 and again in 1981, 1983, and 1985, I returned to the Sambia. Their society was now changing faster than ever. And I had changed too.

Anthropology has afforded me the best of two worlds: a highly privileged Western education and scientific training, and the wonderful experience of living with a non-Western people full and rich with life in a forgotten corner untrampled until recently by our sophisticated corruptions. It also has provided a life-style that well suits me. This includes direct contact with the wholeness of people (which I need and enjoy) and, through my field materials and reflection upon another culture, the opportunity to contemplate humankind and reflect upon myself. All anthropologists' studies comment not only upon other cultures and upon theory and method, but as well upon the choices they made in and on behalf of their own cultures, their science, and themselves—the latter all silent objects of reflection. Thus, in anthropology we proceed from outside of ourselves, via another culture, to return to self-discovery.

During the last 10 years, between my first visit to the Sambia and the writing of this book, the world has changed. My years in the village have shown me a day-to-day side of how life is lived there that is more subtle than the staged, formal rites of initiation. And of course Sambia society is changing in ways that affect village life. How do we take account of these changes in our ethnographies? Anthropology is done by people, subjective human reporters. Even though we are scientifically trained, our method of participant-observation is essentially a subjective method. It is open to our own personalities, our biases, our special interests and individual talents. Our ethnographies are not facts, hard as stone, but observations and interpretations that involve us in making abstractions that go beyond the facts. So we are vulnerable to error. The best insurance against mistakes is to keep checking what we think we know; to keep trying to understand what we see and to keep listening to what people say; and to keep doubting that we know the truth. The wonder is that in spite of all these pitfalls, anthropology is a young science that has already made great discoveries.

In these 10 years I went from being a graduate student to teaching in a university. I was influenced by psychoanalysis and clinical work in psychiatry. This made me aware of how people internalize and adapt uniquely to their cultures. It made me look more at my own personal conflicts and their conscious and unconscious sources. That is hard to do sometimes; it is easier to coast along and avoid the conflicts. But the self-discovery results in feeling more real, more alive. I moved from New Guinea and returned to Australia, my second home. Then I came back to the United States, and these cultural changes made me aware more than ever of my Americanness. My research turned to gender identity. When I went back to the village in 1979 I felt that my original research was sound. Yet, by studying and talking with women and people like Sakulambei, I found that my views began to change. I was no longer as tolerant of Weiyu's constant put-downs of women or the way he treated his wife. He sometimes made me annoyed and angry. And women friends such as Kaiyunango made me see their side of things: the frustrations and hardships of secrecy and the men's sexism. Kanteilo has gotten older and slowed down; I contemplate his death. Moondi has gotten married. Now when I pass through Port Moresby I visit his family in their apartment, and I never cease to be amazed by how we have wound up *there*, so far, far away from the days of slogging through the secret forest rituals up in the mountains. He talks about seeing movies in the local theater and I feel the world is shrinking too fast. I am getting older. I see the world move to its own crazy rhythm and I realize that social change is difficult, unpredictable, and not based on the ideals I imagined as a 25-year-old greenhorn anthropologist. This has all affected the perspective I bring to this book.

We anthropologists are (notwithstanding our critics' opinions) largely a powerless, poorly paid lot, as professions go. But we are lucky to have had that great intellectual experience—fieldwork—which, of all other training experiences, only psychoanalysis matches in depth and complexity and far-reaching discovery of self. Nevertheless, where the anthropologist works through another society back into insight about culture, the psychoanalyst works through past experience to the patient's personal insight. The process of discovery in both is similar, yet analysis is more focused on self-insight as its end product. Psychoanalysis seems culture-bound. What psychoanalysis needs is our cross-cultural experience. What we need are its insights into the self. The two types of insight must go together for they are of a piece, and one is damaged without the other. Have we anthropologists not reached a cul-de-sac without this necessary self-insight? Have we not merely begun the exploration of our true object: the possibilities of human existence? I must say yes. Will we also have the courage to look more deeply at ourselves, even when it is sometimes difficult to do so? For we must realize that if we do not take courage in that scientific discovery of insight, who will?

What I have called "Sambia culture" is therefore an abstraction, an interpretation of the accumulated product of all I have described as filtered through me. When Western contact occurred it froze and compressed the culture as it was at the time. Thereafter Sambia reflected not only upon their own history and culture; they had to respond to the colonizing Australians too. The end of warfare came as a process of social change drilling backward and forward unevenly into the Sambia, as one tiny outpost of a broader world itself divided. So the awareness of the individual Sambia has changed over these critical 20 years. History has altered their identities—a fact easily forgotten when we read of their exotic initiations staged as if they were a movie from the ancient past. But the change is all around and inside of them too. The younger generation is forgetting their past, the traditional culture. Society has a short memory.

It is hard for us to fully understand how much the Australians' jailing of the warriors has changed Sambia masculinity. It does so in subtle, yet profound, ways—trauma and humiliation corrupting traditional male identity. Anger breaks into despair. The men momentarily try to protest that they are all the more masculine, but to no avail. Warfare, the main context to show off in, is gone. When one controls one's own destiny, even though the cost is war and constant danger and maybe premature death, it is hard to surrender independence. Political dependence through colonization is no great bargain. National independence is little different: the Sambia do not know the New Guinea bureaucrats who control them from a desk hundreds of miles away. The men's existential states cannot be the same. These changes affect everything—marriage, gender roles, initiation—as well as their perceptions of the future. And yet, people are in many ways happier because war is gone. The old ones tell war tales to amuse themselves, not to bring back the real thing. It is one thing to glance back at the past; it is quite another to stare.

So far there has been no resurgence of warfare among the Sambia. Their neighboring tribe, the Baruya, have time and again experienced open bow-fighting in recent years. Last year several deaths occurred from warfare there. But this is insignificant compared to the fierce neotraditional warfare in the Western Highlands that has made the news in America and which Mervyn Meggitt has vividly described in *Blood is Their Argument* (1977). I hope that such conflict does not destroy the recent peace among Sambia.

Peace has reduced sexual antagonism. Where before men constantly exaggerated the differences between the sexes, I see the younger generation recently being kinder and more open to each other. Women have more freedom. They can travel about. They are beginning to have a say in who they want to marry. The local dispute-settlement system gives women a voice to air their gripes. The patrol officer listens, and therefore the elders must listen. Boys and girls play together now. There is more warmth in marital relationships, especially as couples get older. Men's aggressiveness seems to be decreasing. In 1983 I even saw a man of the neighboring Baruya tribe holding hands with his wife in public! Perhaps Sambia will do that too. Still, the initiations remain. They were done again in 1983 and I was truly astonished at how little the key rituals had changed at all. Ritual homosexuality is still taught and lives on. The men's identity contexts still require ritual. The power of tradition cannot be underestimated.

But how long will their remarkable secret society live on? Soon roads and an airstrip will penetrate the area. The pressures to build an elementary school grew, until the opening of one in 1985. I was there with the politicians and elders and teachers. Some missionaries want people to stop the initiations. But so far the elders and the adults have firmly resisted. "Not on your life," is their usual attitude. What they mean is: "Not as long as we are alive." They seem distressed and pessimistic, fearing the cult cannot survive forever. The men feel it will die with the elders, the last generation to have known the great and colorful drama of months-long initiations before the Australians came. We cannot be sure of the durability of such a fragile ritual cult, for while its ceremonies and notions are old-fashioned (one might even say archaic), it has survived these 20-odd years of change. The human will to perpetuate identity rituals is a mighty thing. And the Sambia have a strong will. They have yet to show us how they will play their last hand.

Glossary

Aamooluku: war leader; the highest ideal of masculine achievement.

Age-mate: a person initiated into an age-set with a group of others similarly aged.

Bisexuality: expressed sexual behavior with people of the same or opposite sex.

Composite hamlet: a village formed from the union of two previously separate hamlets of the same phratry.

Confederacy, danceground: political alignment between different villages who initiate their sons together and intermarry; identified with a ritual danceground. Confederacies are usually composed of same-phratry villages, but those of the Sambia Valley are interphratry in makeup.

Danceground: *see* Confederacy.

Enculturation: the transmission of cultural knowledge, rules, and attitudes across generations.

Erotic: that which stimulates sexual desire and behavior.

Ethos: the culturally patterned form of emotional expressions characteristic of a group.

Gender: cultural behaviors, skills, ideas, and feelings associated with "masculinity" and "femininity."

Gender identity: the sense of belonging to the male or female sex, and of being masculine or feminine.

Gender roles: typical behavioral patterns expected of men or women in various status positions (e.g., "elder," "shaman," "man," "woman," etc.).

Gender signs: symbolic emblems or tokens of one's gender status in culture (e.g., noseplugs, mustaches).

Great clan: the widest form of patrilineal affiliation between people descended from common fictitious ancestors. The great clan is composed of two or more component clans, which usually reside together but who may have *dispersed clan* segments elsewhere.

Hamlet: a village community defined by Sambia as a mutually supporting extended-family residential unit.
See also Composite hamlet.

Havalt-nunta: the principle of sameness or likeness between age-mates or others who are culturally identified as belonging to one category.

Homosexuality: a generalized category referring to sexual links between people of the same sex. This is made up of: homosexual identity—an identification with habitualized same-sex roles and sexual activities; and homosexual behavior—same-sex sexual relations.

Jerungdu: the principle of male strength, virility, and manliness associated with semen and warrior prowess in Sambia culture.

Learning, symbolic: understanding that stems from exposure to rituals and symbols and which occurs at conscious and unconscious levels.

Marriage, forms of: infant-betrothal (delayed exchange) marriage is assignment at birth of a girl to a boy of another clan for future marriage as adults; sister-exchange (direct exchange) marriage occurs when two adult males agree to exchange their sisters to each other for marriage.

Patriclan: people tied by bonds of demonstrable patrilineal descent from a common real ancestor. These people recognize common rights and duties as a corporate group in marriage, land tenure, ritual, and village defense.

Patrilineal: a kinship descent principle linking people, especially men, by descent from common male ancestors, real or fictitious.

Patrilocal: a principle of residence that requires or encourages people, especially men, to set up residences as adults in the same place or village as their fathers.

Phallic: symbols, rituals, or cults modelled on the penis or related to maleness.

Phratry: a kin grouping recognized by Sambia as the widest related set of people linked by blood relation to fictitious ancestors, by common geographic origins in myth, and by ritual customs practiced in common and demarcators of ethnic distinctiveness.

Resocialization, radical: discontinuity with and unlearning of early training, and the use of ritual ordeals (i.e., brainwashing techniques) to modify boys' behaviors and gender identities to conform with adult standards.

Secret society: ritual and political organization requiring initiation for membership and adequate cultural knowledge.

Sex: refers to biological attributes associated with being either male or female.

Sexual behavior: any sexual activity.

Sexual orientation: habitualized and enduring preference for a certain sex object choice (male or female, young or old, passive or aggressive).

Shaman (*kwooluku*):   religious healer and ritual specialist able to engage in "magical flight" and control trance and spirit familiars for the good of society.

Socialization: the teaching of social roles and performative skills necessary for social behavior.

Socialization group, primary: early caretakers, especially the family, who teach language and early skills.

Socialization group, secondary: later role training, associated with initiation and resocialization, for behavior in wider social institutions beyond the family.

Spirit familiars (*numelyu*):   "magical" counterparts of one's soul substance which aid health, longevity, and, in shamans, trance and healing ceremonies.

Subtribe: *see* Phratry.

Transitional object: a symbolic process involving attachment to a person or a thing (e.g., doll) halfway between a loved person and the self; associated with the development of independence in the person.

Tribe: a social grouping identified by common language, cultural traditions, and some sense of a recognized territory defended against outside groups.

Warfare, Sambia forms of: bow-fighting—intratribal feuding between villages that uses bows and arrows, with more deadly technology forbidden; war-raiding—intertribal stealthful raids launched against outside groups to destroy and loot; all forms of technology are used here.

Wogaanyu: the principle of weakness and unmasculineness (opposed to *jerungdu*) in Sambia culture.

Worlds (men's and women's):   men's and women's "worlds" and their forms of sex-distinctive world views, as defined below.

World view: shared understandings, beliefs, and orientations about the world, including notions of space, time, and the person's place and spirituality in the cosmos.

Wusaatu: rubbish man; the lowest form of masculinity.

References Cited

Adam, B. D.
1986   Age, structure, and sexuality: Reflections on homosexual relations. In E. Blackwood (Ed.), *Anthropology and Homosexual Behavior* (pp. 19–34). New York: Haworth Press.

Barry, H., I. L. Child, and M. K. Bacon
1959   Relation of child training to subsistence economy. *American Anthropologist*, 61: 51–63

Bateson, G.
1958   *Naven*. 2nd ed. Stanford: Stanford University Press.

Bell, A. and Weinberg, M.
1978   *Homosexualities*. New York: Simon and Schuster.

Boswell, J.
1980   *Christianity, Social Tolerance, and Homosexuality*. Chicago: University of Chicago Press.

Bowers, N.
1965   Permanent bachelorhood in the Upper Kaugel Valley of Highland New Guinea. *Oceania*, 36: 27–37.

Bowra, C. M.
1957   *The Greek Experience*. London: Methuen.

Brookfield, H.
1964   The ecology of Highlands settlement: Some suggestions. *American Anthropologist*, 66 (Part 2): 20–38.

Brookfield, H. and D. Hart
1971   *Melanesia: A Geographic Interpretation of an Island World*. London: Methuen.

Brown, P.
1978   *Highland Peoples of New Guinea*. New York: Cambridge University Press.

Carrier, J.
1980   Homosexual behavior in cross-cultural perspective. In J. Marmor (Ed.), *Homosexual Behavior: A Modern Reappraisal* (pp. 100–22). New York: Basic Books.

Deacon, A. B.
1934   *Malekula: A Vanishing People in the New Hebrides*. London: Routledge.

Dover, K. J.
1978   *Greek Homosexuality*. Cambridge, Mass.: Harvard University Press.

Dundes, A.
1976   A psychoanalytic study of the bull-roarer. *Man*, 11: 220–38.

Evans-Pritchard, E. E.
    1970   Sexual inversion among the Azande. *American Anthropologist*, 72: 1428–34.
    1971   *The Azande.* Oxford: Claveudor.
Ford, D. S., and Beach, F.
    1951   *Patterns of Sexual Behavior.* New York: Harper and Bros.
Freeman, D.
    1983   *Margaret Mead and Samoa.* Cambridge, Mass.: Harvard University Press.
Freud, S.
    1961   The future of an illusion, In J. Strachey (Ed. and Trans.), *The Standard Edition of the Complete Psychological Works of Sigmund Freud.* 21: 3–57. London: Hogarth Press. (Original work published 1927)
    1962   *Three Essays on the Theory of Sexuality.* J. Strachey. (Trans.), New York: Basic Books. (Original work published 1905).
Godelier, M.
    1969   Land tenure among the Baruya of New Guinea. *Journal of the Papua New Guinea Society*, 3: 17–23.
    1971   'Salt currency' and the circulation of commodities among the Baruya of New Guinea, In *Studies in Economic Anthropology* (pp. 53–73). Washington, D.C.: American Anthropological Association.
    1982   Social hierarchies among the Baruya of New Guinea, In *Inequality in New Guinea Highland Societies*. A. Strathern (Ed.), (pp. 3–34). Cambridge: Cambridge University Press.
Goffman, E.
    1961   *Asylums.* New York: Doubleday.
Greenberg, D. F., and Bystryn, M. H.
    1982   Christian intolerance of homosexuality. *American Journal of Sociology*, 88: 515–48.
Hallpike, C. R.
    1973   Functionalist interpretations of primitive warfare. *Man*, 8(3): 451–70.
Harris, M.
    1981   *America Now: The Anthropology of a Changing Culture.* New York: Simon and Schuster.
Harrison, T.
    1937   *Savage Civilization.* London: Victor Gollancz Ltd.
Hart, C. W. M., and Pilling, A. R.
    1979   *The Tiwi of North Australia.* New York: Holt, Rinehart and Winston.
Heider, K. G.
    1979   *Grand Valley Dani: Peaceful Warriors.* New York: Holt, Rinehart and Winston.
Herdt, G. H.
    1977   The shaman's 'calling' among the Sambia of New Guinea. *Journal de la Societe des Oceanistes*, 56–57; 153–67.
    1980   Semen depletion and the sense of maleness. *Ethnopsychiatrica*, 3: 79–116.
    1981   *Guardians of the Flutes: Idioms of Masculinity.* New York: McGraw-Hill.
    1982a   Editor's preface, In G. H. Herdt (Ed.), *Rituals of Manhood* (pp. ix–xxvi). Berkeley: University of California Press.
    1982b   "Fetish and fantasy in Sambia initiation," In G. H. Herdt (Ed.), *Rituals of Manhood* (pp. 44–98). Berkeley: University of California Press.

1982c   Sambia nose-bleeding rites and male proximity to women. *Ethos*, 10(3): 189–231

1984   *Ritualized Homosexuality in Melanesia.* (Ed.) Berkeley: University of California Press.

Herdt, G. H. and Stoller, R. J.
1985   Sakulambei—A hermaphrodite's secret: An example of clinical ethnography. *The Psychoanalytic Study of Society*, 11: 115–56.

Hoffman, R. J.
1984   Vices, gods, and virtues: Cosmology as a mediating factor in attitudes toward male homosexuality. *Journal of Homosexuality*, 9: 27–44.

Hoult, T. F.
1984   Human sexuality in biological perspective: Theoretical and methodological considerations. *Journal of Homosexuality*, 9(2/3): 137–55.

Ihara, S.
1972   *Comrade Loves of the Samurai.* Trans. Ronald Shively. Rutland, Vt.: Charles E. Tuttle.

Koch, K. F.
1974   *War and Peace in Jalemo.* Cambridge, Mass: Harvard University Press.

Langness, L. L.
1967   Sexual antagonism in the New Guinea Highlands: A Bena Bena example. *Oceania*, 37: 161–77.

1972   Political organization, In *Encyclopedia of Papua New Guinea*, pp. 922–35. Melbourne: Melbourne University Press.

Lawrence, P.
1966   The Garia of the Madang district. *Anthropological Forum*, 1: 371–92.

LeVine, R. A.
1973   *Culture, Behavior and Personality.* Chicago: Aldine.

Levy, R. I.
1973   *The Tahitians: Mind and Experience in the Society Islands.* Chicago: University of Chicago Press.

Lidz, R. W., and Lidz, T.
1977   Males' menstruation: A ritual alternative to the Oedipal transition. *International Journal of Psycho-Analysis*, 58: 17–31.

Lidz, T.
1976   *The Person.* New York: Basic Books.

Lindenbaum, S.
1979   *Kuru Sorcery.* Palo Alto: Mayfield Publishing Co.

Luria, Z.
1979   Psychosocial determinants of gender identity, role and orientation. In H. A. Katchadourian, (Ed.), *Human Sexuality: A Comparative and Developmental Perspective.* (pp. 163–93). Berkeley: University of California Press.

Malcolm, L. A.
1968   Determination of the growth curve of the Kukukuku people of New Guinea from dental eruption in children and adult height. *Archeological and Physiological Anthropology in Oceania*, 4: 72–78.

1970   Growth, malnutrition and mortality of the infant and toddler in the Asai Valley of the New Guinea Highlands. *American Journal of Clinical Nutrition*, 23: 1090–95.

Mead, M.
  1928   *Coming of Age in Samoa.* New York: William Morrow.
  1930   *Growing Up in New Guinea.* New York: William Morrow.
  1935   *Sex and Temperament.* New York: William Morrow.
Meggitt, M.
  1974   'Pigs are our hearts!' The Te exchange cycle among the Mae Enga of New Guinea. *Oceania*, 44: 165–203.
  1977   *Blood is Their Argument.* Palo Alto: Mayfield.
Meigs, A. S.
  1984   *Food, Sex, and Pollution.* Rutgers, N. J.: Rutgers University Press.
Milgram, S.
  1974   *Obedience to Authority: An Experimental View.* New Haven: Yale University Press.
Minturn, L., et al.
  1969   Cultural patterning of sexual beliefs and behavior. *Ethnology*, 8: 301–17.
Murphy, Y. and Murphy, R.
  1974   *Women of the Forest.* New York: Columbia University Press.
Newman, P. L.
  1962   Supernaturalism and Ritual among the Gururumba. University of Washington, Ph.D. dissertation.
Paul, J.
  1985   Bisexuality: Reassessing our paradigms of sexuality. *Journal of Homosexuality*, 11: 21–34.
Poole, F. J. P.
  1981   Transforming 'natural' woman: Female ritual leaders and gender ideology among Bimin-Kuskusmin. In S. B. Ortner and H. Whitehead (Eds.), *Sexual Meanings* (pp. 116–65). Cambridge: Cambridge University Press.
  1982   The ritual forging of identity: Aspects of person and self in Bimin-Kuskusmin male intiation. In G. H. Herdt (Ed.), *Rituals of Manhood: Male Initiation in Papua New Guinea* (pp. 100–54). Berkeley: University of California Press.
Rappaport, R.
  1968   *Pigs for the Ancestors.* New Haven: Yale University Press.
Read, K. E.
  1954   Cultures of the central Highlands. *Southwestern Journal of Anthropology*, 10: 1–43.
  1955   Morality and the concept of the person among the Gahuku-Gama. *Oceania*, 25: 233–82.
  1959   Leadership and consensus in a New Guinea society. *American Anthropologist*, 61: 425–36.
  1965   *The High Valley.* New York: Scribner's.
Reay, M.
  1959   *The Kuma.* Melbourne: Melbourne University Press.
Roheim, G.
  1932   Psycho-analysis of primitive cultural types. *International Journal of Psycho-Analysis*, 13: 1–224.
  1950   *Psychoanalysis and Anthropology.* New York: International University Press.
Rosaldo, M. Z.
  1974   Women, culture, and society: A theoretical overview, In M. Z. Rosaldo and L. Lamphere, (Eds.), *Woman, Culture, and Society.* pp. 17–42. Stanford: Stanford University Press.

Sargent, W.
1957   Battle for the Mind: A Physiology of Conversion and Brain Washing. Melbourne: Heinemann.
Schwartz, T.
1973   Cult and context: The paranoid ethos in Melanesia. Ethos, 1: 153–74.
Serpenti, L. M.
1965   Cultivators in the Swamps: Social Structure and Horticulture in a New Guinea Society. Assen: Van Gorcum.
Sillitoe, P.
1978   Big men and war in New Guinea. Man, 13: 252–71.
Spindler, G., and Spindler, L.
1982   Do anthropologists need learning theory? Anthropology and Education Quarterly, 13: 109–24.
Spiro, M. E.
1979   Whatever happened to the id? American Anthropologist, 81: 5–13.
1982   Oedipus in the Trobriands. Chicago: University of Chicago Press.
Stoller, R. J.
1968   Sex and Gender, Volume I: On the Development of Masculinity and Femininity. New York: Science House.
Stoller, R. J., and Herdt, G. H.
1982   The development of masculinity: A cross-cultural contribution. Journal of the American Psychoanalytic Association, 30: 29–59.
Strathern, A. J.
1971   The Rope of Moku. Cambridge: Cambridge University Press.
1972   One Father, One Blood. Camberra: A.N.U. Press.
Strathern, M.
1979   The self in self-decoration." Oceania, 49: 241–57.
Strehlow, C.
1913   Die Aranda-und Loritja-Stämme in Zentral Australien.4,1, Das Sociale Leben der Aranda-und Loritja-Stämme. Frankfurt: Joseph Baer.
Turner, V. W.
1967   "Betwixt and between: The liminal period in Rites de Passage," in The Forest of Symbols (pp. 93–111). Ithaca: Cornell University Press.
1971   The Ritual Process. Chicago: Aldine.
Tuzin, D. F.
1980   The Voice of the Tambaran: Truth and Illusion in Ilahita Arapesh Religion. Berkeley: University of California Press.
Van Baal, J.
1966   Dema. The Hague: Martinus Nijhoff.
Van Gennep, A.
1909   Les Rites de Passage. Paris: E. Nourry.
Vanggard, T.
1972   Phallos. New York: International University Press.
Westermarck, E.
1917   The Origin and Development of the Moral Ideas. Vol. 2. 2nd ed. London: Macmillan.
Whiting, J. W. M., et al.
1958   The function of male initiation ceremonies at puberty, In E. E. Maccoby et al, (Eds.), Readings in Social Psychology (pp. 359–70). New York: Holt.

Whiting, J. W. M., and Whiting, B. B.
   1975   Aloofness and intimacy of husbands and wives: A cross-cultural study. *Ethos*, 3: 183–207.
Williams, F. E.
   1936   *Papuans of the Trans-Fly*. Oxford: Oxford University Press.